𝔖𝔱𝔞𝔫𝔡𝔞𝔯𝔡 𝔏𝔦𝔟𝔯𝔞𝔯𝔶 𝔈𝔡𝔦𝔱𝔦𝔬𝔫

# AMERICAN STATESMEN

IN FORTY VOLUMES
VOLUME XVIII

DOMESTIC POLITICS: THE TARIFF
AND SLAVERY

MARTIN VAN BUREN

M Van Buren

# American Statesmen

STANDARD LIBRARY EDITION

*The Home of Martin Van Buren*

HOUGHTON MIFFLIN COMPANY

American Statesmen

# MARTIN VAN BUREN

BY

EDWARD M. SHEPARD

Tout bien ou rien
The Riverside Press

BOSTON AND NEW YORK
HOUGHTON MIFFLIN COMPANY
The Riverside Press Cambridge

The Riverside Press
CAMBRIDGE · MASSACHUSETTS
PRINTED IN THE U.S.A

# PREFACE TO THE REVISED EDITION

Since 1888, when this Life was originally published, the history of American Politics has been greatly enriched. The painstaking and candid labors of Mr. Fiske, Mr. Adams, Mr. Rhodes, and others have gone far to render unnecessary the *caveat* I then entered against the unfairness, or at least the narrowness, of the temper with which Van Buren, or the school to which he belonged, had thus far been treated in American literature, and which had prejudicially misled me before I began my work. Such a *caveat* is no longer necessary. Even now, when the political creed of which Jefferson, Van Buren, and Tilden have been chief apostles in our land, seems to suffer some degree of eclipse, — only temporary, it may well be believed, but nevertheless real, — those who, like myself, have undertaken to present the careers of great Americans who held this faith need not fear injustice or prejudice in the field of American literature.

In this revised edition I have made a few corrections and added a few notes; but the generous

treatment which has been given to the book has
confirmed my belief that historic truth requires no
material change.

A passage from the diary of Charles Jared
Ingersoll (Life by William M. Meigs, 1897)
tempts me, in this most conspicuous place of the
book, to emphasize my observation upon one injustice often done to Van Buren.  Referring, on May
6, 1844, to his letter, then just published, against
the annexation of Texas, Mr. Ingersoll declared
that, in view of the fact that nearly all of Van
Buren's admirers and most of the Democratic press
were committed to the annexation, Van Buren had
committed a great blunder and become *felo de se.*
The assumption here is that Van Buren was a politician of the type so painfully familiar to us, whose
sole and conscienceless effort is to find out what is
to be popular for the time, in order, for their own
profit, to take that side.  That Van Buren was
politic there can be no doubt.  But he was politic
after the fashion of a statesman and not of a dema-
gogue.  He disliked to commit himself upon issues
which had not been fully discussed, which were not
ripe for practical solution by popular vote, and
which did not yet need to be decided.  Mr. Ingersoll should have known that the direct and simple
explanation was the true one, — that Van Buren
knew the risk and meant to take it.  His letter

against the annexation of Texas, written when he knew that it would probably defeat him for the presidency, was but one of several acts performed by him at critical periods, wherein he deliberately took what seemed the unpopular side in order to be true to his sense of political and patriotic duty. The crucial tests of this kind through which he successfully passed must, beyond any doubt, put him in the very first rank of those American statesmen who have had the rare union of political foresight and moral courage.

EDWARD M. SHEPARD.

January, 1899.

# CONTENTS

# ILLUSTRATIONS

# MARTIN VAN BUREN

## CHAPTER I

AMERICAN POLITICS WHEN VAN BUREN'S CAREER
BEGAN. — JEFFERSON'S INFLUENCE

It sometimes happened during the anxious years
when the terrors of civil war, though still smoul-
dering, were nearly aflame, that on Wall Street or
Nassau Street, busy men of New York saw Martin
Van Buren and his son walking arm in arm.
" Prince John," tall, striking in appearance, his
hair divided at the middle in a fashion then novel
for Americans, was in the prime of life, resolute
and aggressive in bearing. His father was a white-
haired, bright-eyed old man, erect but short in
figure, of precise though easy and kindly polite-
ness, and with a touch of deference in his manner.
His presence did not peremptorily command the
attention of strangers ; but to those who looked attentively there was plain distinction in the refined
and venerable face. Passers-by might well turn
back to see more of the two men thus affection-
ately and picturesquely together. For they were

famous characters, — the one in the newer, the
other in the older politics of America. John Van
Buren, fresh from his Free Soil battle and the tus-
sles of the Hards and Softs, was striving, as a
Democrat, to serve the cause of the Union, though
conscious that he rested under the suspicion of the
party to whose service, its divisions in New York
now seemingly ended, he had reluctantly returned.
But he still faced the slave power with an independence only partially abated before the exigencies of party loyalty. The ex-President, definitely withdrawn from the same Free Soil battle,
a struggle into which he had entered when the
years were already heavy upon him, had survived
to be once more a worthy in the Democratic party,
again to receive its formal veneration, but never
again its old affection. In their timid manoeuvres
with slavery it was perhaps with the least possible
awkwardness that the northern Democrats sought
to treat him as a great Democratic leader; but
they did not let it be forgotten that the leader
was forever retired from leadership. While the
younger man was in the thick of political encoun-
ters which the party carried on in blind futility,
the older man was hardly more than an historical
personage. He was no longer, his friends strove
to think, the schismatic candidate of 1848, but
rather the ally and friend of Jackson, or, better
still and further away, the disciple of Jefferson.

For, more than any other American, Martin Van
Buren had succeeded to the preaching of Jeffer-

son's political doctrines, and to his political power as well, that curious and potent mingling of philosophy, statesmanship, and electioneering. The Whigs' distrust towards Van Buren was still bitter; the hot anger of his own party over the blow he had dealt in 1848 was still far from subsided; the gratitude of most Free Soil men had completely disappeared with his apparent acquiescence in the politics of Pierce and Buchanan. Save in a narrow circle of anti-slavery Democrats, Van Buren, in these last days of his, was judged at best with coldness, and most commonly with dislike or even contempt. Not much of any other temper has yet gone into political history; its writers have frequently been content to accept the harshness of partisan opinion, or even the scurrility and mendacity visited upon him during his many political campaigns, and to ignore the positive records of his career and public service. The present writer confesses to have begun this Life, not indeed sharing any of the hatred or contempt so commonly felt towards Van Buren, but still given to many serious depreciations of him, which a better examination has shown to have had their ultimate source in the mere dislike of personal or political enemies, — a dislike to whose expression, often powerful and vivid, many writers have extended a welcome seriously inconsistent with the fairness of history.

When Abraham Lincoln was chosen president in 1860, this predecessor of his by a quarter century was a true historical figure. The bright, genial old man connected, visibly and really, those stirring and dangerous modern days with the first political struggles under the American Constitution, struggles then long passed into the quiet of history, to leave him almost their only living reminiscence. Martin Van Buren was a man fully grown and already a politician when in 1801 the triumph of Thomas Jefferson completed the political foundation of the United States. Its profound inspiration still remained with him on this eve of Lincoln's election. Under its influence his political career had begun and had ended.

At Jefferson's election the aspiration and fervor which attended the first, the new-born sense of American national life, had largely worn away. The ideal visions of human liberty had long before grown dim during seven years of revolutionary war, with its practical hardships, its vicissitudes of meanness and glory, and during the four years of languor and political incompetence which followed. In the agitation for better union, political theories filled the minds of our forefathers. Lessons were learned from the Achæan League, as well as from the Swiss Confederation, the German Empire, and the British Constitution. Both history and speculation, however, were firmly subordinated to an extraordinary common sense, in part flowing from, as it was most finely exhibited in, the luminous and powerful, if unexalted, genius of Franklin. From the open beginning of constitution-making at Annapolis in 1786 until the inauguration of John

Adams, the American people, under the masterful governing of Washington, were concerned with the framework upon which the fabric of their political life was to be wrought. The framework was doubt-less in itself of a vast and enduring importance. If the consolidating and aristocratic schemes of Hamilton had not met defeat in the federal convention, or if the separatist jealousies of Patrick Henry and George Clinton had not met defeat in Virginia and New York after the work of the convention was done, there would to-day be a different American people. Nor would our history be the amazing story of the hundred years past. But upon the governmental framework thus set up could be woven political fabrics widely and essentially different in their material, their use, and their enduring virtue. For quite apart from the framework of government were the temper and traditions of popular politics out of which comes, and must always come, the essential and dominant nature of public institutions. In this creative and deeper work Jefferson was engaged during his struggle for political power after returning from France in 1789, during his presidential career from 1801 to 1809, and during the more extraordinary, and in American history the unparalleled, supremacy of his political genius after he had left office. In the circumstances of our colonial life, in our race extractions, in our race fusion upon the Atlantic seaboard, and in the moral effect of forci-ble and embittered separation from the parent country, arose indeed, to go no further back, the political instincts of American men. It is, however, fatal to adequate conception of our political development to ignore the enormous formative influence which the twenty years of Jefferson's rule had upon American political character. But so partial and sometimes so partisan have been the historians of our early national politics in their treatment of that great man, that a just appreciation of the political atmosphere in which Van Buren began his career is exceedingly difficult.

There was an American government, an American nation, when Washington gladly escaped to Mt. Vernon from the bitterly factional quarrels of the politicians at Philadelphia. The government was well ordered ; the nation was respectable and dignified. But most of the people were either still colonial and provincial, or were rushing, in turbulence and bad temper, to crude speculations and theories. Twenty-five years later, Jefferson had become the political idol of the American people, a people completely and forever saturated with democratic aspirations, democratic ideals, what John Marshall called "political metaphysics," a people with strong and lasting characteristics, no longer either colonial or provincial, but profoundly national. The skill, the industry, the arts of the politician, had been used by a man gifted with the genius and not free from the faults of a philosopher, to plant in American usages, prejudices, and traditions, — in the very fibre of American political life, a cardinal and fruitful idea. The work was done for all time. For Americans, government was thenceforth to be a mere instrument. No longer a symbol, or an ornament or crown of national life, however noble and august, it was a simple means to a plain end; to be always, and if need be rudely, tested and measured by its practical working, by its service to popular rights and needs. In those earlier days, too, there had been "classes and masses," the former of whom held public service and public policy as matters of dignity and order and high assertion of national right and power, requiring in their ministers peculiar and esoteric light, and an equipment of which common men ought not to judge, because they could not judge aright. Afterward, in Monroe's era of good feeling, the personal rivalries of presidential candidates were in bad temper enough; but Americans were at last all democrats. Whether for better or worse, the nation had ceased to be either British or colonial, or provincial, in its character. In the delightful Rip Van Winkle of a later Jefferson, during the twenty years' sleep, the old Dutch house has gone, the peasant's dress, the quaint inn with its village tapster, all the old scene of loyal provincial life. Rip returns to a noisy, boastful, self-assertive town full of American "push" and "drive," and profane disregard of superiors and everything ancient. It was hardly a less change which spread through the United States in the twenty years of Jefferson's unrivaled and fruitful leadership. Superstitious regard for the " well-born," for institutions of government as images of veneration apart from their immediate and practical use ; the faith in government as essentially a financial establishment which ought to be on peculiarly friendly relations with banks and bankers ; the treatment and consideration of our democratic organization as an experiment to be administered with deprecatory deference to European opinion ; the idea that upon the great, simple elements of political belief and practice, the mass of men could not judge as wisely and safely as the opulent, the cultivated, the educated ; the idea that it was a capital feature of political art to thwart the rashness and incompetence of the lower people, — all these theories and traditions, which had firmly held most of the disciplined thought of Europe and America, and to which the lurid horrors of the French Revolution had brought apparent consecration, — all these had now gone ; all had been fatally wounded, or were sullenly and apologetically cherished in the aging bitterness of the Federalists. There was an American people with as distinct, as powerful, as characteristic a polity as belonged to the British islanders. In 1776 a youthful genius had seized upon a colonial revolt against taxation as the occasion to make solemn declaration of a seeming abstraction about human rights. He had submitted, however, to subordinate his theory during the organization of national defense and the

strengthening of the framework of government.
Nor did he shine in either of those works. But
with the nation established, with a union secured
so that its people could safely attend to the simpler
elements of human rights, Jefferson and his disciples were able to lead Americans to the temper,
the aspirations, and the very prejudices of essential democracy. The Declaration of Independence, the ten amendments to the Constitution
theoretically formulating the rights of men or of
the States, sank deep into the sources of American
political life. So completely indeed was the work
done, that in 1820 there was but one political party
in America; all were Jeffersonian Republicans;
and when the Republican party was broken up in
1824, the only dispute was whether Adams or
Jackson or Crawford or Clay or Calhoun best represented the political beliefs now almost universal.
It seemed to Americans as if they had never
known any other beliefs, as if these doctrines of
their democracy were truisms to which the rest
of the world was marvelously blind.

Nothing in American public life has, in prolonged anger and even savage desperation, equaled
the attacks upon Jefferson during the steady
growth of his stupendous influence. The hatred
of him personally, and the belief in the wickedness of his private and public life, survive in our
time. Nine tenths of the Americans who then
read books sincerely thought him an enemy of
mankind and of all that was sacred. Nine tenths

of the authors of American books on history or politics have to this day written under the influence which ninety years ago controlled their predecessors. And for this there is no little reason. As the American people grew conscious of their own peculiar and intensely active political force, there came to them a period of national and popular life in which much was unlovely, much was crude, much was disagreeably vulgar. Books upon America written by foreign travelers, from the days of Jefferson down to our civil war, superficial and offensive as they often were, told a great deal of truth. We do not now need to wince at criticisms upon a rawness, an insolent condescension towards the political ignorance of foreigners and the unhappy subjects of kings, a harshness in the assertion of the equality of Caucasian men, and a restless, boastful manner. The criticisms were in great measure just. But the critics were stupid and blind not to see the vast and vital work and change going on before their eyes, to chiefly regard the trifling and incidental things which disgusted them. Their eyes were open to all our faults of taste and manner, but closed to the self-dependent and self-assertive energy the disorder of whose exhibition would surely pass away. In every democratic experiment, in every experiment of popular or national freedom, there is almost inevitable a vulgarizing of public manners, a lack of dignity in details, which disturbs men who find restful delight in orderly and decorous public life;

and their disgust is too often directed against beneficent political changes or reforms. If one were
to judge the political temper of the American people from many of our own writers, and still more
if he were to judge it from the observations even
of intelligent and friendly foreigners prior to 1861,
he would believe that temper to be sordid, mean,
noisy, boastful, and even cruel. But from the war
of 1812 with England to the election of Buchanan
in 1856, the American people had been doing a
profound, organic, democratic work. Meantime
many had seen no more than the unsightly, the
mean and trivial, the malodorous details, which
were mere incidents and blemishes of hidden and
dynamic operations. Unimaginative minds usually
fail to see the greater and deeper movements of
politics as well as those of science. In the public
virtues then maturing there lay the ability long
and strenuously to conduct an enterprise the
greatest which modern times have known, and
an extraordinary popular capacity for restraint
and discipline. In those virtues was sleeping a
tremendously national spirit which, with cost and
sacrifice not to be measured by the vast figures of
the statistician, on one side sought independence,
and on the other saved the Union, — an exalted
love of men and truth and liberty, which, after all
the enervations of pecuniary prosperity, endured
with patience hardships and losses, and the less
heroic but often more dangerous distresses of taxation, — at the North a magnanimity in victory

unequaled in the traditions of men, and at the
South a composure and dignity and absence of
either bitterness or meanness which brought out
of defeat far larger treasures than could have
come with victory. But these were not effects
without a cause. In them all was only the fruit,
the normal fruit, of the political habits, ideals,
traditions, whose early and unattractive disorders
had chagrined many of the best of Americans, and
had seemed so natural to foreigners who feared or
distrusted a democracy. There had been forming, during forty or fifty years of a certain raw
unloveliness, the peculiar and powerful self-reliance
of a people whose political independence meant far
more than a mere separate government.   ·

In these years Van Buren was one of the chief
men in American public life. He and his political
associates had been profoundly affected by the Jeffersonian philosophy of government. They robustly
held its tenets until the flame and vengeance of the
slavery conflict drove them from political power.
In our own day we have, in the able speeches with
which Samuel J. Tilden fatigued respectful though
often unsympathetic hearers at Democratic meetings, heard something of the same robust political
philosophy, brought directly from intercourse with
his famous neighbor and political master. Van
Buren himself breathed it as the very atmosphere
of American public life, during his early career
which had just begun when Jefferson, his robes
of office dropped and his faults of administration

forgotten, seemed the serene, wise old man presiding over a land completely won to his ideals of democracy. Under this extraordinary influence and in this political light, there opened with the first years of the century the public life to be narrated in this volume.

# CHAPTER II

AT the close of the American Revolution, Abraham Van Buren was a farmer on the east bank of the Hudson River, New York. He was of Dutch descent, as was his wife, whose maiden name Hoes, corrupted from Goes, is said to have had distinction in Holland. But it would be mere fancy to find in the statesman particular traits brought from the dyked swamp lands whence some of his ancestors came. Those who farmed the rich fields of Columbia county were pretty thorough Americans; their characteristics were more immediately drawn from the soil they cultivated and from the necessary habits of their life than from the lands, Dutch or English, from which their forefathers had emigrated. Late in the eighteenth century they were no longer frontiersmen. For a century and more this eastern Hudson River country had been peacefully and prosperously cultivated. There was no lack of high spirit; but it was shown in lawsuits and political feuds rather than in skirmishes with red men. It was close to the old town of Albany with its official and not undignified life, and had comparatively easy access to New York by sloop or

the post-road. It had been an early settlement of
the colony. Within its borders were now the estates and mansions of large landed proprietors, who
inherited or acquired from a more varied and afflu-
ent life some of the qualities, good and bad, of a
country gentry. It was a region of easy, orderly
comfort, sound and robust enough, but not sharing
the straight and precise, though meddling, puritan-
ical habits which a few miles away, over the high
Berkshire hills, had come from the shores of New
England.

The elder Van Buren was said by his son's enemies to have kept a tavern; and he probably did.
Farming and tavern-keeping then were fairly in-
terchangeable; and the gracious manner, the tact
with men, which the younger Van Buren developed
to a marked degree, it is easy to believe came
rather from the social and varied life of an inn
than from the harsher isolation of a farm. The
statesman's boyish days were at any rate spent
among poor neighbors. He was born at Kinderhook, an old village of New York, on the 5th of
December, 1782. The usual years of schooling
were probably passed in one of the dilapidated,
weather-beaten schoolhouses from which has come
so much of what is best in American life. He
studied later in the Kinderhook Academy, one of
the higher schools which in New York have done
good work, though not equaling the like schools in
Massachusetts. Here he learned a little Latin.
But when at fourteen years of age he entered a

law office, he had of course the chief discipline of book-learning still to acquire. In 1835 his campaign biographer rather rejoiced that he had so little systematic education, fearing that "from the eloquent pages of Livy, or the honeyed eulogiums of Virgil, or the servile adulation of Horace, he might have been inspired with an admiration for regal pomp and aristocratic dignity uncongenial to the native independence of his mind," and have imbibed a "contempt for plebeians and common people," unless, perhaps, the speeches of popular leaders in Livy "had kindled his instinctive love of justice and freedom," or the sarcastic vigor of Tacitus "had created in his bosom a fixed hatred of tyranny in every shape." At an early age, however, it is certain that Van Buren, like many other Americans of original force and with instinctive fondness for written pictures of human history and conduct, acquired an education which, though not that of a professional scholar, was entirely appropriate to the skillful man of affairs or the statesman to be set in conspicuous places. This work must have been largely done during the comparative leisure of his legal apprenticeship.

It was in 1796 that he entered the law office of Francis Sylvester at Kinderhook, where he remained until his twentieth year. He there read law. It is safe to say besides that he swept the office, lighted the fires in winter, and, like other law students in earlier and simpler days, had to do the work of an office janitor and errand boy, as well as to serve papers and copy the technical forms of the common law, and the tedious but often masterly pleadings of chancery. That his work as a student was done with great industry and thoroughness is demonstrated by the fact that at an early age he became a successful and skillful advocate in arguments addressed to courts as distinguished from juries, a division of professional work in which no skill and readiness will supply deficiencies in professional equipment. His early reputation for cleverness is illustrated by the story that when only a boy he successfully summed up a case before a jury against his preceptor Sylvester, being made by the justice to stand upon a bench because he was so small, with the exhortation, " There, Mat, beat your master."

In 1802 Van Buren entered the office of William P. Van Ness, in the city of New York, to complete his seventh and final year of legal study. Van Ness was himself from Columbia county and an eminent lawyer. He was afterwards appointed United States district judge by Madison ; and was then an influential Republican and a close friend and defender of Aaron Burr, then the vice-president. The native powers and fascination of Burr were at their zenith, though his political character was blasted. Van Buren made his acquaintance, and was treated with the distinguished and flattering attention which the wisest of public men often show to young men of promise. Van Buren's enemies were absurdly fond of the fancy that in this

slight intercourse he had acquired the skill and
grace of his manner, and the easy principles and
love of intrigue which they ascribe to him. Burr,
for years after he was utterly disabled, inspired a
childish terror in American politics. The mystery
and dread about him were used by the opponents
of Jackson because Burr had early pointed him
out for the presidency, and by the opponents of
Clay because in early life he had given Burr professional assistance. But upon Burr's candidacy
for governor in 1804 Van Buren's freedom from
his influence was clearly enough exhibited.

In 1803 Van Buren, being now of age and admitted as an attorney, returned to Kinderhook and
there began the practice of his profession. The
rank of counsellor-at-law was still distinct and
superior to that of attorney. His half-brother on
his mother's side, James J. Van Alen, at once admitted the young attorney to a law partnership.
Van Alen was considerably older and had a practice already established. Van Buren's career as a
lawyer was not a long one, but it was brilliant and
highly successful. After his election to the United
States Senate in 1821 his practice ceased to be
very active. He left his profession with a fortune
which secured him the ease in money matters so
helpful and almost necessary to a man in public
life. Merely professional reputations disappear
with curious and rather saddening promptness and
completeness. Of the practice and distinction
reached by Van Buren before he withdrew from

the bar, although they were unsurpassed in the State, no vestige and few traditions remain beyond technical synopses of his arguments in the instructive but hardly succulent pages of Johnson's, Wendell's, and Cowen's reports.

At an early day the legal profession reached in our country a consummate vigor. Far behind as Americans were in other learning and arts, they had, within a few years after they escaped colonial dependence, judges, advocates, and commentators of the first rank. Marshall, Kent, and Story were securely famous when hardly another American of their time not in public and political life was known. In the legal art Americans were even more accomplished than in its science; and Columbia county and the valley of the Hudson were fine fields for legal practice. Many animosities survived from revolutionary days. The landed families, long used to administer the affairs of others as well as their own, saw with jealousy and fear the rapid spread of democratic doctrines and of leveling and often insolent manners. Political feuds were rife, and frequently appeared in the professionally profitable collisions of neighbors with vagrant cows, or on watercourses insufficient for the needs of the up-stream and the down-stream proprietors. There were slander suits and libel suits, and suits for malicious prosecution. Into the most legitimate controversies over doubts about property there was driven the bitterness which turns a lawsuit from a process to ascertain a right into a weapon of revenge.

Van Buren's political opinions were strong and clear from the beginning of his law practice; but he was in a professional minority among the rich Federalists of the county. The adverse discipline was invaluable. Through zeal and skill and large industry, he soon led the Republicans as their ablest lawyer, and the lawyers of Columbia county were famous. William W. Van Ness, afterwards a judge of the supreme court of the State, Grosvenor, Elisha Williams, and Jacob R. Van Rensselaer were active at the bar. Williams, although his very name is nowadays hardly known, we cannot doubt from the universal testimony of contemporaries, had extraordinary forensic talents. He was a Federalist; and the most decisive proof of Van Buren's rapid professional growth was his promotion to be Williams's chief competitor and adversary. Van Buren's extraordinary application and intellectual clearness soon established him as the better and the more successful lawyer, though not the more powerful advocate. Williams at last said to his rival, "I get all the verdicts, and you get all the judgments." A famous pupil of Van Buren both in law and in politics, Benjamin F. Butler, afterwards attorney-general in his cabinet, finely contrasted them from his own recollection of their conflicts when he was a law student. "Never," he said, "were two men more dissimilar. Both were eloquent; but the eloquence of Williams was declamatory and exciting, that of Van Buren insinuating and delightful. Williams had the live lier imagination, Van Buren the sounder judgment. The former presented the strong points of his case in bolder relief, invested them in a more brilliant coloring, indulged a more unlicensed and magnificent invective, and gave more life and variety to his arguments by his peculiar wit and inimitable humor. But Van Buren was his superior in analyzing, arranging, and combining the insulated materials, in comparing and weighing testimony, in unraveling the web of intricate affairs, in eviscerating truth from the mass of diversified and conflicting evidence, in softening the heart and moulding it to his purpose, and in working into the judgments of his hearers the conclusions of his own perspicuous and persuasive reasonings." Most of this is applicable to Van Buren's career on the wider field of politics; and much here said of his early adversary on the tobacco-stained floors of country court-houses might have been as truly said of a later adversary of his, the splendid leader who, rather than Harrison, ought to have been victor over Van Buren in 1840, and over whom Van Buren rather than Polk ought to have been victor in 1844.

In a few years Van Buren outgrew the professional limitations of Kinderhook. In February, 1807, he had been admitted as a counsellor of the supreme court; and this promotion he most happily celebrated by marrying Hannah Hoes, a young lady of his own age, and also of Dutch descent, a kinswoman of his mother, and with whom he had been intimate from his childhood. In 1808, the council of appointment becoming Republican, he was made surrogate of Columbia county, succeeding his partner and half-brother Van Alen, a Federalist in politics, who was, however, returned to the place in 1815, when the Federalists regained the council. The office was a respectable one, concerned with the probate of wills, and the ordering of estates of deceased persons. Within a year after this appointment, Van Buren removed to the new and bustling little city of Hudson, directly on the river banks. Here he practiced law with rapidly increasing success for seven years. His pecuniary thrift now enabled him to purchase what was called " a very extensive and well-selected library." With this advantage he applied himself to " a systematic and extended course of reading," which left him a well, even an amply, educated man. His severity in study did not, however, exclude him from the social pleasures of which he was fond, and for which he was perfectly fitted. He learned men quite as fast as he learned books. A country surrogate, though then enjoying fees, since commuted to a salary, had only a meagre compensation. But the duties of Van Buren's office did not interfere with his activity in the private practice of the law. On the contrary, the office enabled him to make acquaintances, a process which, even without adventitious aid, he always found easy and delightful.

In 1813, having been elected a member of the

Senate of the State, he became as such a member of the court for the correction of errors. This was the court of last resort, composed, until 1847, of the chancellor, the judges of the supreme court, the lieutenant-governor, and the thirty-two senators. The latter, though often laymen, were members of the court, partly through a curious imitation of the theoretical function of the British House of Lords, and partly under the idea, even now feebly surviving in some States, that some besides lawyers ought to sit upon the bench in law courts to contribute the common sense which it was fancied might be absent from their more learned associates. It was not found unsuitable for members of this, the highest court, to be active legal practitioners. While Van Buren held his place as a member he was, in February, 1815, made attorney-general, succeeding Abraham Van Vechten, one of the famous lawyers of the State. Van Buren was then but thirty-two years old, and the professional eminence accorded to the station was greater than now. Among near predecessors in it had been Aaron Burr, Ambrose Spencer and Thomas Addis Emmett; among his near successors were Thomas J. Oakley, Samuel A. Talcott, Greene C. Bronson and Samuel Beardsley, — all names of the first distinction in the professional life of New York. The office was of course political, as it has always been, both in the United States and the mother country. But Van Buren's appointment, if it were made because he was an active and influential Re-

publican in politics, would still not have been made
unless his professional reputation had been high.
The salary was $5.50 a day, with some costs, —
not an unsuitable salary in days when the chancellor was paid but $3000 a year.  He held the office
until July, 1819, when, upon the capture of the
council of appointment by a coalition of Clintonian
Republicans and Federalists, he was removed to
give place to Oakley, the Federalist leader in the
State Assembly.

In 1816 Van Buren, now rapidly reaching professional eminence, removed to Albany, the capital
of New York.  Though then a petty city of mean
buildings and about 10,000 inhabitants, it had a
far larger relative importance in the professional
and social life of the State than has the later city
of ten times the population, with its costly and
enormous state-house, its beautiful public buildings,
and its steep and numerous streets of fine resi-
dences.  In 1820 he purposed removing to New
York ; but, for some reason altering his plans, continued to reside at Albany until appointed secretary
of state in 1829.  His professional career was there
crowned with most important and lucrative work.
Soon after moving to Albany, he took into partnership Butler, just admitted to the bar.  Between
the two men there were close and life-long relations.
The younger of them, also a son of Columbia
county, reached great professional distinction, became a politician of the highest type, and remained
steadfast in his attachment to Van Buren's political

fortunes, and to the robust and distinctly marked political doctrines and practices of the Albany Regency.

The law reports give illustrations of Van Buren's precision, his clear and forcible common-sense, and his aptitude for that learning of the law in which the great counsel of the time excelled. In 1813, soon after his service began as state senator, he delivered an opinion in a case of "escape;" and in very courteous words exhibited a bit of his dislike for Kent, then chief justice of the supreme court, whose judgment he helped to reverse, as well as his antipathy to imprisonment for debt, which he afterwards helped to abolish. It was a petty suit against the sureties upon the bond given by a debtor. Under a relaxation of the imprisonment for debt recently permitted, the debtor was, on giving the bond, released from jail, but upon the condition that he should keep within the "jail liberties," which in the country counties was a prescribed area around the jail. His bond was to be forfeit if he passed the "liberties." While the debtor was driving a cow to or from pasture, the latter contemptuously deviated "four, six, or ten feet" from the liberties. The driver, yielding to inevitable bucolic impulse and forgetting his bond, leaped over the imaginary line to bring back the cow. He was without the liberties but a moment, and afterwards duly kept within them. But the creditor was watchful, and for the technical "escape" sued the sureties. Although the debtor was within the limits

when suit was brought, the lower court refused to
pardon the debtor's technical and unintentional
fault. At common law the creditor was entitled to
satisfaction of the debtor's body ; and the milder
statute establishing jail liberties was, the court said,
to be strictly construed against the debtor ; it was
not enough that the creditor had the debtor's body
when he called for it. The supreme court, headed
by Kent, affirmed this curiously harsh decision. In
the court of errors, Van Buren joined Chancellor
Lansing in reversing the rule upon an elaborate review of the law, which to this day is important authority, and which could not have been more carefully done had something greater seemed at stake
than a bovine vagary and a few dollars. The young
lawyer, wearing for a time the judicial robes, now
sat in a review, by no means unpleasant, of the utterances of magistrates before whom he had until
then stood in considerable awe ; and seized the opportunity, doubtless with a keen perception of the drift
of popular sentiment on matters of personal liberty,
to enlarge the mild policy of the later law. When
it was urged that, if the law were not technically administered, imprisoned debtors would of a Sunday
wander beyond the " limits," securely able to return
before Monday, when the creditor could sue, — Van
Buren, with a contemptuous fling at the supreme
court, confessed in Johnsonian sentences his lenient
temper towards these " stolen pleasures," — his
willingness that debtors should snatch the " few
moments of liberty which, although soured by con-

stant perturbation and alarm, are, notwithstanding, deemed fit subjects for judicial animadversion." His rhetoric was rather agreeably florid when he declared the law establishing "jail liberties" to be a concession for humane purposes made by the inflexible spirit which authorized imprisonment for debt. He strongly intimated his sympathy to be with "the exertions of men of intelligence, reflection, and philanthropy to mitigate its rigor; of men who viewed it as a practice fundamentally wrong, a practice which forces their fellow-creatures from society, from their friends, and their agonized families into the dreary walls of a prison; which compels them to leave all those fascinating endearments to become an inmate with vermin;" and all this, not for crime or frauds, "but for the misfortune of being poor, of being unable to satisfy the all-digesting stomach of some ravenous creditor." The practice was one "confounding virtue and vice, and destroying the distinction between guilt and innocence which should unceasingly be cherished in every well-regulated government." Democrats rejoiced over this passage when Van Buren was a candidate for the presidency. Richard M. Johnson, then his associate upon the Democratic ticket, had successfully led an agitation for the abolition of such imprisonment upon judgments rendered in the federal courts.

Van Buren's professional life terminated with his election as governor in 1828. In 1830, while secretary of state at Washington, he is said to have

appeared before the federal supreme court in the
great litigation between Astor and the Sailors' Snug
Harbor, in which he had been counsel below; but
no record is preserved of his argument there.   His
last well-known argument was before the court of
errors at Albany in Varick *v.* Jackson, a branch of
the famous Medcef Eden litigation.  This long and
highly technical battle was lighted up by the fame
and competitions of the counsel.  It arose upon the
question whether a will of Eden which gave a landed
estate to his son Joseph, but if Joseph died without
children, then to his surviving brother, Medcef Eden
the younger, created for Joseph the old lawyers'
delight of an " estate tail."    If it were an " estate
tail," then the law of 1782, which, in the general
tendency of American legislation after the Revolution, was directed against the entailing of property,
would have made the first brother, Joseph, the absolute owner, and have defeated the later claim of
Medcef.   Joseph had failed while in possession of
the property.   His creditors, accepting the opinion
of Alexander Hamilton, then the head of the bar,
insisted that he had been the absolute owner, that
the provision for his brother Medcef's accession to
the property was nugatory as an attempt to entail
the estate ; and upon this view the creditors sold
the lands, which by the rapid growth of the city
soon became of large value.   Hamilton's opinion
for years daunted the younger Medcef and his children from asserting the right which it was morally
plain his father had intended for him.   Aaron Burr,

not less Hamilton's rival at the bar than in the politics of New York, gave a contrary opinion; but after killing Hamilton in 1804 and yielding up the vice-presidency in 1805, his brilliant professional gifts were exiled from New York. On his return in 1812 from years of conspiracy, adventure, and romance, he took up the discredited Medcef Eden claim; and in the judicial test of the question he, and not Hamilton, proved to have been correct. The struggle went on in a number of suits; and when in 1823 the question was to be finally settled in the court of last resort, Burr, fearing, as he himself intimated to the court, lest the profound suspicion under which he rested might obscure and break the force of his legal arguments, or conscious that his past twenty years had dimmed his faculties, called to his aid Van Buren, then United States senator and a chief of the profession. As Van Buren and Burr attended together before the court of errors, they doubtless recalled their meetings in Van Ness's office twenty years before, when Burr, still a splendid though clouded figure in American life, hoped, by Federalist votes added to the Republican secession which he led, to reach the governorship and recover his prestige; those days in which the unknown but promising young countryman had interested a vice-president and enjoyed the latter's skillful and not always insincere flattery. The firm and orderly procedure of Van Buren's life was now well contrasted with the discredited and profligate ability of the returned wanderer. Against this

earlier but long deposed, and against this later and
regnant chief in the Republican politics of New
York, were ranged in these cases David B. Ogden,
the famous lawyer of the Federalist ranks, Samuel
A. Talcott, and Samuel Jones. In Van Buren's
long, masterly, and successful argument there was
again an edge to the zeal with which he attacked
the opinion of Kent, the Federalist chancellor, who
asked the court of errors to overrule its earlier decisions, and the chancellor's own decision as well,
and defeat the intention of the elder Medcef Eden.

Van Buren's professional career was most enviable. It lasted twenty-five years. It ended before
he was forty-six, when he was in the early ripeness
of his powers, but not until a larger and more shining career seemed surely opened before him. He
left the bar with a competence fairly earned, which
his prudence and skill made grow into an ample
fortune, without even malicious suggestion in the
scurrility of politics that he had profited out of
public offices. In money matters he was more
thrifty and cautious than most Americans in public
places. His enemies accused him of meanness and
parsimony, but apparently without other reason
than that he did not practice the careless and useless profusion and luxury which many of his countrymen in political life have thought necessary to
indulge even when their own tastes were far simpler.
In the course of professional employment he acquired an important estate near Oswego, whose
value rapidly enhanced with the rapid growth of

western New York and the development of the lake commerce from that port.

The chief interest now found in Van Buren's professional career lies in its relation to his political life. He was the only lawyer of conspicuous and practical and really great professional success who has reached the White House. In the long preparation for the bar, in the many hours of leisure at Kinderhook and Hudson and even Albany permitted by the methods of practice in vogue before there were railways or telegraphs, and when travel was costly and slow and postage a shilling or more, he gained the liberal education more difficult of access to the busier young attorney and counsel of these crowded days. Great lawyers were then fond of illustrations from polite literature ; they loved to set off their speeches with quotations from the classics, and to give their style finish and ornament not practicable to the precise, prompt methods which their successors learn in the driving routine of modern American cities. Van Buren did not, however, become a great orator at the bar. His admirer, Butler, upon returning to partnership with him in 1820, wrote indeed to an intimate friend, Jesse Hoyt (destined afterwards to bring grief and scandal upon both the partners), that if he were Van Buren he " would let politics alone," and become, as Van Buren might, the " Erskine of the State." But though his success, had he continued in the profession, would doubtless have been of the very first order, his oratory would never have reached the warm and virile splendor of Erskine, or the weighty magnificence of Webster. Van Buren's work as a lawyer brought him, however, something besides wealth and the education and refinement of books, and something which neither Erskine nor Webster gained. The profession afforded him an admirable discipline in the conduct of affairs ; and affairs, in the law as out of it, are largely decided by human nature and its varying peculiarities. The preparation of details ; the keen and far-sighted arrangement óf the best, because the most practicable, plan ; the refusal to fire off ammunition for the popular applause to be roused by its noise and flame ; the clear, steady bearing in mind of the end to be accomplished, rather than the prolonged enjoyment or systematic working out of intermediate processes beyond a utilitarian necessity, — all these elements Van Buren mastered in a signal degree, and made invaluable in legal practice. To men more superbly equipped for *tours de force*, who ignored the uses of long, attentive, varied, painstaking work, there was nothing admirable in the methods which Van Buren brought into political life out of his experience in the law. He was, to undisciplined or envious opponents, a " little magician," a trickster. The same thing appears, in every department of human activity, in the anger which failure often flings at success.

The predominance of lawyers in our politics was very early established, and has been a characteristic distinction between politics in England and politics

in America. Conspicuous as lawyers have been in
the politics of the older country, they have rarely
been figures of the first rank. They have served
in all its modern ministries, and sometimes in
other than professional stations; but, with the
unimportant exception of Perceval, not as the
chief. English opinion has not unjustly believed
its greater landed proprietors to be animated with
a strong and peculiar desire for English greatness
and renown ; nor has the belief been destroyed by
their frequent opposition to the most beneficent
popular movements. Among these proprietors and
those allied with them, even when not strictly in
their ranks, England has found her statesmen. To
this day, the speech of a lawyer in the British
House of Commons is fancied to show the narrowness of technical training, or is treated as a bid
for promotion to some of the splendid seats open
to the English bar. In America, the great landed
proprietor very early lost the direction of public
affairs. All the members of the " Virginian dy-
nasty " were, it is true, large land-owners, and in
the politics of New York there were several of
them. But land-ownership was to Jefferson, Madison, and Monroe simply a means of support while
they attended to public affairs ; it was not one of
their chief recommendations to the landed interest
throughout the country. For a time in the early
politics of New York the landed wealth of the
Schuylers, Van Rensselaers, and Livingstons was
of itself a source of strength ; but in the spread of

democratic sentiment it was found that to be a great landlord was entirely consistent with dullness, narrowness, and timid selfishness. Among the landlords there soon and inevitably decayed that sense of public obligation belonging to exalted position and leadership which sometimes brings courage, high public spirit, and even a sound and active political imagination, to those who preside over bodies of tenants. The laws were changed which facilitated family accumulations of land. Since these early years of the century a great land-owner has been in politics little more than any other rich man. Both have had advantages in that as in any other field of activity. Certain easy graces not uncommon to inherited wealth have often been popular, — not, however, for the wealth, but for themselves. Where these graces have existed in America without such wealth, they have been none the less popular; but in England a lifetime of vast public service and the finest personal attainments have failed to overcome the distrust of a landless man as a sort of adventurer.

When Van Buren's career began, the men who were making money in trade or manufactures were generally too busy for the anxious and busy cares of public life; the tradesmen and manufacturers who had already made money were past the time of life when men can vigorously and skillfully turn to a new and strange calling. There was no leisure class except land-owners or retired men of business. Lawyers, far more than those of any other calling, became public men, and naturally enough. Their experience of life and their knowledge of men were large. The popular interest in their art of advocacy; their travels from county seat to county seat; their speeches to juries in towns where no other secular public speaking was to be heard; the varieties of human life which lawyers came to know, — varieties far greater where the same men acted as attorneys and advocates than in England where they acted in only one of these fields, — these and the like, combined with the equipment for the forms of political and governmental work which was naturally gained in legal practice and the systematic study of law, gave to distinguished lawyers in America their large place in its political life. For this place the liberality of their lives helped, besides, to fit them. They had ceased to be disqualified for it by their former close alliance, as in England, with the landed aristocracy; and they had not yet begun to suffer a disqualification, frequently unjust, for their close relations with corporate interests, between which and the public there often arises an antagonism of interests. De Tocqueville, after his visit in 1832, said that lawyers formed in America its highest political class and the most cultivated circle of society; that the American aristocracy was not composed of the rich, but that it occupied the judicial bench and the bar. And the descriptions of the liberal and acute though theoretical Frenchman are generally trustworthy, however often his striking generalizations are at fault. Such, then, was the intimacy of relations between the professions of law and politics when Van Buren shone in both. And when, in his early prime, he gave up the law, neither forensic habits nor those of the attorney were yet too strongly set to permit the easy and complete diversion of his powers to the more generous and exalted activity of public life.

It is simpler thus separately to treat Van Buren's life as a lawyer, because in a just view of the man it must be subordinate to his life as a politician. It is to be remembered, however, that in his earlier years his progress in politics closely attended in time, and in much more than time, his professional progress. When, at thirty, he sat as an appellate judge in the court of errors, he was already powerful in politics; when, at thirty-two, he was attorney-general, he was the leader of his party in the state senate; when, at forty-five, he had perhaps the most lucrative professional practice in New York, he was the leader of his party in the United States Senate. But it will be easier to follow his political career without interruption from his work as a lawyer, honorable and distinguished as it was, and much of his political ability as he owed to its fine discipline.

Van Buren's domestic life was broken up by the death of his wife at Albany, in February, 1819, leaving him four sons. To her memory Van Buren remained scrupulously loyal until his own death forty-three years afterwards. We may safely believe political enemies when, after saying of him many dastardly things, they admitted that he had been an affectionate husband. Nor were accusations ever made against the uprightness and purity of his private life

# CHAPTER III

THE politics of New York State were never more
bitter, never more personal, than when Van Buren
entered the field in 1803. The Federalists were
sheltered by the unique and noble prestige of
Washington's name; and were conscious that in
wealth, education, refinement, they far excelled the
Republicans. They were contemptuously suspi-
cious of the unlettered ignorance, the intense and
exuberant vanity, of the masses of American men.
It was by that contempt and suspicion that they
invited the defeat which, protected though they
were by the property qualifications required of
voters in New York, they met in 1800 at the hands
of a people in whom the instincts of democracy
were strong and unsubmissive. This was in our
history the one complete and final defeat of a great
national party while in power. The Federalists
themselves made it final, — by their silly and unworthy anger at a political reverse; by their profoundly immoral efforts to thwart the popular will
and make Burr president; by their fatal and
ingrained disbelief in common men, who, they

thought, foolishly and impiously refused to accept
wisdom and guidance from the possessors of learning and great estates; and finally by their unpatriotic opposition to Jefferson and Madison in the
assertion of American rights on the seas during
the Napoleonic wars. All these drove the party,
in spite of its large services in the past and its
eminent capacity for service in the future, forever
from the confidence of the American people. The
Federalists maintained, it is true, a party organization in New York until after the second war with
England; but their efforts were rather directed to
the division and embarrassment of their adversaries
than to victories of their own strength or upon
their own policy. They carried the lower house
of the legislature in 1809, 1812, and 1813. There
were among them men of the first rank, who retained a strong hold on popular respect, among
whom John Jay and Rufus King were deservedly
shining figures. But never after 1799 did the
Federalists elect in New York a governor, or control both legislative houses, or secure any solid
power, except by coalition with one branch or another of the Republicans.

Van Buren's fondness for politics was soon developed. His father was firmly attached to the
Jeffersonians or Republicans, — a rather discredited minority among the Federalists of Columbia
county and the estates of the Hudson River aristocracy. Inheriting his political preferences, Van
Buren, with a great body of other young Ameri-

cans, caught the half-doctrinaire enthusiasm which
Jefferson then inspired, an enthusiasm which in
Van Buren was to be so enduring a force, and to
which sixty years later he was still as loyal as he
had been in the hot disputes on the sanded floors
of the village store or tavern.   During these boyish
years he wrote and spoke for his party ; and before
he was eighteen he was formally appointed a delegate to a Republican convention for Columbia and
Rensselaer counties.

Van Buren returned from New York to Columbia county late in 1803, just twenty-one years old.
At once he became active in politics.   The Republican party, though not strong in his county, was
dominant in the State; and the game of politics
was played between its different factions, the Federalists aiding one or the other as they saw their
advantage.   The Republicans were Clintonians,
Livingstonians, or Burrites.   George Clinton, in
whose career lay the great origin of party politics
of New York, was the Republican leader.   The
son of an Irish immigrant, he had, without the aid
of wealth or influential connections, made himself
the most popular man in the State.   He was the
first governor after colonial days were over, and
was repeatedly reëlected.   It was his opposition
which most seriously endangered New York's adoption of the Federal Constitution.   But in spite of
the wide enthusiasm which the completed Union
promptly aroused, this opposition did not prevent
his reëlection in 1789 and 1792.   The majorities

were small, however, it being even doubtful whether
in the latter year the majority were fairly given
him.    In 1795 he declined to be a candidate, and
Robert R. Livingston, the Republican in his place,
was defeated.    In 1801 Clinton was again elected.
Later he was vice-president in Jefferson's second
term and Madison's first term ; and his aspiration
to the presidency in 1808 was by no means unreasonable.    He was a strong party leader and a
sincerely patriotic man.    The Livingston family
interest in New York was very great.    The chancellor, Robert R. Livingston, who nowadays is
popularly associated with the ceremony of Washington's inauguration, had been secretary for foreign affairs under the Articles of Confederation,
and had left the Federalists in 1790.    After his
sixty years had under the law disqualified him for
judicial office, he became Jefferson's minister to
France and negotiated with Bonaparte the Louisiana treaty.    Brockholst Livingston was a judge
of the Supreme Court of New York in 1801.    In
1807 Jefferson promoted him to the federal Supreme Court.    Edward Livingston, younger than
his brother, the chancellor, by seventeen years,
was long after to be one of the finest characters in
our politics.    Early in Washington's administration
he had become a strong pro-French Republican,
and had opposed Jay's treaty with Great Britain ;
though forty years later, when Jackson brought
him from Louisiana to be secretary of state, he
was sometimes reminded of his still earlier Federal-

ism. Morgan Lewis, judge of the Supreme Court and afterwards chief justice, and still later governor, was a brother-in-law of the chancellor. Smith Thompson, also a judge and chief justice, and later secretary of the navy under Monroe and a judge of the federal Supreme Court, and Van Buren's competitor for governor in 1828, was a connection of the family. There were sneers at the Livingston conversion to Democracy as there always are at political conversions. But whether or not Chancellor Livingston's Democracy came from jealousy of Hamilton in 1790, it is at least certain that he and his family connections rendered political services of the first importance during a half century. The drafting of Jackson's nullification proclamation in 1833 by Edward Livingston was one of the noblest and most signal services which Americans have had the fortune to render to their country.

The best offices were largely held by the Clinton and Livingston families and their connections, an arrangement very aristocratic indeed, but which did not then seem inconsistent with efficient and decorous performance of the public business. Burr naturally gathered around him those restless, speculative men who are as immoral in their aspirations as in their conduct, and whose adherence has disgraced and weakened almost every democratic movement known to history. Burr had been attorney-general; he had refused a seat in the Supreme Court; he had been United States senator; and now in the second office of the nation he presided with distinguished grace over the Federal Senate. His hands were not yet red with Hamilton's blood when Van Buren met him at New York in 1803; but Democratic faces were averted from the man who, loaded with its honors and enjoying its confidence, had intrigued with its enemies to cheat his exultant party out of their choice for president. In tribute to the Republicans of New York, George Clinton had already been selected in his place to be the next vice-president. While Van Buren was near the close of his law studies at New York, Burr was preparing to restore his fortunes by a popular election, for which he had some Republican support, and to which the fatuity of the defeated party, again rejecting Hamilton's advice, added a considerable Federalist support. William P. Van Ness, as "Aristides," one of the classical names under which our ancestors were fond of addressing the public, had in the Burr interest written a bitter attack on the Clintons and Livingstons, accusing them, and with reason, of dividing the offices between themselves.

Van Buren was easily proof against the allurements of Burr, and even the natural influence of so distinguished a man as Van Ness, with whom he had been studying a year. Sylvester, his first preceptor, was a Federalist. So was Van Alen, his half-brother, soon to be his partner, who in May, 1806, was elected to Congress. But Van Buren was firm and resolute in party allegiance.

In the election for governor in April, 1804, Burr was badly beaten by Morgan Lewis, the Clinton-Livingston candidate, whom Van Buren warmly supported, and Burr's political career was closed. The successful majority of the Republicans was soon resolved into the Clintonians, led by Clinton and Judge Ambrose Spencer, and the Livingstonians, led by Governor Lewis. The active participation of judges in the bitter politics of the time illustrates the universal intensity of political feeling, and goes very far to justify Jefferson's and Van Buren's distrust of judicial opinions on political questions. Brockholst Livingston, Smith Thompson, Ambrose Spencer, Daniel D. Tompkins, — all judges of the State Supreme Court, — did not cease when they donned the ermine to be party politicians; neither did the chancellors Robert R. Livingston and Lansing. Even Kent, it is pretty obvious, was a man of far stronger and more openly partisan feelings than we should to-day think fitting so great a judicial station as he held. The quarrels over offices were strenuous and increasing from the very top to the bottom of the community.

The Federalists in 1807 generally joined the Lewisites, or "Quids." Governor Lewis, finding that the jealousy of the Livingston interests would defeat his renomination by the usual caucus of Republican members of the legislature, became the candidate of a public meeting at New York, and of a minority caucus, and asked help from the

Federalists. Such an alliance always seemed monstrous only to the Republican faction that felt strong enough without it. The regular legislative caucus, controlled by the Clintonians, nominated Daniel D. Tompkins, then a judge of the Supreme Court, and for years after the Republican " war-horse." Van Buren adhered to the purer, older, and less patrician Democracy of the Clintonians. Tompkins was elected, with a Clintonian legislature ; and the result secured Van Buren's first appointment to public office. A Clintonian council of appointment was chosen. The council, a complex monument of the distrust of executive power with which George III. had filled his revolted subjects, was composed of five members, being the governor and one member from each of the four senatorial districts, who were chosen by the Assembly from among the six senators of the district. The four senatorial members of the council were always, therefore, of the political faith of the Assembly, except in cases where all the senators from a district belonged to the minority party in the Assembly. To this council belonged nearly every appointment in the State, even of local officers. Prior to 1801 the governor appointed, with the advice and consent of the council. After the constitutional amendment of that year, either member of the council could nominate, the appointment being made by the majority. Van Buren became surrogate of Columbia county on February 20, 1808. There was no prescribed term of office, the commission really running until the opposition party secured the council of appointment. Van Buren held the office about five years and until his removal on March 19, 1813, when his adversaries had secured control of the council.

At this time the system of removing the lesser as well as the greater officers of government for political reasons was well established in New York. It is impossible to realize the nature of Van Buren's political education without understanding this old system of proscription, whose influence upon American public life has been so prodigious. The strife over the Federal Constitution had been fierce. Its friends, after their victory, sought, neither unjustly nor unnaturally, to punish Governor Clinton for his opposition. Although Washington wished to stand neutral between parties, he still believed it politically suicidal to appoint officers not in sympathy with his administration.[1] Hamilton undoubtedly determined the New York appointments when the new government was launched, and they were made from the political enemies of Governor Clinton, — a course provoking an animosity which not improbably appeared

[1] " I shall not, whilst I have the honor to administer the government, bring a man into any office of consequence, knowingly, whose political tenets are adverse to the measures which the general government are pursuing ; for this, in my opinion, would be a sort of political suicide." —Washington to Pickering, secretary of war, September 27, 1795. Vol. 11 of Sparks's edition of *Washington's Writings*, 74.

in the more numerous state appointments controlled by Clinton and the Republican council.   After the excesses of the French Revolution the Republicans were denounced as Jacobins and radicals, danger-ous in politics and corrupt in morals.   The family feuds aided and exaggerated the divisions in this small community of freehold voters.   Appointments were made in the federal and state services for political reasons and for family reasons, precisely as they had long been made in England.   Especially along the rich river counties from New York to the upper Hudson were so distributed the lucrative offices, which were eagerly sought for their profit as well as for their honor.

The contests were at first for places naturally vacated by death or resignation ; the idea of the property right of an incumbent actually in office lingered until after the last century was out.   It is not clear when the first removals of subordinate officers took place for political reasons.   Some were made by the Federalists during Governor Jay's administration ; but the first extensive re-movals seem to have occurred after the elections of 1801.   For this there were two immediate causes. In that year the exclusive nominating power of the governor was taken from him.   Each of the other four members of the council of appointment could now nominate as well as confirm.   Appointments and removals were made, therefore, from that year until the new Constitution of 1821, by one of the worst of appointing bodies, a commission of several men whose consultations were secret and whose responsibility was divided. Systematic abuse of the power of appointment became inevitable. There was, besides, a second reason in the anger against Federalists, which they had gone far to provoke, and against their long and by no means gentle domination. This anger induced the Republicans to seek out every method of punishment. But for this, the abuse might have been long deferred. Nor is it unlikely that the refusal of Jefferson, inaugurated in March of that year, to make a "clean sweep" of his enemies, turned the longing eyes of embittered Republicans in New York more eagerly to the fat state offices enjoyed by their insolent adversaries of the past twelve years.

The Clintons and Livingstons had led the Republicans to a victory at the state election in April, 1801. Later in that year George Clinton, now again governor, called together the new council with the nominating power vested in every one of its five members. This council acted under distinguished auspices, and it deserves to be long remembered. Governor Clinton presided, and his famous nephew, De Witt Clinton, was below him in the board. The latter represented the Clintonian Republicans.[1] Ambrose Spencer, a man of great parts and destined to a notable career, repre-

[1] I use the political name then in vogue. The greater part of the Republicans have, since the rearrangement of parties in John Quincy Adams's time, or rather since Jackson's time, been known as Democrats.

sented the Livingstons, of whom he was a family connection. Roseboom, the other Republican, was easily led by his two abler party associates. The fifth member did not count, for he was a Federalist. Two of the three really distinguished men of this council, De Witt Clinton and Ambrose Spencer, it is not unjust to say, first openly and responsibly established in New York the "spoils system" by removals, for political reasons, of officers not political. The term of office of the four senatorial members of this council had commenced while the illustrious Federalist John Jay was governor; but they rejected his nominations until he was tired of making them, and refused to call them together. When Clinton took the governor's seat, he promptly summoned the board, and in August, 1801, the work began. De Witt Clinton publicly formulated the doctrine, but it did not yet reach its extreme form. He said that the principal executive offices in the State ought to be filled by the friends of the administration, and the more unimportant offices ought to be proportionately distributed between the two parties. The council rapidly divided the chief appointments among the Clintons and Livingstons and their personal supporters. Officers were selected whom Jay had refused to appoint. Edward Livingston, the chancellor's brother, was given the mayoralty of New York, a very profitable as well as important station; Thomas Tillotson, a brother-in-law of Chancellor Livingston, was made secretary of state, in

place of Daniel Hale, removed; John V. Henry, a
distinguished Federalist lawyer, was removed from
the comptrollership; the district attorney, the clerk
and the recorder of New York were removed;
William Coleman, the founder of the "Evening
Post," and a strong adherent of Hamilton, was
turned out of the clerkship of the Circuit Court.
And so the work went on through minor offices.
New commissions were required by the Constitution to be issued to the puisne judges of the county
courts and to justices of the peace throughout the
State once in three years. Instead of renewing
the commissions and preserving continuity in the
administration of justice, the council struck out
the names of Federalists and inserted those of Republicans. The proceedings of this council of 1801
have profoundly affected the politics of New York
to this day. Few political bodies in America have
exercised as serious and lasting an influence upon
the political habits of the nation. The tradition
that Van Buren and the Albany Regency began
political proscription is untrue. The system of
removals was thus established several years before
Van Buren held his first office. Its founders, De
Witt Clinton and Ambrose Spencer, were long his
political enemies. Governor Clinton, whose honorable record it was that during the eighteen years
of his governorship he had never consented to a
political removal, entered his protest — not a very
hearty one, it is to be feared — in the journal of
the council; but in vain. In the next year the two

chief offenders were promoted, — De Witt Clinton to be United States senator in the place of General Armstrong, a brother-in-law of Chancellor Livingston, and Ambrose Spencer to be attorney-general; and two years later Spencer became a judge of the Supreme Court.

After the removals there began a disintegration of the party hitherto successfully led by Burr, the Clintons, and the Livingstons. Colonel Swartwout, Burr's friend, was called by De Witt Clinton a liar, scoundrel and villain; although, after receiving two bullets from Clinton's pistol in a duel, he was assured by the latter, with the courtesy of our grandfathers, that there was no personal animosity. Burr's friends had of course to be removed. But in 1805, after the Clintons and the Livingstons had united in the election of Lewis as governor over Burr, they too quarreled, — and naturally enough, for the offices would not go around. So, after the Clintonians on the meeting of the legislature early in 1806 had captured the council, they turned upon their recent allies. Maturin Livingston was removed from the New York recordership, and Tillotson from his place as secretary of state. The work was now done most thoroughly. Sheriffs, clerks, surrogates, county judges, justices of the peace, had to go. But at the corporation election in New York in the same year, the Livingstonians and Federalists, with a majority of the common council, in their fashion righted the wrong, and, with a vigor not excelled by their successors a half century later, removed at once all the subordinate municipal officers subject to their control who were Clintonians. In 1807 the Livingstonian Republicans, or, as they were now called from the governor, the Lewisites, with the Federalists and Burrites, secured control of the state council; and proceeded promptly to the work of removals, defending it as a legitimate return for the proscriptive course of their predecessors. In 1808 the Clintonians returned to the council, and, through its now familiar labors, to the offices from which the Lewisites were in their turn driven. In 1810 the Federalists controlled the Assembly which chose the council; and they enjoyed a " clean sweep " as keenly as had the contending Republican factions. But the election of this year, the political record tells us, taught a lesson which politicians have ever since refused to learn, perhaps because it has not always been taught. The removal of the Republicans from office " had the natural tendency to call out all their forces." The Clintonians in 1811, therefore, were enabled by the people to reverse the Federalist proscription of 1810. The Federalists, again in power in 1813, again followed the uniform usage then twelve years old. Political removals had become part of the unwritten law.

At this time Van Buren suffered the loss of his office as surrogate, but doubtless without any sense of private or public wrong. It was the customary fate of war. In 1812 he was nominated for state senator from the middle district, composed of

Columbia, Dutchess, Orange, Ulster, Delaware, Chenango, Greene, and Sullivan counties, as the candidate of the Clintonian Republicans against Edward P. Livingston, the candidate of the Lewisites or Livingstonians and Burrites as well as the Federalists. Livingston was the sitting member, and a Republican of powerful family and political connections. Van Buren, not yet thirty, defeated him by a majority of less than two hundred out of twenty thousand votes. In November, 1812, he took his seat at Albany, and easily and within a few months reached a conspicuous and powerful place in state politics.

These details of the establishment of the " spoils system " in New York politics seem necessary to be told, that Van Buren's own participation in the wrong may be fairly judged. It is a common historical vice to judge the conduct of men of earlier times by standards which they did not know. Van Buren found thoroughly and universally established at Albany, when he entered its life, the rule that, upon a change in the executive, there should be a change in the offices, without reference to their political functions. He had in his own person experienced its operation both to his advantage and to his disadvantage. Federalists and Republicans were alike committed to the rule. The most distinguished and the most useful men in active public life, whatever their earlier opinion might have been, had acquiesced and joined in the practice. Nor was the practice changed or extended after Van

Buren came into state politics. It continued as it had thus begun, until he became a national figure. Success in it required an ability and skill of which he was an easy master ; nor does he seem to have shrunk from it. But he was neither more nor less reprehensible than the universal public sense about him. For it must be remembered that the " spoils system " was not then offensive to the more enlightened citizens of New York. The system was no excess of democracy or universal suffrage. It had arisen amidst a suffrage for governor and senators limited to those who held in freehold land worth at least £100, and for assemblymen limited to those who held in freehold land worth £20, or paid a yearly rent of forty shillings, and who were rated and actually paid taxes. It was practiced by men of aristocratic habits chosen by the well-to-do classes. It grew in the disputes of great family interests, and in the bitterness of popular elements met in a new country, still strange or even foreign to one another, and permitted by their release from the dangers of war and the fear of British oppression to indulge their mutual dislikes.

The frequent " rotation " in office which was soon to be pronounced a safeguard of republican institutions, and which Jackson in December, 1829, told Congress was a " leading principle in the Republicans' creed," was by no means an unnatural step towards an improvement of the civil service of the State. Reformers of our day lay great stress upon the fundamental rule of democratic government, that a public office is simply a trust for the people; and they justly find the chief argument against the abuses of patronage in the notorious use of office for the benefit of small portions of the people, to the detriment of the rest. In England, however, for centuries (and to some extent the idea survives there in our own time), there was in an office a quality of property having about it the same kind of sacred immunity which belongs to real or personal estate. There were reversions to offices after the deaths of their occupants, like vested remainders in lands. It was offensive to the ordinary sense of decency and justice that the right of a public officer to appropriate so much of the public revenue should be attacked. It did not offend the public conscience that great perquisites should belong to officers performing work of the most trifling value or none at all. The same practices and traditions, weakened by distance from England and by the simpler life and smaller wealth of the colonists, came to our forefathers. They existed when the democratic movement, stayed during the necessities of war and civil reconstruction, returned at the end of the last century and became all-powerful in 1801. To break this idea of property and right in office, to make it clear that every office was a mere means of service of the people at the wish of the people, there seemed, to very patriotic and generally very wise men, no simpler way than that the people by their elections should take away and distribute offices in utter disregard of the

interests of those who held them. The odious result to which this afterwards led, of making offices
the mere property of influential politicians, was but
imperfectly foreseen. Nor did that result, inevitable as it was, follow for many years. There seems
no reason to believe that the incessant and extensive changes in office which began in 1801, seriously lowered the standard of actual public service
until years after Van Buren was a powerful and
conspicuous politician. Political parties were pretty
generally in the hands of honest men. The prosti-
tuted and venal disposition of "spoils," though a
natural sequence, was to come long after. Rotation
was practiced, or its fruits were accepted and enjoyed with satisfaction, by public men of the State
who were really statesmen, who had high standards
of public honor and duty, whose minds were directed
towards great and exalted public ends. If it seemed
right to De Witt Clinton, Edward Livingston,
Robert R. Livingston, and Ambrose Spencer, surely
lesser gods of our early political Olympus could not
be expected to refuse its advantages or murmur at
its hardships. Nor was the change distasteful to
the people, if we may judge by their political behavior. No faction or party seems to have been
punished by public sentiment for the practice except in conspicuous cases like those of De Witt
Clinton and Van Buren, where sometimes blows
aimed at single men roused popular and often an
undeserved sympathy. The idea that a public officer should easily and naturally go from the ranks

of the people without special equipment, and as easily return to those ranks, has been popularly agreeable wherever the story of Cincinnatus has been told. Early in this century the closeness of offices to ordinary life, and the absence of an organized bureaucracy controlling or patronizing the masses of men, seemed proper elements of the great democratic reform. There had not yet arisen the very modern and utilitarian and the vastly better conception of a service, the responsible directors of whose policy should be changed with popular sentiment, but whose subordinates should be treated by the public as any other employer would treat them, upon simple and unsentimental rules of business. Another practical consideration makes more intelligible the failure of our ancestors to perceive the dangers of the great change they permitted. Offices were not nearly as technical, their duties not nearly as uniform, as they have grown to be in the more complex procedures of our enormously richer and more populous time. Every officer did a multitude of things. Intelligent and active men in unofficial life shifted with amazing readiness and success from one calling to another. A general became a judge, or a judge became a general, — as, indeed, we have seen in later days. A merchant could learn to survey ; a farmer could keep or could learn to keep fair records.

In the art of making of the lesser offices ammunition with which to fight great battles over great questions, Van Buren became a master. His im-

perturbable temper and patience, his keen reading
of the motives and uses of men, gave him so firm
a hold upon politicians that it has been common to
forget the undoubted hold he long had upon the
people. In April, 1816, he was reëlected senator
for a second term of four years. His eight years
of service in the senate expired in 1820.

In November, 1812, the first session of the new
legislature was held to choose presidential electors.
Not until sixteen years later were electors chosen
directly by the people. Van Buren voted for the
candidates favorable to De Witt Clinton for president as against Madison. In the successful struggle of the Clintonians for these electors, he is said
in this, his first session, to have shown the address
and activity which at once made him a Republican
leader. For his vote against Madison Van Buren's
friends afterwards made many apologies; his adversaries declared it unpardonable treachery to
one of the revered Democratic fathers. But the
young politician was not open to much condemnation. De Witt Clinton, though he had but just
reached the beginning of middle life, was a very
able and even an illustrious man. He had been
unanimously nominated in an orderly way by a
caucus of the Republican members of the legislature of 1811 and 1812 of which Van Buren was
not a member. He had accepted the nomination
and had declined to withdraw from it. There was
a strong Republican opposition to the declaration
of war at that time, because preparation for it had

not been adequately made. Most of the Republican members of Congress from New York had voted against the declaration. The virtues and abilities of Madison were not those likely to make a successful war, as the event amply proved. There was natural and deserved discontent with the treatment by Jefferson's administration, in which Madison had charge of foreign relations, and by Madison's own administration, of the difficulties caused by the British Orders in Council, the Berlin and Milan decrees of Napoleon, and the unprincipled depredations of both the great belligerents. Van Buren is said by Butler, then an inmate of his family, to have been an open and decided advocate of the embargo, and of all the strong measures proposed against Great Britain and of the war itself. Nor was this very inconsistent with his vote for Clinton. He had a stronger sense of allegiance to his party in the State than to his party at Washington; and the Republican party of New York had regularly declared for Clinton. For once at least Van Buren found himself voting with the great body of the Federalists, men who had not, like John Quincy Adams, become reconciled to the strong and obvious, though sometimes ineffective, patriotism of Jefferson's and Madison's administrations. But whatever had been the motives which induced Van Buren to support Clinton, they soon ceased to operate. Within a few months after this the political relations between the two men were dissolved; and they were

politically hostile, until Clinton's death fourteen
years afterwards called from Van Buren a pathetic
tribute.

Although the youngest man but one, it was said,
until that time elected to the state senate, Van
Buren was in January, 1814, chosen to prepare
the answer then customarily made to the speech of
the governor. In it he defended the war, which
had been bitterly assailed in the address to the
governor made by the Federalist Assembly. Political divisions even when carried to excess were,
he said, inseparable from the blessings of freedom;
but such divisions were unfit in their resistance of
a foreign enemy. The great body of the New York
Republicans, with Governor Tompkins at their
head, now gave Madison vigorous support; although their defection in 1812 had probably made
possible the Federalist success at the election for
the Assembly in 1813, which embarrassed the national administration. Van Buren warmly supported Tompkins for his reëlection in April, 1813,
and prepared for the legislative caucus a highly
declamatory, but clear and forcible, address to Republican electors in his behalf. The provocations
to war were strongly set out. It was declared that
"war and war alone was our only refuge from
national degradation;" the "two great and crying
grievances" were "the destruction of our commerce, and the impressment of our seamen;" for
Americans did not anticipate the surrender at
Ghent two years later to the second wrong. While

American sailors' "deeds of heroic valor make old Ocean smile at the humiliations of her ancient tyrant," the address urged Americans to mark the man, meaning the trading Federalist, who believed "in commuting our sailors' rights for the safety of our merchants' goods." In the sophomoric and solemn rhetoric of which Americans, and Englishmen too, were then fond, it pointed out that the favor of citizens was not sought "by the seductive wiles and artful blandishments of the corrupt minions of aristocracy," who of course were Federalists, but that citizens were now addressed "in the language which alone becomes freemen to use, — the language to which alone it becomes freemen to listen."

In the legislative sessions of 1813 and 1814 Van Buren gave a practical and skillful support to administration measures. But many of them were balked by the Federalists, until in the election of April, 1814, the rising patriotism of the country, undaunted by the unskillful and unfortunate conduct of the war, pronounced definitely in favor of a strong war policy. The Republicans recovered control of the Assembly; and there were already a Republican governor and Senate. An extra session was summoned in September, 1814, through which exceedingly vigorous measures were carried against Federalist opposition. Van Buren now definitely led. Appropriations were made from the state treasury for the pay of militia in the national service. The State undertook to enlist twelve thousand men for two years, a corps of sea fencibles consisting of twenty companies, and two regiments of colored men; slaves enlisting with the consent of their masters to be freed. Van Buren's "classification act" Benton afterwards declared to be the "most energetic war measure ever adopted in this country." By it the whole military population was divided into 12,000 classes, each class to furnish one able-bodied man, making the force of 12,000 to be raised. If no one volunteered from a class, then any member of the class was authorized to procure a soldier by a bounty, the amount of which should be paid by the members of the class according to their ability, to be determined by assessors. If no soldier from the class were thus procured, then a soldier was to be peremptorily drafted from each class. Van Buren was proud enough of this act to file the draft of it in his own handwriting with the clerk of the Senate, indorsed by himself: "The original Classification Bill, to be preserved as a memento of the patriotism, intelligence, and firmness of the legislature of 1814–15. M. V. B. Albany, Feb. 15, 1815."

Cheered, after many disasters, by the victory at Plattsburg and the creditable battle of Lundy's Lane, the Senate, in Van Buren's words, congratulated Governor Tompkins upon "the brilliant achievements of our army and navy during the present campaign, which have pierced the gloom that for a time obscured our political horizon." The end of the war left in high favor the Republicans who had supported it. The people were good-humoredly willing to forget its many inefficiencies, to recall complacently its few glories, and to find little fault with a treaty which, if it established no disputed right, at least brought peace without surrender and without dishonor. Jackson's fine victory at New Orleans after the treaty was signed, though it came too late to strengthen John Quincy Adams's dauntless front in the peace conference, was quickly seized by the people as the summing up of American and British prowess. The Republicans now had a hero in the West, as well as a philosopher at Monticello. Van Buren drafted the resolution giving the thanks of New York "to Major-General Jackson, his gallant officers and troops, for their wonderful and heroic victory."

In the method then well established the Republicans celebrated their political success in 1814. Among the removals, Abraham Van Vechten lost the post of attorney-general, which on February 17, 1815, was conferred upon Van Buren for his brilliant and successful leadership in the Senate. He remained, however, a senator of the State. At thirty-two, therefore, he was, next to the governor, the leader of the Tompkins Republicans, now so completely dominant; he held two political offices of dignity and importance; and he was conducting besides an active law practice.

De Witt Clinton, after his defeat for the presidency, suffered other disasters. It was in January,

1813, that he and Van Buren broke their political relations; and the Republicans very largely fell off from him. The reasons for this do not clearly appear; but were probably Clinton's continuance of hostility to the national administration, which seemed unpatriotic to the Republicans, and some of the mysterious matters of patronage in which Clinton had been long and highly proscriptive. In 1815 the latter was removed from the mayoralty of New York by the influence of Governor Tompkins in the council. He had been both mayor and senator for several years prior to 1812. He was mayor and lieutenant-governor when he was a candidate for the presidency.

In 1816 the Republicans in the Assembly, then closely divided between them and the Federalists (who seemed to be favored by the apportionment), sought one of those immoral advantages whose wrong in times of high party feeling seems invisible to men otherwise honorable. In the town of Pennington a Federalist, Henry Fellows, had been fairly elected to the Assembly by a majority of 30; but 49 of his ballots were returned as reading "Hen. Fellows;" and his Republican competitor, Peter Allen, got the certificate of appointment. The Republicans, acting, it seems, in open conference with Van Buren, insisted not only upon organizing the house, which was perhaps right, but upon what was wrong and far more important. They elected the council of appointment before Fellows was seated, as he afterwards was by an

almost unanimous vote. The "Peter Allen legislature" is said to have become a term of reproach.
But, as with electoral abuses in later days, the
Federalists were not as much aided as they ought
to have been by this sharp practice of their rivals;
the people perhaps thought that, as they were in
the minority everywhere but in the Assembly, they
ought not to have been permitted, by a capture of
the council, to remove the Republicans in office.

At any rate the election in April, 1816, while
the "Peter Allen legislature" was still in office,
went heavily in favor of the Republicans, Van
Buren receiving his second election to the Senate.
On March 4, 1816, he was chosen by the legislature a regent of the University of the State of New
York, an office which he held until 1829. The
University was then, as now, almost a myth, being
supposed to be the associated colleges and aca-
demies of the State. But the regents have had a
varying charge of educational matters.

In 1817 the agitation, so superbly and with such
foresight conducted by De Witt Clinton, resulted
in the passage of the law under which the construction of the Erie Canal began. Van Buren's
enmity to Clinton did not cause him to oppose
the measure, of which Hammond says he was an
"early friend." With a few others he left his
party ranks to vote with Clinton's friends; and
this necessary accession from the "Bucktails" is
said by the same fair historian to have been produced by Van Buren's "efficient and able efforts."

In his speech favoring it he declared that his vote for the law would be " the most important vote he ever gave in his life ; " that " the project, if executed, would raise the State to the highest possible pitch of fame and grandeur," an expression not discredited by the splendid and fruitful result of the enterprise. Clinton, after hearing the speech, forgot for a moment their political collisions, and personally thanked Van Buren.

In April, 1817, Clinton was elected governor by a practically unanimous vote. His resolute courage and the prestige of the canal policy compelled this tribute from the Republicans, in spite of his sacrilegious presidential aspiration in 1812, and his dismissal from the mayoralty of New York in 1815. Governor Tompkins, now vice-president, was Clinton's only peer in New York politics. The popular tide was too strong for the efforts of Tompkins, Van Buren, and their associates. In the eagerness to defeat Clinton, it was even suggested that Tompkins should serve both as governor and vice-president; should be at once ruler at Albany and vice-ruler at Washington. Van Buren did not, however, go with the hot-heads of the legislature in opposing a bill for an election to fill the vacancy left by the resignation, which it was at last thought necessary for Tompkins to make, of the governorship. No one dared run against Clinton ; and he triumphantly returned to political power. Under this administration of his, the party feud took definite form. Clinton's Republican adversaries were dubbed "Bucktails" from the ornaments worn on ceremonial occasions by the Tammany men who had long been Clinton's enemies. The Bucktails and their successors were the "regular" Republicans, or the Democrats as they were later called; and they kept their regularity until, long afterwards, the younger and greater Bucktail leader, when venerable and laden with honors, became the titular head of the Barnburner defection. The merits of the feud between Bucktails and Clintonians it is now difficult to find. Each accused the other of coquetting with the Federalists; and the accusation was nearly always true of one or the other of them. Politics was a highly developed and extremely interesting game, whose players, though really able and patriotic men, were apparently careless of the undignified parts they were playing. Nor are Clintonians and Bucktails alone in political history. Cabinets of the greatest nations have, in more modern times, broken on grounds as sheerly personal as those which divided Clinton and Van Buren in 1818. British and French ministries, as recent memoirs and even recent events have shown, have fallen to pieces in feuds of as little essential dignity as belonged to those of New York seventy years ago.

In 1819 the Bucktails suffered the fate of war; and Van Buren, their efficient head, was removed from the attorney-general's office. Thurlow Weed, then a country editor, grotesquely wrote at the time that "rotation in office is the most striking

and brilliant feature of excellence in our benign
form of government; and that by this doctrine,
bottomed, as it is, upon the Magna Charta of our
liberties, Van Buren's removal was not only sanctioned, but was absolutely required." The latter
still remained state senator, and soon waged a
short and decisive campaign to recover political
mastery. He now came to the aid of Governor
Tompkins, who during the war with England had
borrowed money for public use upon his personal
responsibility, and in the disbursement of several
millions of dollars for war purposes had, through
carelessness in bookkeeping or clerical detail, apparently become a debtor of the State. The comptroller, in spite of a law passed in 1819 to indem-
nify Tompkins for his patriotic services, took a
hostile attitude which threatened the latter with
pecuniary destruction. In March, 1820, Van
Buren threw himself into the contest with a skill
and generous fervor which saved the ex-governor.
Van Buren's speech of two days for the old chief
of the Bucktails, is described by Hammond, a
political historian of New York not unduly friendly
to Van Buren, to have been "ingenious, able, and
eloquent."

It was also in 1820 that Van Buren promoted
the reëlection of Rufus King, the distinguished
Federalist, to the United States Senate. His motives in doing this were long bitterly assailed; but
as the choice was intrinsically admirable, Van
Buren was probably glad to gratify a patriotic

impulse which was not very inconsistent with party
advantage. In 1819 the Republican caucus, the
last at which the Bucktails and Clintonians both
attended, was broken up amid mutual recrimina-
tions. John C. Spencer, the son of Ambrose
Spencer, and afterwards a distinguished Whig, was
the Clintonian candidate, and had the greater
number of Republican votes. In the legislature
there was no choice, Rufus King having fewer
votes than either of the Republicans. When the
legislature of 1820 met, there appeared a pamphlet
skillfully written in a tone of exalted patriotism.
This decided the election for King. Van Buren
was its author, and was said to have been aided by
William L. Marcy. Both had suffered at the
hands of Clinton. However much they may have
been so influenced in secret, they gave in public
perfectly sound and weighty reasons for returning
this old and distinguished statesman to the place
he had honored for many years. In 1813 King
had received the votes of a few Republicans, without whom he would have been defeated by a Republican competitor. The Clintonians and their
adversaries had since disputed which of them had
then been guilty of party disloyalty. But it can
hardly be doubted that King's high character and
great ability, with the revolutionary glamour about
him, made his choice seem patriotic and popular,
and therefore politically prudent.

Van Buren's pamphlet of 1820 was addressed
to the Republican members of the legislature by a

" fellow-member " who told them that he knew and
was personally known to most of them, and that
he had, " from his infancy, taken a deep interest
in the honor and prosperity of the party." This
anonymous " fellow-member " pronounced the support of King by Republicans to " be an act honorable to themselves, advantageous to the country,
and just to him." He declared that the only reluctance Republicans had to a public avowal of
their sentiments arose from a " commendable apprehension that their determination to support him
under existing circumstances might subject them
to the suspicion of having become a party to a
political bargain, to one of those sinister commu-
tations of principle for power, which they think
common with their adversaries, and against which
they have remonstrated with becoming spirit." He
showed that there were degrees even among Federalists ; that some in the war had been influenced
by " most envenomed malignity against the administration of their own government ; " that a second
and " very numerous and respectable portion " had
been those " who, inured to opposition and heated
by collision, were poorly qualified to judge dispas-
sionately of the measures of government," who
thought the war impolitic at the time, but who
were ignorantly but honestly mistaken ; but that a
third class of them had risen " superior to the prejudices and passions of those with whom they once
acted." In the last class had been Rufus King ;
at home and in the Senate he had supported the

administration; he had helped procure loans to the
State for war purposes. The address skillfully
recalled his Revolutionary services, his membership
in the convention which framed the Federal Constitution, his appointment by Washington as minister to the English court, and his continuance there
under Jefferson. He was declared to be opposed
to Clinton. The address concluded by reciting that
there had been in New York " exceptionable and
unprincipled political bargains and coalitions,"
which with darker offenses ought to be proved, to
vindicate the great body of citizens " from the
charge of participating in the profligacy of the few,
and to give rest to that perturbed spirit which now
haunts the scenes of former moral and political
debaucheries; " but added that the nature of a vote
for King precluded such suspicions.

The last statement was just. King's return was
free from other suspicion than that he probably
preferred the Van Buren to the Clinton Republicans. Van Buren, seeing that the Federalist
party was at an end, was glad both to do a public
service and to ally with his party, in the divisions
of the future, some part of the element so finely
represented by Rufus King. In private Van Buren
urged the support of King even more emphatically.
" We are committed," he wrote, " to his support.
It is both wise and honest, and we must have no
fluttering in our course. Mr. King's views towards
us are honorable and correct. . . . Let us not,
then, have any halting. I will put my head on its

propriety." Van Buren's partisanship always had
a mellow character. He practiced the golden rule
of successful politics, to foresee future benefits
rather than remember past injuries. Indeed, it is
just to say more. In sending King to the Senate
he doubtless experienced the lofty pleasure which
a politician of public spirit feels in his occasional
ability to use his power to reach a beneficent end,
which without the power he could not have reached,
— a stroke which to a petty politician would seem
dangerous, but which the greater man accomplishes
without injury to his party standing. A year or
two after King's election, when Van Buren joined
him at Washington, there were established the
most agreeable relations between them. The refinement and natural decorum of the younger man
easily fell in with the polished and courtly manner
of the old Federalist. Benton, who had then just
entered the Senate, said it was delightful to behold
the deferential regard which Van Buren paid to his
venerable colleague, a regard always returned by
King with marked kindness and respect.

In this year the era of good feeling was at its
height. Monroe was reëlected president by an
almost unanimous vote, with Tompkins again as
vice-president. The good feeling, however, was
among the people, and not among the politicians.
The Republican party was about to divide by reason of the very completeness of its supremacy.
The Federalist party was extinguished and its
members scattered. The greater number of them

in New York went with the Clintonian Republicans, with whom they afterwards formed the chief
body of the Whig party. A smaller number of
them, among whom were James A. Hamilton and
John C. Hamilton, the sons of the great founder
of the Federalist party, William A. Duer, John A.
King (the son of the reëlected senator), and many
others of wealth and high social position, ranged
themselves for a time in the Bucktail ranks under
Van Buren's leadership. In the slang of the day,
they were the "high-minded Federalists," because
they had declared that Clinton's supporters practiced a personal subserviency "disgusting to high-
minded and honorable men." With this addition,
the Bucktails became the Democratic party in New
York. In April, 1820, the gubernatorial election
was between the Clintonians supporting Clinton,
and the Bucktails supporting Tompkins, the Vice-
President. Clinton's recent and really magnificent
public service made him successful at the polls, but
his party was beaten at other points.

Rufus King's reëlection to the Senate was believed to have some relation to the Missouri question, then agitating the nation. In one of his letters urging his Republican associates to support
King, Van Buren declared that the Missouri question concealed no plot so far as King was concerned,
but that he, Van Buren, and his friends, would
"give it a true direction." King's strong opposition to the admission of Missouri as a slave State
was, however, perfectly open. If he returned to

the Senate, it was certain he would steadily vote against any extension of slavery. Van Buren knew all this, and doubtless meant that King was bargaining away none of his convictions for the senatorship. But what the "true direction" was which was to be given the Missouri question, is not clear. About the time of King's reëlection Van Buren joined in calling a public meeting at Albany to protest against extending slavery beyond the Mississippi. He was absent at the time of the meeting, and refused the use of his name upon the committee to send the anti-slavery resolutions to Washington. Nor is it clear whether his absence and refusal were significant. He certainly did not condemn the resolutions; and in January, 1820, he voted in the state Senate for an instruction to the senators and representatives in Congress " to oppose the admission, as a State in the Union, of any territory not comprised within the original boundary of the United States, without making the prohibition of slavery therein an indispensable condition of admission." This resolution undoubtedly expressed the clear convictions of the Republicans in New York, whether on Van Buren's or Clinton's side, as well as of the remaining Federalists.

Van Buren's direct interest in national politics had already begun. In 1816 he was present in Washington (then a pretty serious journey from Albany) when the Republican congressional caucus was held to nominate a president. Governor

Tompkins, after a brief canvass, retired; and Crawford, then secretary of war, became the candidate
against Monroe, and was supported by most of the
Republicans from New York. Van Buren's preference was not certainly known, though it is supposed he preferred Monroe. In 1820 he was
chosen a presidential elector in place of an absen-
tee from the electoral college, and participated in
the all but unanimous vote for Monroe. He voted
with the other New York electors for Tompkins
for the vice-presidency. In April, 1820, he wrote
to Henry Meigs, a Bucktail congressman then at
Washington, that the rascality of some of the deputy postmasters in the State was intolerable, and
cried aloud for relief; that it was impossible to
penetrate the interior of the State with friendly
papers; and that two or three prompt removals
were necessary. The postmaster-general was to be
asked " to do an act of justice and render us a partial service " by the removal of the postmasters
at Bath, Little Falls, and Oxford, and to appoint
successors whom Van Buren named. In January,
1821, Governor Clinton sent this letter to the legislature, with a message and other papers so numerous as to be carried in a green bag, which gave
the name to the message, in support of a charge
that the national administration had interfered in
the state election. But the " green-bag message "
did Van Buren little harm, for Clinton's own proscriptive rigor had been great, and it was only
two years before that Van Buren himself had been

removed from the attorney-generalship. In 1821 the political division of the New York Republicans was carried to national politics. When a speaker was to be chosen in place of Clay, Taylor of New York, the Republican candidate, was opposed by the Bucktail congressmen, because he had supported Clinton.

In February, 1821, Van Buren gained the then dignified promotion to the federal Senate. He was elected by the Bucktails against Nathan Sanford, the sitting senator, who was supported by the Clintonians and Federalists. Van Buren was now thirty-eight years old, and in the early prime of his powers. He had run the gauntlet of two popular elections; he had been easily first among the Republicans of the state Senate; he had there shown extraordinary political skill and an intelligent and public spirit; he had ably administered the chief law office of the State which was not judicial. Though not yet keenly interested in any federal question, — for his activity and thought had been sufficiently engaged in affairs of his own State, — he turned to the new field with an easy confidence, amply justified by his mastery of the problems with which he had so far grappled. He reached Washington the undoubted leader of his party in the State. The prestige of Governor Tompkins, although just reëlected vice-president, had suffered from his recent defeat for the governorship, and from his pecuniary and other difficulties; and besides, he obviously had not Van Buren's unrivaled equipment for political leadership.

Before Van Buren attended his first session in the federal capital he performed for the public most honorable service in the state constitutional convention which sat in the autumn of 1821. This body illustrated the earnest and wholesome temper in which the most powerful public men of the State, after many exhibitions of partisan, personal, and even petty animosities, could treat so serious and abiding a matter as its fundamental law. The Democrats sent Vice-President Tompkins, both the United States senators, King and Van Buren, the late senator, Sanford, and Samuel Nelson, then beginning a long and honorable career. The Clintonians and Federalists sent Chancellor Kent and Ambrose Spencer, the chief justice. Van Buren was chosen from Otsego, and not from his own county, probably because the latter was politically unfavorable to him.

This convention was one of the steps in the democratic march. It was called to broaden the suffrage, to break up the central source of patronage at Albany, and to enlarge local self-administration. The government of New York had so far been a freeholders' government, with those great virtues, and those greater and more enduring vices, which were characteristic of a government controlled exclusively by the owners of land. The painful apprehension aroused by the democratic resolution to reduce, if not altogether to destroy, the exclusive privileges of land-owners, was expressed in the convention by Chancellor Kent.

He would not " bow before the idol of universal suffrage ; " this extreme democratic principle, he said, had " been regarded with terror by the wise men of every age ; " wherever tried, it had brought " corruption, injustice, violence, and tyranny ; " if adopted, posterity would " deplore in sackcloth and ashes the delusion of the day." He wished no laws to pass without the free consent of the owners of the soil. He did not foresee English parliaments elected in 1885 and 1886 by a suffrage not very far from universal, or a royal jubilee celebrated by democratic masses, or the prudent conservatism in matters of property of the enfranchised French democracy, — he foresaw none of these when he declared that England and France could not sustain the weight of universal suffrage ; that " the radicals of England, with the force of that mighty engine, would at once sweep away the property, the laws, and the liberty of that island like a deluge." Van Buren distinguished himself in the debate. Upon this exciting and paramount topic he did not share the temper which possessed most of his party. His speech was clear, explicit, philosophical, and really statesmanlike. It so impressed even his adversaries ; and Hammond, one of them, declared that he ought for it to be ranked " among the most shining orators and able statesmen of the age."

In reading this, or indeed any of the utterances of Van Buren where the occasion required distinctness, it is difficult to find the ground of the charge

of " noncommittalism " so incessantly made against
him.   He doubtless refrained from taking sides on
questions not yet ripe for decision, however clear,
and whatever may have been his speculative opinions.   But this is the duty of every statesman ; it
has been the practice of every politician who has
promoted reform.   Van Buren now pointed out
how completely the events of the forty years past
had discredited the grave speculative fears of
Franklin, Hamilton, and Madison as to the result
of some provisions of the Federal Constitution.
With Burke he believed experience to be the only
unerring touchstone.   He conclusively showed that
property had been as safe in those American communities which had universal suffrage as in the
few which retained a property qualification ; that
venality in voting, apprehended from the change,
already existed in the grossest forms at the parliamentary elections of England.   Going to the truth
which is at the dynamic source of democratic institutions, he told the chancellor that when among
the masses of America the principles of order and
good government should yield to principles of anarchy and violence and permit attacks on private
property or an agrarian law, all constitutional provisions would be idle and unavailing, because they
would have lost all their force and influence.
With a true instinct, however, Van Buren wished
the steps to be taken gradually.   He was not yet
ready, he said, to admit to the suffrage the shifting
population of cities, held to the government by no

other ties than the mere right to vote. He was
not ready for a really universal suffrage. The
voter ought, if he did not participate in the government by paying taxes or performing militia
duty, to be a man who was a householder with
some of the elements of stability, with something
at stake in the community. Although they had
reached "the verge of universal suffrage," he
could not with his Democratic friends take the
"one step beyond ; " he would not cheapen the invaluable right by conferring it with indiscrimina-
ting hand "on every one, black or white, who
would be kind enough to condescend to accept it."
Though a Democrat he was opposed, he said, to
a "precipitate and unexpected prostration of all
qualifications ; " he looked with dread upon increasing the voters in New York city from thirteen
or fourteen thousand to twenty-five thousand, believing (curious prediction for a father of the
Democratic party !) that the increase "would render their elections rather a curse than a blessing,"
and "would drive from the polls all sober-minded
people."

The universal suffrage then postponed was wisely
adopted a few years later. Democracy marched
steadily on ; and Van Buren was willing, probably very willing, to be guided by experience. He
opposed in the convention a proposal supported
by most of his party to restrict suffrage to white
citizens, but favored a property qualification foɪ
black men, the $250 freehold ownership until then

required of white voters. He would not, he said, draw from them a revenue and yet deny them the right of suffrage. Twenty-five years later, in 1846, nearly three-fourths of the voters of the State refused equal suffrage to the blacks; and even in 1869, six years after the emancipation proclamation, a majority still refused to give them the same rights as white men.

The question of appointments to office was the chief topic in the convention. Van Buren, as chairman of the committee on this subject, made an interesting and able report. It was unanimously agreed that the use of patronage by the council of appointment had been a scandal. Only a few members voted to retain the council, even if it were to be elected by the people. He recommended that military officers, except the highest, be elected by the privates and officers of militia. Of the 6663 civil officers whose appointment and removal by the council had for twenty years kept the State in turmoil, he recommended that 3643, being notaries, commissioners, masters and examiners in chancery, and other lesser officers, should be appointed under general laws to be enacted by the legislature; the clerks of courts and district attorneys should be appointed by the common pleas courts; mayors and clerks of cities should be appointed by their common councils, except in New York, where for years afterwards the mayors were appointed; the heads of the state departments should be appointed by the legislature; and all other officers, including surrogates and justices of the peace as well as the greater judicial officers, should be appointed by the governor upon the confirmation of the Senate. Van Buren declared himself opposed, here again separating himself from many of his party associates, to the popular election of any judicial officers, even the justices of the peace. Of all this he was long after to be reminded as proof of his aristocratic contempt for democracy. His recommendations were adopted in the main ; although county clerks and sheriffs, whom he would have kept appointive, were made elective. Upon this question he was in a small minority with Chancellor Kent and Rufus King, having most of his party friends against him. Thus was broken up the enormous political power so long wielded at Albany, and the patronage distributed through the counties. The change, it was supposed, would end a great abuse. It did end the concentration of patronage at the capital ; but the partisan abuses of patronage were simply transferred to the various county seats, to exercise a different and wider, though probably a less dangerous, corruption.

The council of revision fell with hardly a friend to speak for it. It was one of those checks upon popular power of which Federalists had been fond. It consisted of the governor with the chancellor and the judges of the Supreme Court, and had a veto power upon bills passed by the legislature. As the chancellor and judges held office during good behavior until they had reached the limit of age, the council was almost a chamber of life peers. The exercise of its power had provoked great animosity. The chief judicial officers of the State, judges, and chancellors, to whom men of our day look back with a real veneration, had been drawn by it into a kind of political warfare, in which few of our higher magistrates, though popularly elected and for terms, would dare to engage. An act had been passed by the legislature in 1814 to promote privateering; but Chancellor Kent as a member of the council objected to it. Van Buren maintained with him an open and heated discussion upon the propriety of the objections, — a discussion in which the judicial character justly enough afforded no protection. Van Buren's feeling against the judges who were his political adversaries was often exhibited. He said in the convention : " I object to the council, as being composed of the judiciary, who are not directly responsible to the people. I object to it because it inevitably connects the judiciary — those who, with pure hearts and sound heads, should preside in the sanctuaries of justice — with the intrigues and collisions of party strife ; because it tends to make our judges politicians, and because such has been its practical effect." He further said that he would not join in the rather courtly observation that the council was abolished because of a personal regard for the peace of its members. He would have it expressly remembered that the council had served the ends

of faction; though he added that he should regard
the loss of Chancellor Kent from his judicial station as a public calamity. In his general position
Van Buren was clearly right. Again and again
have theorists, supposing judges to be sanctified
and illumined by their offices, placed in their hands
political power, which had been abused, or it was
feared would be abused, by men fancied to occupy
less exalted stations. Again and again has the result shown that judges are only men, with human
passions, prejudices, and ignorance ; men who, if
vested with functions not judicial, if freed from the
checks of precedents and law and public hearings
and appellate review, fall into the same abuses and
act on the same motives, political and personal,
which belong to other men. In the council of revision before 1821 and the electoral commission of
1877 were signally proved the wisdom of restrict-
ing judges to the work of deciding rights between
parties judicially brought before them.

Van Buren's far from "non-committal" talk
about the judges was not followed by any support
of the proposal to "constitutionize" them out of
office. The animosity of a majority of the members against the judges then in office was intense ;
and they were not willing to accept the life of the
council of revision as a sufficient sacrifice. Nor
was the animosity entirely unreasonable. Butler,
in one of his early letters to Jesse Hoyt, described
the austerity with which Ambrose Spencer, the
chief justice, when the young lawyer sought to

address him, told him to wait until his seniors had been heard. In the convention there were doubtless many who had been offended with a certain insolence of place which to this day characterizes the bearing of many judges of real ability; and the opportunity of making repayment was eagerly seized. Nor was it unreasonable that laymen should, from the proceedings of judges when acting upon political matters which laymen understood as well as they, make inferences about the fairness of their proceedings on the bench upon which laymen could not always safely speak. By a vote of 66 to 39, the convention refused to retain the judges then in office, — a proceeding which, with all the faults justly or even naturally found with them, was a gross violation of the fundamental rule which ought to guide civilized lands in changing their laws. For the retention of the judges was perfectly consistent with the judicial scheme adopted. Van Buren put all this most admirably before voting with the minority. He told the convention, and doubtless truly, that from the bench of judges, whose official fate was then at their mercy, he had been assailed " with hostility, political, professional, and personal, — hostility which had been the most keen, active, and unyielding ; " but that he would not indulge individual resentment in the prostration of his private and political adversary. The judicial officer, who could not be reached by impeachment or the proceeding for removal by a two-thirds vote, ought not to be disturbed. They should amend the constitution, he told the convention, upon general principles, and not descend to pull down obnoxious officers. He begged it not to ruin its character and credit by proceeding to such extremities. But the removal of the judges did not prove unpopular. Only eight members of the convention voted against the Constitution; only fifteen others did not sign it. And the freeholders of the State, while deliberately surrendering some of their exclusive privileges, adopted it by a vote of 75,422 to 41,497.

Van Buren's service in this convention was that of a firm, sensible, far-seeing man, resolute to make democratic progress, but unwilling, without further light from experience, to take extreme steps difficult to retrace. With a strong inclination towards great enlargement of the suffrage, he pointed out that a mistake in going too far could never be righted "except by the sword." The wisdom of enduring temporary difficulties, rather than to make theoretical changes greater than were necessary to obviate serious and great wrongs, was common to him with the highest and most influential type of modern law-makers. With some men of the first rank, the convention had in it very many others crudely equipped for its work; and it met in an atmosphere of personal and political asperity unfavorable to deliberations over organic law. Van Buren was politically its most powerful member. It is clear that his always conservative temper, aided by his tact and by his temperate and persuasive eloquence, held back his Democratic associates, headed by the impetuous and angered General Root, from changes far more radical than those which were made. Though eminent as a party man, he showed on this conspicuous field undoubted courage and independence and high sense of duty. Entering national politics he was fortunate therefore to be known, not only as a skillful and adroit and even managing politician, as a vigorous and clear debater, as a successful leader in popular movements, but also as a man of firm and upright patriotism, with a ripe and educated sense of the complexity of popular government, and a sober appreciation of the kind of dangers so subtly mingled with the blessings of democracy.

## CHAPTER IV

In December, 1821, Van Buren took his seat in
the United States Senate. The " era of good feeling " was then at its height. It was with perfect
sincerity that Monroe in his message of the preceding year had said : " I see much cause to rejoice in
the felicity of our situation." He had just been
reëlected president with but a single vote against
him. The country was in profound peace. The
burdens of the war with England were no longer
felt ; and its few victories were remembered with
exuberant good-nature. Two years before, Florida
had been acquired by the strong and persisting
hand of the younger Adams. Wealth and comfort
were in rapid increase. The moans and rage of the
defeated and disgraced Federalists were suppressed,
or, if now and then feebly heard, were complacently
treated as outbursts of senility and impotence.
People were not only well-to-do in fact, but, what
was far more extraordinary, they believed themselves to be so. In his great tariff speech but three
or four years later, Hayne called it the " period of
general jubilee." Every great public paper and

speech described the " felicity " of America. The
president pointed out to his fellow-citizens " the
prosperous and happy condition of our country in
all the great circumstances which constitute the
felicity of a nation ; " he told them that they were
" a free, virtuous, and enlightened people ; " the
unanimity of public sentiment in favor of his
" humble pretensions " indicated, he thought, " the
great strength and stability of our Union." And
all was reciprocated by the people. This modest,
gentle ruler was in his very mediocrity agreeable
to them. He symbolized the comfort and order, the
supreme respectability of which they were proud.
When in 1817 he made a tour through New England, which had seen neither Jefferson nor Madison
as visitors during their terms of office, and in his
military coat of domestic manufacture, his light
small-clothes and cocked hat, met processions and
orators without end, it was obvious that this was
not the radical minister whom Washington had recalled from Jacobin Paris for effusively pledging
eternal friendship and submitting to fraternal embraces in the National Convention. Such youthful
frenzy was now long past. America was enjoying
a great national idyl. Even the Federalists, except
of course those who had been too violent or who
were still unrepentant, were not utterly shut out
from the light of the placid high noon. Jackson
had urged Monroe in 1816 "to exterminate that
monster called party spirit," and to let some Federalists come to the board. Monroe thought, how-

ever, "that the administration should rest strongly
on the Republican party," though meaning to bring
all citizens " into the Republican fold as quietly as
possible." Party, he declared, was unnecessary to
free government; all should be Republicans. And
when Van Buren reached the sprawling, slatternly
American capital in 1821, all were Republicans.

There were of course personal feuds in this great
political family. Those of New York were the
most notorious; but there were many others. But
such rivalries and quarrels were only a proof of the
political calm. When families are smugly prosperous they indulge petty dislikes, which disappear
before storm or tragedy. The halcyon days could
not last. Monroe's dream of a country with but
one party, and that basking in perpetual " felicity,"
was, in spite of what seemed for the moment a close
realization, as far from the truth as the dreams of
later reformers who would in politics organize all
the honest, respectable folk together against all the
dishonest.

The heat of the Missouri question was ended at
the session before Van Buren's senatorial term began. It seemed only a thunder-storm passing across
a rich, warm day in harvest time, angry and agitating for the moment, but quickly forgotten by
dwellers in the pastoral scene when the rainbow of
compromise appeared in the delightful hues of
Henry Clay's eloquence. The elements of the tremendous struggle yet to come were in the atmosphere, but they were not visible. The slavery

question had no political importance to Van Buren until fourteen years afterwards. In judging the men of that day we shall seriously mistake if we set up our own standards among their ideas. The moral growth in the twenty-five years since the emancipation makes it irksome to be fair to the views of the past generation, or indeed to the former views of half of our present generation. Slavery has come to seem intrinsically wicked, hideous, to be hated everywhere. But sixty-five years ago it still lingered in several of the Northern States. It was wrong indeed; but the temper of condemnation towards it was Platonic, full of the unavailing and unpoignant regret with which men hear of poverty and starvation and disease and crime which they do not see and which they cannot help. Nor did slavery then seem to the best of men so very great a wrong even to the blacks; there were, it was thought, many ameliorations and compensations. Men were glad to believe and did believe that the human chattels were better and happier than they would have been in Africa. The economic waste of slavery, its corrupting and enervating effect upon the whites, were thought to be objections quite as serious. Besides, it was widely fancied to be at worst but a temporary evil. Jefferson's dislike of it was shared by many throughout the South as well as the North. The advantages of a free soil were becoming so apparent in the strides by which the North was passing the South in every material advantage, that the latter, it seemed, must surely learn the lesson. For the institution within States already admitted to the Union, anti-slavery men felt no responsibility. Forty years later the great leader of the modern Republican party would not, he solemnly declared in the very midst of a pro-slavery rebellion, interfere with slavery in the States if the Union could be saved without disturbing it. If men in South Carolina cared to maintain a ruinous and corrupting domestic institution, even if it were a greater wrong against the slaves than it was believed to be, or even if it were an injury to the whites themselves, still men of Massachusetts and New York ought, it seemed to them, to be no more disturbed over it than we feel bound to be over polygamy in Turkey.

But as to the territory west of the Mississippi not yet formed into States, there was a different sentiment held by a great majority at the North and by many at the South. Slavery was not established there. The land was national domain, whose forms of political and social life were yet to be set up. Why not, before the embarrassments of slave settlement arose, devote this new land to freedom, — not so much to freedom as that shining goddess of mercy and right and justice who rose clear and obvious to our purged vision out of the civil war, as to the less noble deities of economic well-being, thrift, and industrial comfort? Democrats at the North, therefore, were almost unanimous that Missouri should come in free or not at all; and so with the rest of the territory beyond

the Mississippi, except the old slave settlement of
Louisiana, already admitted as a State. The resolution in the legislature of New York in January,
1820, supported by Van Buren, that freedom be
" an indispensable condition of admission " of new
States, was but one of many exhibitions of feeling
at the North. Monroe and the very best of Americans did not, however, think the principle so sacred
or necessary as to justify a struggle. John Quincy
Adams, hating slavery as did but few Americans,
distinctly favored the compromise by which Missouri came in with slavery, and by which the other
new territory north of the present southern line of
Missouri extended westward was to be free, and the
territory south of it slave. With no shame he acquiesced in the very thing about which forty years
later the nation plunged into war. " For the present," he wrote, " this contest is laid asleep." So
the stream of peaceful sunshine and prosperity returned over the land.

Van Buren's views at this time were doubtless
clear against the extension of slavery. He disliked
the institution ; and in part saw how inconsistent
were its odious practices with the best civic growth,
how debasing to whites and blacks alike. In
March, 1822, he voted in the Senate, with Harrison
Gray Otis of Massachusetts and Rufus King, for
a proviso in the bill creating the new Territory of
Florida by which the introduction of slaves was
forbidden except by citizens removing there for
actual settlement, and by which slaves introduced

in violation of the law were to be freed. But he was in a minority. Northern senators from Rhode Island, New Jersey, and Indiana refused to interfere with free trade in slaves between the Southern States and this southernmost territory.

Among the forty-eight members of the Senate which met in December, 1821, neither Clay nor Calhoun nor Webster had a seat. The first was restless in one of his brief absences from official life; the second was secretary of war; and Webster, out of Congress, was making great law arguments and greater orations. Benton was there from the new State of Missouri, just beginning his thirty years. The warm friendship and political alliance between him and Van Buren must have soon begun. During all or nearly all Van Buren's senatorship the two occupied adjoining seats. Two years later Andrew Jackson was sent to the Senate by Tennessee, as a suitable preliminary to his presidential canvass. During the next two sessions Van Buren, Benton, and Jackson were thrown together; and without doubt the foundations were laid of their lifelong intimacy and political affection. Benton and Jackson, personal enemies years before, had become reconciled. Among these associates Van Buren adhered firmly enough to his own clear views; he did not turn obsequiously to the rising sun of Tennessee. William H. Crawford, the secretary of the treasury, had, in the Republican congressional caucus of 1816, stood next Monroe for the presidential nomination. For

reasons which neither history nor tradition seems
sufficiently to have brought us, he inspired a strong
and even enthusiastic loyalty among many of his
party. His candidacy in 1824 was more " regular "
than that of either Adams, Jackson, or Clay, whose
friends combined against him as the strongest
of them all. Though Crawford had been prostrated by serious disease in 1823, Van Buren remained faithful to him until, in 1825, after refusing
a seat in Adams's cabinet, he retired from national
public life a thoroughly broken man.

The first two sessions of Congress, after Van
Buren's service began, seemed drowsy enough.
French land-titles in Louisiana, the settlement of
the accounts of public officers, the attempt to abolish imprisonment for debt, the appropriation for
money for diplomatic representatives to the new
South American states and their recognition, —
nothing more exciting than these arose, except
Monroe's veto, in May, 1822, of the bill authorizing the erection of toll-gates upon the Cumberland road and appropriating $9000 for them.
This brought distinctly before the public the great
question of internal improvements by the federal
government, which Van Buren, Benton, and Jackson afterwards chose as one of the chief battle-
grounds for their party. For this bill Van Buren
indeed voted, while Benton afterwards boasted that
he was one of the small minority of seven who dis-
cerned its true character. But this trifling appropriation was declared by Barbour, who was in

charge of the measure, not to involve the general
question; it was said to be a mere incident necessary to save from destruction a work for which
earlier statesmen were responsible. Monroe, though
declaring in his veto that the power to adopt and
execute a system of internal improvements national
in their character would have the happiest effect on
all the great interests of the Union, decided that
the Constitution gave no such power. Six years
later, in a note to his speech upon the power of the
Vice-President to call to order for words spoken in
debate in the Senate, Van Buren apologized for his
vote on the bill, because it was his first session, and
because he was sincerely desirous to aid the Western country and had voted without full examination. He added that if the question were again
presented to him, he should vote in the negative;
and that it had been his only vote in seven years
of service which the most fastidious critic could
torture into an inconsistency with his principles
upon internal improvements. In January, 1823,
during his second session, Van Buren spoke and
voted in favor of the bill to repair the road, but
still took no decided ground upon the general
question. He said that the large expenditure already made on the road would have been worse
than useless if it were now suffered to decay; that
the road, being already constructed, ought to be
preserved; but whether he would vote for a new
construction he did not disclose. Even Benton,
who was proud to have been one of the small

minority against the bill of the year before for toll-gates upon the road, was now with Van Buren, constitutional scruples yielding to the statesman-like reluctance to waste an investment of millions of dollars rather than spend a few thousands to save it.

In January, 1824, Van Buren proposed to solve these difficulties by a constitutional amendment. Congress was to have power to make roads and canals, but the money appropriated was to be apportioned among the States according to population. No road or canal was to be made within any State without the consent of its legislature; and the money was to be expended in each State under the direction of its legislature. This proposal seems to have fallen still-born and deservedly. It illustrated Van Buren's jealousy of interference with the rights of States. But the right of each State to be protected, he seemed to forget, involved its right not to be taxed for improvements in other States which it neither controlled nor promoted. Van Buren's speech in support of the proposal would to-day seem very heretical to his party. A dozen years later he himself would probably have admitted it to be so. He then believed in the abstract proposition that such funds of the nation as could be raised without oppression, and as were not necessary to the discharge of indispensable demands upon the government, should be expended upon internal improvements under restrictions guarding the sovereignty and equal interests of the

States.   Henry Clay would not in theory have gone
much further.   But to this subject in its national
aspect Van Buren had probably given but slight
attention.   The success of the Erie Canal, with
him doubtless as with others, made adverse theories
of government seem less impressive.   But Van
Buren and his school quickly became doubtful and
soon hostile to the federal promotion of internal
improvements.   The opposition became popular on
the broader reasoning that great expenditures for
internal improvements within the States were not
only, as the statesmen at first argued, violations
of the letter of the Constitution, whose sanctity
could, however, be saved by proper amendment,
but were intrinsically dangerous, and an unwholesome extension of the federal power which ought
not to take place whether within the Constitution or by amending it.   Aided by Jackson's
powerful vetoes, this sentiment gained a strength
with the people which has come down to our day.
We have river and harbor bills, but they are supposed to touch directly or indirectly our foreign
commerce, which, under the Constitution and upon
the essential theory of our confederation, is a subject proper to the care of the Union.

In the same session Van Buren spoke at length
in favor of the bill to abolish imprisonment for
debt, and drew with precision the distinction wisely
established by modern jurisprudence, that the property only, and not the body of the debtor, should
be at the mercy of his creditor, where the debt involved no fraud or breach of trust.

The session of 1823–1824 was seriously influenced by the coming presidential election. The protective tariff of 1824 was christened with the absurd name of the "American system," though it was American in no other or better sense than foreign war to protect fancied national rights is an American system, and though the system had come from the middle ages in the company of other restrictions upon the intercourse of nations. It was carried by the factitious help of this designation and the fine leadership of Clay. With Jackson and Benton, Van Buren voted for it, against men differing as widely from each other as his associate, the venerable Federalist Rufus King, differed from Hayne, the brilliant orator of South Carolina. Upon the tariff Van Buren then had views clearer, at least, than upon internal improvements. In 1824 he was unmistakably a protectionist. The moderation of his views and the pressure from his own State were afterwards set up as defenses for this early attitude of his. But he declared himself with sufficient plainness not only to believe in the constitutionality of a protective tariff, but that 1824 was a fit year in which to extend its protective features. He acted, too, with the amplest light upon the subject. The dislike of the Holy Alliance, the hated recollections of the Orders in Council and the Napoleonic decrees, the idea that, for self-defense in times of war, the country must be forced to produce many goods not already produced, — these considerations had great weight, as very well

appears in the speech for the bill delivered by
Richard M. Johnson of Kentucky, afterwards
Van Buren's associate on the presidential ticket.
" When the monarchs of Europe are assembled
together, do you think," he asked, " that we are
not a subject of their holy consultations? " But
the support of the bill was upon broader considerations. The debates upon the tariff in the House
of Representatives in February, March, and April,
and in the Senate in April, 1824, were admirable
presentations of the subject. Webster in the
House and Hayne in the Senate put the free
trade side. The former, still speaking his own
sentiments, declared that " the best apology for laws
of prohibition and laws of monopoly will be found
in that state of society, not only unenlightened but
sluggish, in which they are most generally established." But now, he said, " competition comes in
place of monopoly, and intelligence and industry
ask only for fair play and an open field." He
repudiated the principle of protection. " On the
contrary," said he, " I think freedom of trade to
be the general principle, and restriction the exception."

Nor was Van Buren then left without the light
which afterwards reached him on the constitutional
question. Rufus King said that, if gentlemen
wished to encourage the production of hemp and
iron, they ought to bring in a bill to give bounties
on those articles; for there was the same constitutional right to grant bounties as to levy restrictive

duties upon foreign products. Hayne made the really eloquent and masterly speech for which he ought to stand in the first rank of orators, and which summed up as well for free-traders now as then the most telling arguments against artificial restrictions. He skillfully closed with Washington's words : " Our commercial policy should hold an equal and impartial hand, neither seeking nor granting exclusive favors or preferences ; consulting the natural course of things ; diffusing and diversifying by gentle means the streams of commerce, but forcing nothing." Hayne did not confine himself to the doctrines of Adam Smith, or the hardships which protection meant to a planting region like his own. For the chief interest of the South was in cotton ; and the price of cotton was largely determined by the ability of foreigners to import it from America, — an ability in its turn dependent upon the willingness of America to take her pay, directly or indirectly, in foreign commodities. Hayne, however, went further. He clearly raised the question, whether the encouragement of manufactures could constitutionally be made a Federal object.

Sitting day after day under this long debate in the little senate chamber then in use, where men listened to speeches, if for no other reason, because they were easily heard, Van Buren could not, with his ability and readiness, have misunderstood the general principles involved. Early in the debate, upon a motion to strike out the duty on hemp, he briefly but explicitly said that " he was in favor of increasing the duty on hemp, with a view of affording protection to its cultivation in this country." He voted against limiting the duty on wool to twenty-five per cent., but voted against a duty of twenty-five per cent. on India silks, — a revenue rather than a protective duty. He voted for duties on wheat and wheat flour and potatoes. He voted against striking out the duty on books, in spite of Hayne's grotesque but forcible argument that they were to be considered " a raw material, essential to the formation of the mind, the morals, and the character of the people." It is difficult to under-stand the significance of all Van Buren's votes on the items of the bill; but the record shows them to have been, on the whole, protectionist, with a preference for moderate rates, but a firm assertion of the wool interests of New York. Benton tells us that Van Buren was one of the main speakers for the bill; but the assertion is not borne out by the record. He delivered no general speech upon the subject, as did most of the senators, but seems to have spoken only upon some of the details as they were considered in committee of the whole. The best to be said in Van Buren's behalf is, that his judgment was not yet so ripe upon the matter as not to be still open to great change. He was in his third session, and still new to national politics, and there was before him the plain and strong argument that his State wanted protection. In 1835 Butler, speaking for him as a presidential

candidate, said that his personal feelings had been
" at all times adverse to the high tariff policy."
But " high tariff " was then, as now, a merely relative term. His votes placed him in that year very
near Henry Clay. That from 1824 he grew more
and more averse to the necessary details and results
of a protective policy is probably true. Nor ought
it to be, even from the standpoint of free-traders,
serious accusation that a public man varies his
political utterances upon the tariff question, if the
variation be progressive and steadily towards what
they deem a greater liberality. To Van Buren,
however, the tariff question never had a capital
importance. Even thirty-two years later, while
rehearsing from his retirement the achievements of
his party in excuse of the support he reluctantly
gave Buchanan, he did not name among its services its insistence upon merely revenue duties,
although he had then for years been himself committed to that doctrine.

Van Buren's vote for the tariff of 1824 had no
very direct relation to his political situation. His
own successor was not to be chosen for nearly three
years. Crawford, whom he supported for the presidency, was the only one of the four candidates
opposed to the bill. Adams was consistently a
protectionist; he believed in actively promoting
the welfare of men, though chiefly if not exclusively American men, even when they resisted their
own welfare. He, like his father, was perfectly
ready to use the power of government where it

seemingly promised to be effective, without caring
much for economical theories or constitutional restrictions. Jackson himself was far enough away
from the ranks of strict constructionists on the
tariff. In April, 1824, in the midst of the debate,
and while a presidential candidate, he wrote from
the Senate what free-traders, who afterwards supported him, would have deemed the worst of her-
esies. Like most candidates, ancient and modern,
he was "in favor of a judicious examination and
revision of" the tariff. He would advocate a tariff
so far as it enabled the country to provide itself
with the means of defense in war. But he would
go further. The tariff ought to "draw from agriculture the superabundant labor, and employ it in
mechanism and manufactures;" it ought to "give
a proper distribution to our labor, to take from
agriculture in the United States 600,000 men, women, and children." It is time, he cried, and quite
as extravagantly as Clay, that "we should become
a little more Americanized." How slight a connection the tariff had with the election of 1824 is
further seen in the fact that Jackson, who thus
supported the bill, received the vote of several of
the States which strongly opposed the tariff.

In March, 1824, Van Buren urged the Senate to
act upon a constitutional amendment touching the
election of president. As the amendment could
not be adopted in time to affect the pending canvass, there was, he said, no room for partisan feeling. He insisted that if there were no majority

choice by the electors, the choice should not rest with the house of representatives voting by States, but that the electors should be reconvened, and themselves choose between the highest two candidates. The debate soon became thoroughly partisan. Rufus King, with but thinly veiled reference to Crawford's nomination, denounced the practice by which a caucus at Washington deprived the constitutional electors of any free choice ; members of Congress were attending to president-making rather than to their duties. He thought that the course of events had "led near observers to suspect a connection existing between a central power of this description at the seat of the general government and the legislatures of Georgia, North Carolina, Virginia, and New York, and perhaps of other States." To this it was pointed out with much force that such a caucus had chosen Jefferson, Madison, and Monroe without scandal or injury ; that members of Congress were distinguished and representative persons familiar with national affairs, who might with great advantage respectfully suggest a course of action to their fellow-citizens. Van Buren went keenly to the real point of the belated objection to the system; it lay in the particular action of the recent caucus. He did not think it worth while to consider "those nice distinctions which challenged respect for the proceedings of conventions of one description and denied it to others ; or to detect those still more subtle refinements which regarded meetings of the same character as sometimes proper, and at others destructive of the purity of elections and dangerous to the liberties of the people." After much talk about the will of the people, the Senate by a vote of 30 to 13 postponed the consideration of the amendments until after the election. Benton joined Van Buren in the minority, although they did not agree upon the form of amendment; but Jackson, perhaps because he was a candidate, did not vote.

It was highly probable that there would be embarrassment in choosing the next president. It was already nearly certain that neither candidate would have a majority of the electoral votes. The decision was then, as in our own time, supposed to rest with New York; and naturally therefore Van Buren's prestige was great, gained, as it had been, in that difficult and opulent political field. His attachment to Crawford was proof against the signs of the latter's decaying strength. Crawford was to him the Republican candidate regularly chosen, and one agreeable to his party by the vigorous democracy of his sentiments. His opposition to Jefferson's embargo, and his vote for a renewal of the charter of the Bank of the United States, had been forgotten since his warm advocacy of the late war with England. His formal claims to the nomination were great. For he had been in the Senate as early as 1807, and its president upon the death of Vice-President Clinton in 1812; afterwards he had been minister to France, and was now secretary of the treasury. In the caucus of 1816 he had nearly as many votes as Monroe; and those votes were cast for him, it was said, though without much probability, in spite of his peremptory refusal to compete with Monroe. Moreover, Crawford had a majesty and grace of personal appearance which, with undoubtedly good though not great abilities, had, apart from these details of his career, made him conspicuous in the Republican ranks; and in its chief service he was, after the retirement of Monroe, the senior, except Adams, whose candidacy was far more recent. Crawford's claim to the succession was therefore very justifiable; he was the most obvious, the most "regular," of the candidates.

It has been said that Van Buren was at first inclined to Adams. The latter's unequaled public experience and discipline of intellect doubtless seemed, to Van Buren's precise and orderly mind, eminent qualifications for the first office in the land. Adams at this time, by a coincidence not inexplicable, thought highly of Van Buren. He entered in his diary a remark of his own, in February, 1825, that Van Buren was "a man of great talents and of good principles; but he had suffered them to be too much warped by party spirit." This from an Adams may be taken as extreme praise. It is pretty certain that if Van Buren had reprehensibly shifted his position from Adams to Crawford, we should find a record of it in the vast treasure-house of damnations which Adams left.

Nor is there good reason to suppose that Van Buren
was influenced by the nomination which Crawford's friends in Georgia gave him in 1824 for the
vice-presidency. This showed that New York had
already surrendered her favorite " son to the nation ; " he was now definitely to be counted a power
in national politics, where he was known as the
" Albany director." Crawford's enemies in Georgia, the Clarkites, ridiculed this nomination with
the coarse and silly abuse which active politicians
to this day are always ready to use in their cynical
under-estimate of popular intelligence, — abuse
which they are by and by pretty sure to be glad to
forget. Van Buren was pictured as half man and
half cat, half fox and half monkey, half snake and
half mink. He was dubbed " Blue Whiskey Van "
and " Little Van." The Clarkites, being only a
minority in the Georgia Assembly, delighted to
vote for him as their standing candidate for door-
keeper and the like humbler positions.

New York was greatly disturbed through 1824
over the presidency. Its politics were in the position described by Senator Cobb, one of Crawford's
Georgia supporters. " Could we hit upon a few
great principles," he wrote home from Washington
in January, 1825, " and unite their support with
that of Crawford, we should succeed beyond
doubt." But the great principles were hard to
find. The people and the greater politicians were
therefore swayed by personal preferences, without strong reason for either choice ; and the lesser

politicians were simply watching to see how the tide ran. Adams was the most natural choice of the New York Republicans. The South had had the presidency for six terms. His early secession from the Federalists; his aid in solidifying the Republican sentiment at the North; his support of Jefferson in the patriotic embargo struggle; his long, eminent, and fruitful services; and his place of secretary of state, from which Madison and Monroe had in turn been promoted to the presidency, — all these commended him to Northern Republicans as a proper candidate.

De Witt Clinton admired and supported General Jackson. In 1819 the latter had at a dinner in Tammany Hall amazed and affronted the former's Bucktail enemies by giving as his toast, "De Witt Clinton, the enlightened statesman and governor of the great and patriotic State of New York." In January, 1824, Clinton was the victim of a political outrage which illustrated the harsh partisanship then ruling in New York politics, and may well have determined the choice of president. Clinton had retired from the governor's chair; but he still held the honorary and unpaid office of canal commissioner, to which he brought distinguished honor but which brought none to him, and whose importance he more than any other man had created. The Crawford men in the legislature feared a combination of the men of the new People's party with the Clintonians on the presidential question. Clinton seemed at the time an unpopular character.

To embarrass the People's party, Clinton's enemies suddenly, and just before the rising of the
legislature, offered a resolution removing him from
the canal commissionership.  The People's party,
it was thought, by opposing the resolution, would
incur popular dislike through their alliance with the
few and unpopular Clintonians; while by supporting the resolution they would forfeit the support
of the latter upon which they relied.  In either
case the Crawford men would apparently profit by
the trick.  The People's party men, including those
favoring Adams for president, at once seized the
wrong horn of the dilemma, and voted for Clinton's
removal, which was thus carried by an almost
unanimous vote.  But the people themselves were
underrated; the outrage promptly restored Clinton
to popular favor.  In spite of the resistance of the
politicians, he was, in the fall of 1824, elected by
a large majority to the governor's seat, to which,
or to any great office, it had been supposed he
could never return; and this, although at the same
time and upon the same ticket one of those who
had voted for his removal was chosen lieutenant-
governor.  Van Buren was no party to this removal, although his political friends at Albany were
the first movers in the scheme.  He himself was
far-sighted enough to see the probable effect of so
gross and indecent a use of political power.  Nor
was he so relentless a partisan as to remember in
unfruitful vengeance Clinton's own proscriptive
conduct, or to remove the latter from an honorary

DeWitt Clinton

seat which belonged to him above all other men. By this silly blunder Clinton was again raised to deserved power, which he held until his death.

The popular outburst consequent upon Clinton's removal in January, 1824, made it very dangerous for the Bucktails to leave to the people in the fall the choice of presidential electors. The rise of the People's party for a time seriously threatened Van Buren's influence. Until 1824 the presidential electors of New York had been chosen by its legislature. The opponents of Crawford and Van Buren, fearing that the latter's superior political skill would more easily capture the legislature in November, 1824, raised at the legislative elections of 1823 a cry against the Albany Regency, and demanded that presidential electors should be chosen directly by the people. The Regency, popularly believed to have been founded by Van Buren, consisted of a few able followers of his, residing or in office at Albany. They were also called the " conspirators." Chief among them were William L. Marcy, the comptroller; Samuel A. Talcott, the attorney-general; Benjamin F. Butler, then district attorney of Albany county; Edwin Croswell, the state printer; Roger Skinner, the United States district judge; and Benjamin Knower, the state treasurer. Later there joined the Regency, Silas Wright, Azariah C. Flagg, Thomas W. Olcott, and Charles E. Dudley. Its members were active, skillful, shrewd politicians; and they were much more. They were men of strong political convictions, holding and observing a high standard for the public service, and of undoubted personal integrity. In 1830 John A. Dix gave as a chief reason for accepting office at Albany that he should there be "one of the Regency." His son, Dr. Morgan Dix, describes their aggressive honesty, their refusal "to tolerate in those whom they could control what their own fine sense of honor did not approve;" and he quotes a remark made to him by Thurlow Weed, their long and most formidable enemy, "that he had never known a body of men who possessed so much power and used it so well." In his Memoirs, Weed describes their "great ability, great industry, indomitable courage." Two at least of the original members, Marcy and Butler, afterwards justly rose to national distinction. Even to our own day, the Albany Regency has been a strong and generally a sagacious influence in its party. John A. Dix, Horatio Seymour, Dean Richmond, and Samuel J. Tilden long directed its policy; and from the chief seat in its councils the late secretary of the treasury, Daniel Manning, was chosen in 1885.

In November, 1823, the People's party elected only a minority of the legislature; but many of the Democrats were committed to the support of an electoral law, and the movement was clearly popular. A just, though possibly an insufficient objection to the law was its proposal of a great change in anticipation of a particular election whose candidates were already before the public. But there was no resort to frank argument. Its indirect defeat was proposed by the Democratic managers, and accomplished with the coöperation of many supporters of Adams and Clay. A bill was reported in the Assembly, where the Regency was in a minority, giving the choice of the electors to the people directly, but cunningly requiring a majority instead of a plurality vote to elect. If there were no majority, then the choice was to be left to the legislature. The Adams and Clay men were unwilling to let a plurality elect, lest in the uncertain state of public feeling some other candidate might be at the head of the poll; and they were probably now quite as ·confident as the Bucktails, and with more reason, of their strength upon joint ballot in the legislature. Divided as the people of New York were between the four presidential candidates, it was well known that this device would really give them no choice. The consideration of the electoral law was postponed in the Senate upon a pretense of objection to the form of the bill, and with insincere protestations of a desire to pass it. The outcome of all this was that in the election of November, 1824, the Democrats were punished at the polls both for the wanton attack on Clinton and for their unprincipled treatment of the electoral bill. The Regency got no more than a small minority in the legislature; and De Witt Clinton, as has been said, was chosen governor by a great majority.

Crawford's supporters at Washington believed

that in a congressional caucus he would have a larger vote than any other candidate. His opponents, in the same belief, refused to join in a caucus, in spite of the cry that their refusal was a treason to old party usage. The Republicans at Albany, probably upon Van Buren's advice, had in April, 1823, declared in favor of a caucus, but without effect. Two thirds of Congress would not assent. At last, in February, 1824, a caucus was called, doubtless in the hope that many who had refused their assent would, finding the caucus inevitable, attend through force of party habit. But of the 261 members of Congress, only 66 attended; and they were chiefly from New York, Virginia, North Carolina and Georgia. In the caucus 62 voted for Crawford for president and 57 for Albert Gallatin for vice-president. A cry was soon raised against the latter as a foreigner; so that in spite of his American residence of forty-five years, and his invaluable services to the country and to the Republican party through nearly all this period, he felt compelled to withdraw.

The failure of the caucus almost destroyed Crawford's chances, though Van Buren steadily kept up courage. A few days later he wrote a confidential letter complaining of the subserviency and ingratitude of the non-attendants, who had " partaken largely of the favor of the party; " but despondency, he said, was a weakness with which he was but little annoyed, and if New York should be firm and promptly explicit, the election would be substantially settled. But New York was neither firm nor promptly explicit. Its electoral vote was in doubt until the meeting of the legislature in November. The Adams and Clay forces then united, securing 31 out of the 36 electors, although one of the 31 seems finally to have voted for Jackson. Five Crawford electors were chosen with the help of the Adams men, who wished to keep Clay at the foot of the poll of presidential electors, and thus prevent his eligibility as one of the highest three in the House of Representatives. This device of the Adams men may have deprived Clay of the presidency. Thus Van Buren's New York campaign met defeat even in the legislature, where his friends had incurred odium rather than surrender the choice of electors to the people, while his forces were being thoroughly beaten by the people at the polls. In the electoral college Crawford received only 41 votes ; Adams had 84 and Jackson 99 ; while Clay with only 37 was fourth in the race, and could not therefore enter the contest in the House. Georgia cast 9 electoral votes for Van Buren as vice-president.

Van Buren did not figure in the choice of Adams in the House by the coalition of Adams and Clay forces. Nor does his name appear in the traditions of the manœuvering at Washington in the winter of 1824–25, except in a vague and improbable story that he wished, by dividing the New York delegation in the House on the first vote by States, to prevent a choice, and then to throw the votes of

the Crawford members for Adams, and thus secure
the glory and political profit of apparently electing
him. He did not join in the cry that Adams's
election over Jackson was a violation of the democratic principle. Nor was it a violation of that
principle. Jackson had but a minority of the popular vote. Clay was in political principles and
habits nearer to Adams than Jackson. It was
clearly Clay's duty to take his strength to the candidate whose administration was most likely to be
agreeable to those opinions of his own which had
made him a candidate. The coalition was perfectly natural and legitimate ; and it was wholesome in its consequences. It established the Whig
party; it at least helped to establish the modern
Democratic party. That the acceptance of office
by Clay would injure him was probable enough.
Coalitions have always been unpopular in America
and England, when there has seemed to follow a
division of offices. They offend the strong belief
in party government which lies deep in the political conscience of the two countries.

In the congressional session of 1824–25 president-making in the House stood in the way of
everything else of importance. Van Buren, with
increasing experience, was taking a greater and
greater part in congressional work. He joined far
more frequently in the debates. Again he spoke
for the abolition of imprisonment for debt, his colleague, Rufus King, differing from him on this as
he now seemed to differ from him on most disputed

questions. King had not been reëlected senator, having declined to be a candidate, because, as he said, of his advancing years. But doubtless Van Buren was correct in telling John Quincy Adams, and the latter was correct in believing, as his diary records, that King could not have been re-chosen.

At this session Van Buren took definite stand against the schemes of internal improvement. On February 11, 1825, differing even from Benton, he voted against topographical surveys in anticipation of public works by the Federal government. On February 23 he voted against an appropriation of $150,000 to extend the Cumberland road, while Jackson and Benton both voted for it. So, also, the next day, when Jackson voted for federal subscriptions to help construct the Delaware and Chesapeake Canal and the Dismal Swamp Canal, Van Buren was against him. Two days before the session closed he voted against the bill for the occupation of Oregon, Benton and Jackson voting in the affirmative. Van Buren was one of the senatorial committee to receive the new president upon his inauguration. It was doubtless with the easy courtesy which was genuine with him that he welcomed John Quincy Adams to the political battle so disastrous to the latter.

When Congress met again, in December, 1825, Van Buren took a more important place than ever before in national politics. He now became a true parliamentary leader; for he, like Clay, had the really parliamentary career which has rarely been seen in this country.  Dealing with amorphous political elements, Van Buren created out of them a party to promote his policy, and seized upon the vigor and popular strength of Jackson to lead both party and policy to supreme power.  While, before 1825, Van Buren had not represented in the Senate a party distinctly constituted, from 1825 to 1828 he definitely led the formation of the modern Democratic party.  In this work he was clearly chief. From the floor of the Senate he addressed those of its members inclined to his creed, and the sympathetic elements throughout the country, and firmly guided and disciplined them after that fashion which in very modern days is best familiar to us in the parliamentary conflicts of Great Britain. Since Van Buren wielded this organizing power, there has been in America no equally authoritative and decisive leadership from the Senate; although he has since been surpassed there, not only as an orator, but in other kinds of senatorial work. Seward seemed to exercise a like leadership in the six years or more preceding Lincoln's election ; but he was far more the creature of the stupendous movement of the time than he was its creator.  So, in the two years before General Grant's renomination in 1872, Charles Sumner and Carl Schurz, speaking from the Senate, created a new party sentiment ; but the sentiment died in a "midsummer madness" but for which our later political history might have been materially different.  In the interesting and fruitful three years of Van Buren's senatorial opposition, he showed the same qualities of firmness, supple tact, and distinct political aims which had given him his power in New York; but all now upon a higher plane.

In December, 1825, Jackson was no longer in the Senate. His Tennessee friends had placed him there as in a fitting vestibule to the White House; but it seemed as hard then as it has been since, to go from the Senate over the apparently broad and easy mile to the west on Pennsylvania Avenue. So Jackson returned to the Hermitage, to await, in the favorite American character of Cincinnatus, the popular summons which he believed to be only delayed. Van Buren, now thoroughly acquainted with the general, saw in him the strongest titular leader of the opposition. It is pretty certain, however, that Van Buren's preference was recent. The "Albany Argus," a Van Buren paper, had but lately declared that "Jackson has not a single feeling in common with the Republican party, and makes the merit of desiring the total extinction of it;" while Jackson papers had ridiculed Crawford's

> "Shallow knaves with forms to mock us,
>   Straggling, one by one, to caucus."

It has been the tradition, carefully and doubtless sincerely begun by John Quincy Adams, and adopted by most writers dealing with this period, that Adams met his first Congress in a spirit which should have commanded universal support; and that it was a factious opposition, cunningly led by

Van Buren, which thwarted his patriotic purposes.
But this is an untrue account of the second great
party division in the United States.  The younger
Adams succeeded to an administration which had
represented no party, or rather which had represented a party now become so dominant as to practically include the whole country.  As president
he found himself able to promote opinions with a
weighty authority which he had not enjoyed while
secretary of state in an era of good feeling, and
under a president who was firm, even if gentle.
Nor was it likely that Adams, with his unrivaled
experience, his resolute self-reliance, and his ag-
gressively patriotic feeling, would fail to impress
his own views upon the public service, lest he might
disturb a supposititious unanimity of sentiment.
His first message boldly sounded the notes of party
division.  The second war with England was well
out of the public mind ; and his old Federalist
associations, his belief in a strong, active, beneficent
federal government, his traditional dislike of what
seemed to him extreme democratic tendencies and
constitutional refinings away of necessary federal
power, — all these made him promptly and ably
take an attitude very different from that of his
predecessors.  The compliment was perfectly sincere which, in his inaugural address, he had paid
the Republican and Federalist parties, saying of
them that both had " contributed splendid talents,
spotless integrity, ardent patriotism, and disinterested sacrifices to the formation and administra-

tion" of the government. But it was idle for him to suppose that the successors of these parties, although from both had come his own supporters, and although, as in his offer of the treasury to Crawford, he showed his desire, even in the chief offices, to ignore political differences, would remain united under him, if he espoused causes upon which they widely differed. After recapitulating the tenets of American political faith, and showing that most discordant elements of public opinion were now blended into harmony, he was again perfectly sincere in saying that only an effort of magnanimity needed to be made, that individuals should discard every remnant of rancor against each other. This advice he was himself unable to follow; and so were other men. In his inaugural he distinctly adopted as his own the policy of internal improvements by the federal government, although he knew how wide and determined had been the opposition to it. His own late chief, Monroe, had pronounced the policy unconstitutional. But he now told the people that the magnificence and splendor of the public works, the roads and aqueducts, of Rome, were among the imperishable splendors of the ancient republic. He asked to what single individual our first national road had proved an injury. Of the constitutional doubts which were raised, he said, with a touch of the contempt of a practical administrator: "Every speculative scruple will be solved by a practical blessing." To the self-consecrated guardians of the Constitution this

was as corrupt as offers of largesses to plebeians at
Rome. In his first message he recommended again
the policy of internal improvements, and proposed
the establishment of a national university. Although he admitted the Constitution to be "a
charter of limited powers," he still intimated his
opinion that its powers might " be effectually
brought into action by laws promoting the improvement of agriculture, commerce, and manufactures,
the cultivation and encouragement of the mechanic
and of the elegant arts, the advancement of literature, and the progress of the sciences, ornamental
and profound ; " and that to refrain from exercising
these powers for the benefit of the people themselves, would be to hide the talent in the earth,
and a " treachery to the most sacred of trusts."
Further, he now broached the novel project of the
congress at Panama, — a project surely doubtful
enough to permit conscientious opposition.

All this was widely different from the messages
of content from President Monroe. There was in
these new utterances a clear political diversion,
marked not less by the brilliant and restless genius
of Henry Clay, now the secretary of state, than
by the President's consciousness of his own strong
and disciplined ability. Here was a new policy
formally presented by a new administration ; and
a formal and organized resistance was as sure to
follow as effect to follow cause. Van Buren was
soon at the head of this inevitable opposition. It
is difficult, at least in the records of Congress, to

find any evidence justifying the long tradition that the opposition was factious or unworthy. It was doubtless a warfare, with its surprises, its skirmishes, and its pitched battles. Mistakes of the adversary were promptly used. Debates were not had simply to promote the formal business before the House, but rather to reach the listening voters. But all this belongs to parliamentary warfare. Nor is it inconsistent with most exalted aims and an admirable performance of public business in a free country. Gladstone, the greatest living master in the work of political reform, has described himself as an " old parliamentary hand." Nor in the motions, the resolutions, the debates, led by Van Buren during his three years of opposition, can one find any device which Palmerston or Derby or Gladstone in one forum, and Seward and even Adams himself in his last and best years in another, have not used with little punishment from disinterested and enduring criticism.

Immediately after Adams's inauguration Van Buren voted for Clay's confirmation as secretary of state, while Jackson and fourteen other senators, including Hayne, voted to reject him, upon the unfounded story of Clay's sale of the presidency to Adams for the office to which he was now nominated. Van Buren's language and demeanor towards the new administration were uniformly becoming. He charged political but not personal wrong-doing; he made no insinuation of base motives; and his opposition throughout was the more forcible for its very decorum.

The first great battle between the rapidly dividing forces was over the Panama mission, a creation
of Clay's exuberant imagination. The president
nominated to the Senate two envoys to an American
congress called by the new South American republics of Columbia, Mexico, and Central America,
and in which it was proposed that Peru and Chile
also should participate. The congress was to be
held at Panama, which, in the extravagant rhetoric
of some of the Republicans of the South, would, if
the world had to elect a capital, be pointed out for
that august destiny, placed as it was " in the centre
of the globe." Spain had not yet acknowledged
the independence of her revolted colonies; and it
was clear that the discussions of the congress must
be largely concerned with a mutual protection of
American nations which implied an attitude hostile
to Spain. Adams, in his message nominating the
envoys, declared that they were not to take part in
deliberations of belligerent character, or to contract
alliances or to engage in any project importing
hostility to any other nation. But referring to the
Monroe doctrine, Adams said that the mission
looked to an agreement between the nations represented, that each would guard by its own means
against the establishment of any future European
colony within its borders; and it looked also to an
effort on the part of the United States to promote
religious liberty among those intolerant republics.
The decisive inducement, he added, to join in the
congress was to lay the foundation of future inter-

course with those states " in the broadest principles of reciprocity and the most cordial feelings of fraternal friendship."

This was vague enough. But when the diplomatic papers were exhibited, it was plain that the southern republics proposed a congress looking to a close defensive alliance, a sort of confederacy or Amphictyonic council as Benton described it; and that it was highly improbable that the representatives from one country could responsibly participate in the congress without most serious danger of incurring obligations, or falling into precisely the embarrassments which the well settled policy of the United States had avoided. It was perfectly agreeable to Adams, resolute and aggressive American that he was, that his country should look indulgently upon the smaller American powers, should stand at their head, should counsel them in their difficulties with European nations, and jealously take their side in those difficulties. Clay's eager, enthusiastic mind delighted in the picture of a great leadership of America by the United States, an American system of nations, breathing the air of republicanism, asserting a young and haughty independence of monarchical Europe, and ready for opposition to its schemes. In all this there has been fascination to many American minds, which even in our own day we have seen influence American diplomacy. But it was a step into the entangling alliances against which American public opinion had from Washington's day been set.

When Adams asked an appropriation for the expenses of the mission, he told the House of Representatives that he was hardly sanguine enough to
promise " all or even any of the transcendent benefits to the human race which warmed the conceptions of its first proposer," but that it looked " to
the melioration of the condition of man ; " that it
was congenial with the spirit which prompted our
own declaration of independence, which dictated
our first treaty with Prussia, and " which filled the
hearts and fired the souls of the immortal founders
of our revolution."

Such fanciful speculation the Republicans, led
by Van Buren, opposed with strong and heated
protests, in tone not unlike the Liberal protests of
1878 in England against Disraeli's Jingo policy.
In the secret session of the Senate Van Buren proposed resolutions against the constitutionality of
the mission, reciting that it was a departure from
our wise and settled policy ; that, for the conference
and discussion contemplated, our envoys already
accredited to the new republics were competent,
without becoming involved as members of the congress.   These resolutions, so the President at once
wrote in his opulent and invaluable diary, " are
the fruit of the ingenuity of Martin Van Buren
and bear the impress of his character."   The mission was, the opposition thus insisted, unconstitutional ; a step enlarging the sphere of the federal
government ; a meddlesome and dangerous interference with foreign nations ; and if it lay in the

course of a strong and splendid policy, it was also
part of a policy full of warlike possibilities almost
sure to drag us into old-world quarrels. Clay's
"American system," Hayne said in the senatorial
debate, meant restriction and monopoly when applied to our domestic policy, and "entangling alliances" when applied to our foreign policy.

Van Buren's speech was very able. He did not
touch upon the liberality of the Spanish Americans
towards races other than the Caucasian, which
peered out of Hayne's speech as one of the Southern
objections. After using the wise and seemingly
pertinent language of Washington against such
foreign involvements, Van Buren skillfully referred
to the very Prussian treaty which the President
had cited in his message to the House. The elder
Adams, the Senate was reminded, had departed
from the rule commended by his great predecessor.
He had told his first Congress that we were indeed
to keep ourselves distinct and separate from the
political system of Europe "if we can," but that
we needed early and continual information of political projects in contemplation; that however we
might consider ourselves, others would consider us
a weight in the balance of power in Europe, which
never could be forgotten or neglected; and that it
was natural for us, studying to be neutral, to consult with other nations engaged in the same study.
The younger Adams had been, Van Buren pointed
out, appointed upon the Berlin mission to carry
out these heretical suggestions of his father. The

Republicans of that day had vigorously opposed
the mission; and for their opposition were denounced as a faction, and lampooned and vilified
" by all the presses supporting and supported by
the government, and a host of malicious parasites
generaled by its patronage." But, covered with
Washington's mantle, the Republicans of '98 had
sought to strangle at its birth this political hydra,
this first attempt since the establishment of the
government to subject our political affairs to the
terms and conditions of political connection with a
foreign nation. Probably anticipating the success
of the administration senators by a majority of
five, Van Buren ingeniously reminded the Senate
that those early Republicans had failed with a
majority of four against them. But it was to be
remembered, he continued, that after a few more
such Federalist victories the ruin of Federalism
had been complete. Its doctrines had speedily
received popular condemnation. The new administration under the presidency of that early minister
to Prussia had returned to the practices of the
Federalist party, to which Van Buren with courteous indirection let it be remembered that the
president had originally belonged. Except a guar-
anty to Spain of its dominions beyond the Mississippi, which Jefferson had offered as part of the
price of a cession of the territory between that
river and the Mobile, the administrations of Jefferson, Madison, and Monroe had strictly followed
the admonition of Washington: " Peace, com-

merce, and honest friendship with all nations, entangling alliances with none." If we were asked
to form a connection with European states, such
as was proposed with the southern republics, Van
Buren argued, no American would approve it; and
there was no sound reason, there was nothing but
fanciful sentiment, to induce us to distinguish between the states of Europe and those of South
America. Grant that there was a Holy Alliance
in monarchical Europe, was it not a hollow glory,
inconsistent with a sober view of American interests, to create a holy alliance in republican
America? It might indeed be easy to agree upon
speculative opinions with our younger neighbors at
the south; but we should be humiliated in their
eyes, and difficulties would at once arise, when
means of promoting those opinions were proposed,
and we were then to say we could talk but not
fight. The Monroe doctrine was not to be withdrawn; but we ought to be left free to act upon it
without the burden of promises, express or implied.
The proposed congress was a specious and dis-
guised step towards an American confederacy, full
of embarrassment, full of danger; and the first
step should be firmly resisted. Such was the out-
line of Van Buren's argument; and its wisdom has
commanded a general assent from that day.

Dickerson of New Jersey very well phrased
sound American sentiment when he said in the
debate that, next to a passion for war, he dreaded
a passion for diplomacy. The majestic declama-

tion of Webster, his pathetic picture of a South America once oppressed but now emancipated, his eloquent cry that if it were weak to feel that he was an American it was a weakness from which he claimed no exemption, — all this met a good deal of exuberant response through the country. But it failed, as in our history most such efforts have failed, to convince the practical judgment of Americans, a judgment never long dazzled or inspired by the picture of an America wielding enormous or dominant international power. The Panama congress met in the absence of the American representatives, who had been delayed. It made a treaty of friendship and perpetual confederation to which all other American powers might accede within a year. The congress was to meet annually in time of common war, and biennially in times of peace. But it never met again. The " centre of the world " was too far away from its very neighbors. Even South American republics could not be kept together by effusions of republican glory and international love.

In spite of its victory in Congress, Adams's administration had plainly opened with a serious mistake. The opposition was perfectly legitimate ; and although in the debate it was spoken of as unorganized, it certainly came out of the debate a pretty definite party. Before the debate Adams had written in his diary, and truly, that it was the first subject upon which a great effort had been made " to combine the discordant elements of the

Crawford and Jackson and Calhoun men into a united opposition against the administration." Although some of the Southern opposition was heated by a dislike of States in which negroes were to be administrators, the division was not at all upon a North and South line. With Van Buren voted Findlay of Pennsylvania, Chandler and Holmes of Maine, Woodbury of New Hampshire, Dickerson of New Jersey, Kane of Illinois, making seven Northern with twelve Southern senators. Against Van Buren were eight senators from slave States, Barton of Missouri, Bouligny and Johnston of Louisiana, Chambers of Alabama, Clayton and Van Dyke of Delaware, Richard M. Johnson of Kentucky, and Smith of Maryland. It was an incipient but a true party division.

Throughout this session of 1824–25 Van Buren was very industrious in the Senate, and nearly, if not quite, its most conspicuous member, if account be not taken of Randolph's furious and blazing talents. Calhoun was only in the chair as vice-president; the great duel between him and Van Buren not yet begun. Clay was at the head of the cabinet, and Webster in the lower House. Jackson was in Tennessee, watching with angry confidence, and aiding, the rising tide with the political dexterity in which he was by no means a novice. Having only a minority with him, and with Benton frequently against him, Van Buren gradually drilled his party into opposition on internal improvements, — a most legitimate and im-

portant issue.  In December, 1825, he threw down
the gauntlet to the administration, or rather took
up its gauntlet.  He proposed a resolution " that
Congress does not possess the power to make roads
and canals within the respective States."  At the
same time he asked for a committee to prepare a
constitutional amendment on the subject like his
earlier proposal, saying with a touch of very polite
partisanship that though the President's recent declaration, that the power clearly existed in the Constitution, might diminish, it did not obviate the
necessity of an amendment.  In March, April, and
May, 1826, he opposed appropriations of $110,000
to continue the Cumberland road, and of $50,000
for surveys preparatory to roads and canals, and
subscriptions to stock of the Louisville and Port-
land Canal Company and of the Dismal Swamp
Canal Company.  All these were distinctly administration measures.

Although the principles advanced by Van Buren
in this part of his opposition have not since obtained complete and unanimous affirmance, they
have at least commanded so large, honorable, and
prolonged support, that his attitude can with little
good sense be considered one of factious difference.
Especially wise was he on the question of government subscriptions to private canal companies.
Upon one of these bills he said, in May, 1826,
that he did not believe that the government had
the constitutional power to make canals or to grant
money for them ; but he added that, if he believed

otherwise, the grant of money should, he thought, be made directly, and not by forming a partnership between the government and a private corporation. In 1824 he had voted for the road from Missouri to New Mexico; but this stood, as the Pacific railway later stood, upon a different principle, the former as a road entirely without state limits and a means of international commerce, and the latter a road chiefly through federal territories, and of obvious national importance in the war between the North and the South.

The proposed amendment of the Constitution to prevent the election of president by a vote of States in the House of Representatives, upon which Van Buren had spoken in 1824, had now acquired new interest. Van Buren seized Adams's election in the House as a good subject for political warfare; and it was clearly a legitimate topic for party discussion and division. Van Buren would have been far more exalted in his notions of political agitation than the greatest of political leaders, had he not sought to use the popular feeling, that the American will had been subverted by the decision of the House, to promote his plan of constitutional reform. He told the Senate in May, 1826, that he was satisfied that there was no one point on which the people of the United States were more perfectly united than upon the propriety of taking the choice of president from the House. But Congress was not ready for the change; however much in theory was to be said against the clumsy system which nearly made Burr president in 1801,[1] and which produced in 1825 a choice which Adams himself declared that he would vacate if the Constitution provided a mode of doing it.

As chairman of the judiciary committee, Van Buren participated in a most laborious effort to enlarge the federal judiciary. Upon the question whether the judges of the Supreme Court should be relieved from circuit duty, he made an elaborate and very able speech upon the negative side. The opportunity arose for a disquisition on the danger of centralized government, and for a renewal of the criticisms he had made in the New York Constitutional Convention upon the common and absurd picture of judges as dwellers in an atmosphere above all human infirmity, and beyond the reach of popular impression. Van Buren said, what all sensible men know, that in spite of every effort, incompetent men will sometimes reach the judicial bench. If always sitting among associates *in banc*, their incompetence would be shielded, he said, by their abler brethren. But if regularly compelled to perform their great duties alone and in the direct face of the people, and not in the isolation of Washington, there was another constraint, Van Buren said very democratically and with substantial truth. "There is a power in pub-

[1] The more conspicuous difficulty in 1801 arose from the voting by each elector for two candidates without distinguishing which he preferred for president and which for vice-president. But the awkwardness and not improbable injustice of a choice by the House was also well illustrated in February, 1801.

lic opinion in this country," he declared, "and I thank God for it, for it is the most honest and best of all powers, which will not tolerate an incompetent or unworthy man to hold in his weak or wicked hands the lives and fortunes of his fellow citizens." He added an expression to which he would afterwards have given most narrow interpretation. The Supreme Court stood, he said, "as the umpire between the conflicting powers of the general and state governments." There was in the speech very plain though courteous intimation of that jealousy with which Van Buren's party examined the political utterances of the court from Jefferson's time until, years after Van Buren's retirement, the party found it convenient to receive from the court, with a sanctimonious air of veneration, the most odious and demoralizing of all its expressions of political opinion. In arguing for a close and democratic relation between the judges and the different parts of the country, and against their dignified and exalted seclusion at Washington which was so agreeable to many patriotic Americans, Van Buren said, in a passage which is fairly characteristic of his oratorical manner : —

"A sentiment I had almost said of idolatry for the Supreme Court has grown up, which claims for its members an almost entire exemption from the fallibilities of our nature, and arraigns with unsparing bitterness the motives of all who have the temerity to look with inquisitive eyes into this consecrated sanctuary of the law. So powerful has this sentiment become, such strong hold has it taken upon the press of this country, that it requires not a little share of firmness in a public man, however imperious may be his duty, to express sentiments that conflict with it. It is nevertheless correct, sir, that in this, as in almost every other case, the truth is to be found in a just medium of the subject. To so much of the high-wrought eulogies (which the fashion of the times has recently produced in such great abundance) as allows to the distinguished men who now hold in their hands that portion of the administration of public affairs, talents of the highest order, and spotless integrity, I cheerfully add the very humble testimony of my unqualified assent. That the uncommon man who now presides over the court, and who I hope may long continue to do so, is, in all human probability, the ablest judge now sitting upon any judicial bench in the world, I sincerely believe. But to the sentiment which claims for the judges so great a share of exemption from the feelings that govern the conduct of other men, and for the court the character of being the safest depository of political power, I do not subscribe. I have been brought up in an opposite faith, and all my experience has confirmed me in its correctness. In my legislation upon this subject I will act in conformity to those opinions. I believe the judges of the Supreme Court (great and good men as I cheerfully concede them to be) are subject to the same infirmities, influenced by the same passions, and operated upon by the same causes, that good and great men are in other situations. I believe they have as much of the *esprit de corps* as other men. Those who think [1] otherwise form an erroneous estimate of human

---

[1] Gales and Seaton's Debates in Congress give here the word " act " instead of " think," — but erroneously, I assume.

nature; and if they act upon that estimate, will, soon or late, become sensible of their delusion."

At this session, upon the election by the Senate of their temporary president, Van Buren received the compliment of four votes. In May, 1826, he participated in Benton's report on the reduction of executive patronage, a subject important enough, but there crudely treated. The report strongly exhibited the jealousy of executive power which had long been characteristic of American political thought. By describing the offices within the president's appointment, their numbers and salaries, and the expense of the civil list, a striking picture was drawn — and in that way a striking picture can always be drawn — of the power of any great executive. By imagining serious abuses of power, the picture was darkened with the dangers of patronage, as it could be darkened to-day. The country was urged to look forward to the time when public revenue would be doubled, when the number of public officers would be quadrupled, when the president's nomination would carry any man through the Senate, and his recommendation any measure through Congress. Names, the report said, were nothing. The first Roman emperor was styled Emperor of the Republic; and the late French emperor had taken a like title. The American president, it was hinted, might by his enormous patronage and by subsidies to the press, nominally for official advertisements, subject us to a like danger. But the usefulness of such pictures as these

of Benton and Van Buren depends upon the practical lesson taught by the artists.   If there were
disadvantages and dangers which our ancestors
rightly feared, in placing the federal patronage
under the sole control of the president, so there
are disadvantages and dangers in scattering it by
laws into various hands, or in its subjection to the
traditions of " senatorial courtesy."

Six bills accompanied the report.   Two of them
proposed the appointment of military cadets and
midshipmen, one of each from every congressional
district; and this was afterwards done, giving a
petty patronage to national legislators which public
sentiment has but recently begun to compel them
to use upon ascertained merit rather than in sheer
favoritism.   A third bill proposed that military
and naval commissions should run " during good
behavior " and not " during the pleasure of the
president."   A fourth sought with extraordinary
unwisdom to correct the old but ever new abuse of
government advertising, by depriving the responsible executive of its distribution and by placing it
in the hands of congressmen, perhaps the very
worst to hold it.   Another required senatorial confirmation for postmasters whose emoluments exceeded an amount to be fixed.   The remaining bill
was very wise, and a natural sequence of Benton's
not untruthful though too highly colored picture.
The law of 1820, which fixed at four years the
terms of many subordinate officers, was to be modified so as to limit the terms only for officers who

had not satisfactorily accounted for public moneys. It has been commonly said that this act was a device of Crawford, when secretary of the treasury, more easily to use federal patronage for his presidential canvass. But there seems to be no sufficient reason to doubt that Benton's and Van Buren's committee correctly stated the intent of the authors of the law to have been no more than that the officer should be definitely compelled by the expiration of his term to render his accounts and have them completely audited; that it was not intended that some other person should succeed an officer not found in fault; and that the practice of refusing re-commissions to deserving officers was an unexpected perversion of the law. The committee simply proposed to accomplish the true intent of the law. The same bill required the president to state his reasons for removals of officers when he nominated their successors. The proposals in the last two bills were very creditable to Benton and Van Buren and their coadjutors. It is greatly to be lamented that they were not safely made laws while patronage was dispensed conscientiously and with sincere public spirit by the younger Adams, so far as he could control it. The biographer has more particularly to lament that during the twelve years of Van Buren's executive influence he seemed daunted by the difficulties of voluntarily putting in practice the admirable rules which as a senator he would have imposed by law upon those in executive stations. It was only three years after this report, that the great chieftain, whom Benton and Van Buren helped to the presidency, discredited all its reasoning by proposing "a general extension" of the law whose operation they would have thus limited. The committee also proposed by constitutional amendment to forbid the appointment to office of any senator or representative until the end of the presidential term in which he had held his seat. This was also one of the reforms whose necessity seems plain enough to the reformer, until in office he discovers the conveniences and perhaps the public uses of the practice he has wished to abolish.

In the short session of 1826–1827, little of any importance was done. Van Buren refused to vote with Benton to abolish the duty on salt, a vote doubtless influenced by the apparent interest of New York, which itself taxed the production of salt to aid the State in its internal improvements, and which probably could not maintain the tax if foreign salt were admitted free. Van Buren did not, indeed, avow, nor did he disavow this reason. He was content to point out that the great canals of New York were of national use, though their expense was borne by his State alone. He voted at this session for lower duties on teas, coffees, and wines. He did not join Benton and others in their narrow unwillingness to establish a naval academy. Van Buren's temper was eminently free from raw prejudices against disciplined education. The death of one of the envoys to the Panama congress enabled him again at this session to renew his opposition by a vote against filling the vacancy. Another attempt was made to pass a bankruptcy bill; but again it failed through the natural and wholesome dislike of increasing the powers of the federal judiciary, and the preference that state courts and laws should perform all the work to which they were reasonably competent. The bill did not even pass the Senate, until by Van Buren's opposition it had been reduced to a bill establishing a summary and speedy remedy for creditors against fraudulent or failing traders, instead of a general system of bankruptcy, voluntary and involuntary, for all persons. Van Buren's speech against the insolvency features of the bill was made on January 23, 1827, only a few days before his successor as senator was to be chosen. But the thoughtless popularity which often accompanies sweeping propositions of relief to insolvents did not move him from resolute and successful opposition to what he called (and later experience has most abundantly justified him) "an injurious extension of the patronage of the federal government, and an insupportable enlargement of the range of its judicial power." On February 24, 1827, a few days after his reëlection, he delivered a lucid and elaborate speech on the long-perplexing topic of the restrictions upon American trade with the British colonies, a subject to be afterwards closely connected with his political fortunes.

The agitation of the coming presidential election

left little of its turbulence upon the records of the long session from December, 1827, to May, 1828. Van Buren was doubtless busy enough out of the senate chamber. But he was still a very busy legislator. He spoke at least twice in favor of the bill to abolish imprisonment under judgments rendered by federal courts for debts not fraudulently incurred, the bill which Richard M. Johnson had pressed so long and so honorably ; and at last he saw the bill pass in January, 1828. He spoke often upon the technical bill to regulate federal judicial process. Again he voted, and again in a minority and in opposition to Benton and other political friends, against bills to extend the Cumberland road and for other internal improvements. Besides the usual bills to appropriate lands for roads and canals, and to subscribe to the stock of private canal companies, a step further was now taken in the constitutional change led by Adams and Clay. Public land was voted for the benefit of Kenyon College, in the State of Ohio. There was plainly intended to be no limit to federal beneficence. In this session Van Buren again rushed to defend the salt duty so dear to New York.

At the same session was passed the " tariff of abominations," a measure so called from the oppressive provisions loaded on it by its enemies, but in spite of which it passed. Van Buren, though he sat still during the debate, cast for the bill a protectionist vote, with Benton and several others whose convictions were against it, but who yielded to the supposed public sentiment or the peremptory instructions of their States, or who did not yet dare to make upon the tariff a presidential issue. The votes of the senators were sectionally thus distributed: For the tariff, — New England, 6; Middle States, 8; Louisiana, 1; and the Western States, 11; in all 26. Against it, — New England, 5; Maryland, 2; Southern States, 13; and Tennessee, 1. It was a victory of neither political party, but of the Middle and Western over the Southern States. Only three negative votes were cast by senators who had voted against the administration on the Panama question in 1826; while of the votes for the tariff, fourteen were cast by senators who had then opposed the administration. Of the senators in favor of the tariff, six, Van Buren, Benton, Dickerson of New Jersey, Eaton of Tennessee (Jackson's close friend), Kane of Illinois, and Rowan of Kentucky, had in 1826 been in opposition, while ten of those voting against the tariff had then been with them.[1] The greater number of the opposition senators were therefore against the tariff, though very certainly the votes of Van Buren, Benton, and Eaton prevented the opposition from taking strong ground or suffering injury on the tariff in the election. Van Buren's silence in this debate of 1828 indicated at least a temper now hesitant. But he and his colleague, Sanford, according to the theory then popular that senators

[1] The comparison cannot of course be complete, as some who were senators in 1826 were not senators in 1828.

were simply delegated agents of their States, were constrained, whatever were their opinions, by a resolution of the legislature of New York passed almost unanimously in January, 1828. It stated a sort of *ultima ratio* of protection, commanding the senators "to make every proper exertion to effect such a revision of the tariff as will afford a sufficient protection to the growers of wool, hemp, and flax, and the manufacturers of iron, woolens, and every other article, so far as the same may be connected with the interest of manufactures, agriculture, and commerce." The senators might perhaps have said to this that, if they were to protect not only iron and woolens but also every other article, they ought not to levy prohibitory duties on some and not on other articles; that if they were equally to protect manufactures, agriculture, and commerce, they could do no better than to let natural laws alone. But the silly instruction said what no intelligent protectionist means; his system disappears with an equality of privilege; that equality must, he argues, at some point yield to practical necessities. Van Buren took the resolution, however, in its intended meaning, and not literally. Hayne concluded his fine struggle against the bill by a solemn protest upon its passage that it was a partial, unjust, and unconstitutional measure.

At this session Van Buren, upon the consideration of a rule giving the Vice-President power to call to order for words spoken in debate, made perhaps the most elaborate of his purely political speeches. It was a skillful and not unsuccessful effort to give philosophical significance to the coming struggle at the polls. He spoke of " that collision, which seems to be inseparable from the nature of man, between the rights of the few and the many," of " those never-ceasing conflicts between the advocates of the enlargement and concentration of power on the one hand, and its limitation and distribution on the other." The one party, he said, had " grown out of a deep and settled distrust of the people and of the States : " the other, out of " a jealousy of power justified by all human experience." The advocates of " a strong government," having been defeated in much that they sought in the federal convention, had since, he said, " been at work to obtain by construction what was not included or intended to be included in the grant." He declared the incorporation of the United States Bank to be the " great pioneer of constitutional encroachments." Thence had followed those famous usurpations, the alien and sedition laws of the older Adams's administration. Then came the doctrine that the House of Representatives was bound to make all appropriations necessary to carry out a treaty made by the President and Senate ; and then " the bold avowal that it belonged to the President alone to decide upon the propriety " of a foreign mission, and that it was for the Senate only " to pass on the fitness of the individuals selected as ministers." He

lamented the single lapse of Madison, "one of
the most, if not the most, accomplished statesman
that our country has produced," in signing the bill
to incorporate the new bank. The younger Adams,
Van Buren declared, had "gone far beyond the
utmost latitude of construction " therefore claimed ;
and he added a reference, decorous enough but
neither fair nor gracious, to Adams's own early
entrance in the public service upon a mission un-
authorized by Congress. It was now demonstrated,
he said, that the result of the presidential choice
of 1825 "was not only the restoration of the men
of 1798, but of the principles of that day." The
spirit of encroachment had, it was true, become
more wary ; but it was no more honest. The
system had then been coercion ; now it was seduc-
tion. Then unconstitutional powers had been exercised to force submission ; now they were assumed to purchase golden opinions from the people
with their own means. Isolated acts of the Federalists had not produced an unyielding exclusion
from the confidence of a majority of the people,
for more than a quarter of a century, of large
masses of men distinguished for talent and private
worth. The great and glorious struggle had proceeded from something deeper, an opposition to the
principle of an extension of the constructive powers
of the government. Without harsh denunciation,
and by suggestion rather than assertion, the administration of John Quincy Adams was grouped
with the administration of his father. The earlier

administration had deserved and met the retribution of a Republican victory. The later one now deserved and ought soon to meet a like fate.

The issue was clearly made. The parties were formed. The result rested with the people. On February 6, 1827, Van Buren had been reëlected senator by a large majority in both houses of the New York legislature. In his brief letter of acceptance he said no more on public questions than that it should be his " constant and zealous endeavor to protect the remaining rights reserved to the States by the federal Constitution," and " to restore those of which they have been divested by construction." This had been the main burden of his political oratory from the inauguration of Adams. There are many references in books to doubts of Van Buren's position until 1827 ; but such doubts are not justified in the face of his prompt and perfectly explicit utterances in the session of 1825–1826, and from that time steadily on.

De Witt Clinton's death on February 11, 1828, removed from the politics of New York one of its most illustrious men, a statesman of the first rank, able and passionate, and of the noblest aspirations. The understanding reached between him and Van Buren in 1826, for the support of Jackson, had not produced a complete coalition. In spite of the union on Jackson, the Bucktails nominated and Van Buren loyally supported for governor against Clinton in 1826, William B. Rochester, a warm friend and supporter of Adams and Clay, and one of the members of the very Panama mission against which so strenuous a fight had been made. Clinton was reëlected by a small majority. In a meeting at Washington after his death, Van Buren declared the triumph of his talents and patriotism to be monuments of high and enduring fame. He was glad that, though in their public careers there had been " collisions of opinions and action at once extensive, earnest, and enduring," they had still been " wholly free from that most venomous and corroding of all poisons, personal hatred." These collisions were now " turned to nothing and less than nothing." Speaking of his respect for Clinton's name and gratitude for his signal services, Van Buren concluded with this striking tribute: " For myself, so strong, so sincere, and so engrossing is that feeling, that I, who whilst living, never — no, never, envied him anything, now that he has fallen, am greatly tempted to envy him his grave with its honors."

With this session of 1827–1828 ended Van Buren's senatorial career and his parliamentary leadership. From 1821 to 1828 the Senate was not indeed at its greatest glory. Webster entered it only in December, 1827. Hayne and Benton with Van Buren are to us its most distinguished members, if Randolph's rather indescribable and useless personality may be excepted. But to neither of them has the opinion of later times assigned a place in the first rank of orators, although Hayne's tariff speech in 1824 deserves to be set

with the greatest of American political orations.
The records and speeches of the Senate in which
Van Buren sat have come to us with fine print
and narrow margins; they have not contributed to
the collected works of great men. But the Senate
was then an able body. The principles of American politics were never more clearly stated. When
the books are well dusted, and one has broken
through the starched formality in which the speakers' phrases were set, he finds a copious fund of
political instruction. The federal Senate was more
truly a parliamentary body in those formative days
than perhaps at any other period. Several at least
of its members were in doubt as to the political
course they should follow; they were in doubt
where they should find their party associations.
To them, debates had therefore a real and present
significance. There were some votes to be affected,
there were converts to be gained, by speeches even
on purely political questions; there were some senators whose votes were not inexorably determined
for them by the will of their parties or their constituents. Much that was said had therefore a
genuine parliamentary ring. The orators really
sought to convince and persuade those who heard
them within the easy and almost conversational
limits of the old senate chamber. There was little
of the mere pronouncing of essays or declamations
intended to have their real and only effect elsewhere. In this art of true parliamentary speaking
rather than oratory, Van Buren was a master such

as Lord Palmerston afterwards became. He was not eloquent. His speeches, so far as they are preserved, interest the student of political history and not of literature. They are sensible, clear, practical arguments made in rather finished sentences. One does not find quotations from them in books of school declamation. But they served far more effectively the primary end of parliamentary speaking than did the elaborate and powerful disquisitions of Calhoun, or the more splendid flood of Webster's eloquence. Van Buren's speeches were intended to convince, and they did convince some of the men in the seats about him. They were meant to persuade, and they did persuade. They were lucid exhibitions of political principles, generally practical, and touched sufficiently but not morbidly with the theoretical fears so common to our earlier politics. Some of those fears have since been shown to be groundless; but out of many of them has come much that is best in the modern temper of American political institutions. Van Buren's speeches did not rise beyond the reach of popular understanding, although they never warmly touched popular sympathy. They were intended to formulate and spread a political faith in which he plainly saw that there was the material of a party, — a faith founded upon the jealousy of federal activity, however beneficent, which sought to avoid state control or encourage state dependence. The prolixity which was a grave fault of his state papers and political letters was far less exhibited in his oratorical efforts. His style was generally easy and vigorous, with little of the turgid learning which loaded down many sensible speeches of the time. Now and then, however, he resorted to the sentences of stilted formality which sometimes overtake a good public speaker, as a good actor sometimes lapses into the stage strut.

In Van Buren's senatorial speeches there is nothing to justify the charge of "non-committalism" so much made against him. When he spoke at all he spoke explicitly; and he plainly, though without acerbity, exhibited his likes and dislikes. Jackson was struck with this when he sat in the Senate with him. "I had heard a great deal about Mr. Van Buren," he said, "especially about his non-committalism. I made up my mind that I would take an early opportunity to hear him and judge for myself. One day an important subject was under debate in the Senate. I noticed that Mr. Van Buren was taking notes while one of the senators was speaking. I judged from this that he intended to reply, and I determined to be in my seat when he spoke. His turn came; and he rose and made a clear, straightforward argument, which, to my mind, disposed of the whole subject. I turned to my colleague, Major Eaton, who sat next to me. 'Major,' said I, 'is there anything non-committal about that?' 'No, sir,' said the major." Van Buren scrupulously observed the amenities of debate. He was uniformly courteous towards adversaries; and the calm self-control saved him, as some greater orators were not saved, from a descent to the aspersion of motive so common and so futile in political debate. He could not, indeed, help now and then an allusion to the venality and monarchical tendency of the Federalists and their successors; but this was an old formula which strong haters had years before made very popular in the Republican phrase-book, and which, as to the venality, meant nobody in particular.

# CHAPTER V

WHEN in May, 1828, Van Buren left Washington, the country universally recognized him as the chief organizer of the new party and its congressional leader. As such he turned all his skill and industry to win a victory for Jackson and Calhoun. There was never in the history of the United States a more legitimate presidential canvass than that of 1828. The rival candidates distinctly stood for conflicting principles of federal administration. On the one side, under Van Buren's shrewd management, with the theoretical coöperation of Calhoun, — the natural bent of whose mind was now aided and not thwarted by the exigencies of his personal career, — was the party inclined to strict limitation of federal powers, jealous for local powers, hostile to internal improvements by the federal government, inclined to a lower rather than a higher tariff. On the other side was the party strongly national in temper, with splendid conceptions of a powerful and multifariously useful central administration, impatient of the poverties and meannesses of many of the States. The latter party was led by a president with ampler training

in public life than any American of his time, who
sincerely and intelligently believed the principles
of his party; and his party held those principles
firmly, explicitly, and with practical unanimity.
Jefferson, in almost his last letter, written in December, 1825, to William B. Giles, a venerable
leader of the Democracy, the " Charles James Fox
of Congress," Benton's " statesman of head and
tongue," recalled indeed Adams's superiority over
all ordinary considerations when the safety of his
country had been questioned; but Jefferson declared himself in " the deepest affliction " at the
usurpations by which the federal branch, through
the decisions of the federal court, the doctrines of
the President, and the misconstructions of Congress, was stripping its " colleagues, the state authorities, of the powers reserved to them." The
voice from Monticello, feeble with its eighty-three
years, and secretly uttered though it was, sounded
the summons to a new Democratic battle.

Van Buren and his coadjutors, however, led a
party as yet of inclination to principles rather than
of principles. It was out of power. There was
neither warmth nor striking exaltation in its pro-
gramme. Its philosophical and political wisdom
needed the aid of one of those simple cries for justice which are so potent in political warfare, and
a leader to interest and fire the popular temper.
Both were at hand. The late defeat of the popular will by the Adams-Clay coalition was the cry;
the hero of the military victory most grateful to

Americans was the leader. To this cry and this leader Van Buren skillfully harnessed an intelligible, and at the least a reasonable, political creed. There were thus united nearly all the elements of political strength. Not indeed all, for the record of the leader was weak upon several articles of faith. Jackson had voted in the Senate for internal improvement bills, and among them bills of the most obnoxious character, those authorizing subscriptions to the stocks of private corporations. He had voted against reductions of the tariff. But the votes, it was hoped, exhibited only his inexpertness in applying general principles to actual legislation, or a good-natured willingness to please his constituents by single votes comparatively unimportant. In truth these mistakes were really inconsistencies of the politician, and no more. There had been a long inclination on Jackson's part to the Jeffersonian policy. Over thirty years before, he had in Congress been a strict constructionist and an anti-federalist. In 1801 he had required a candidate desiring his support to be " an admirer of state authority, agreeable to the true literal meaning" of the Constitution, and "banishing the dangerous doctrine of implication." If he were now to have undivided responsibility, this old Democratic trend of his would, it was hoped, be strong enough under Democratic advice. As a candidate, the inconsistencies of a soldier politician were far outweighed by his picturesque and powerful personality. It is commonly thought of Jackson that he was a headstrong, passionate, illiterate man, used and pulled about by a few intriguers. Nothing could be further from the truth. He was himself a politician of a high order. His letters are full of shrewd, vigorous, and even managing suggestions of partisan manœuvres. Their political utterances show a highly active and generally sensible though not disciplined mind. He had had long and important experience of civil affairs, in the lower house of Congress, in the federal Senate when he was only thirty years old, in the constitutional convention of his State, in its Supreme Court, later again in the Senate ; he had been for eight years before the country as a candidate for its first office, and for many years in public business of large importance. There were two of the most distinguished Americans, men of the ripest abilities and amplest experience, and far removed from rashness, who from 1824 or before had steadily preferred Jackson for the presidency. These were Edward Livingston of Louisiana and De Witt Clinton of New York. Daniel Webster described his manners as "more presidential than those of any of the candidates." Jackson was, he wrote, "grave, mild, and reserved." Unless in Jackson's case there were effects without adequate causes, it is very certain that, with faults of most serious character, he still had the ability, the dignity, and the wisdom of a ruler of a high rank. He was, as very few men are, born to rule.

After Crawford's defeat, Van Buren is credited

with a skillful management of the alliance of his
forces with those of Jackson.  There is not yet
public, if it exist, any original evidence as to the
details of this work.  Van Buren's enemies were
fond of describing it as full of cunning and trickery, the work of " the little magician ; " and later
and fairer writers have adopted from these enemies
this characterization.  But all this seems entirely
without proof.  Nor is the story probable.  The
union of the Crawford and Jackson men was perfectly natural.  Crawford was a physical wreck,
out of public life.  Numerous as were the exceptions, his followers and Jackson's included the
great majority of the strict constructionists ; and
but a minority of either of the two bodies held the
opposite views.  Neither of the two men had, at
the last election, been defeated by the other.  That
Van Buren used at Washington his unrivaled skill
in assuaging animosities and composing differences
there can be no doubt.  After the end of the session in March, 1827, together with Churchill C.
Cambreleng, a member of Congress from New
York and a close political friend of his, he made
upon this mission a tour through Virginia, the Carolinas, and Georgia.  They visited Crawford, and
were authorized to declare that he should support
Jackson, but did not wish to aid Calhoun.  At
Raleigh Van Buren told the citizens that the spirit
of encroachment had assumed a new and far more
seductive aspect, and could only be resisted by the
exercise of uncommon virtues.  Passing through

Washington on his way north, he paid a polite
visit to Adams, talking with him placidly about
Rufus King, Monroe, and the Petersburg horse-
races. The President, regarding him as " the
great electioneering manager for General Jackson," promptly noted in his diary, when the interview was over, that Van Buren was now acting the
part Burr had performed in 1799 and 1800 ; and
he found " much resemblance of character, manners, and even person, between the two men."

As early as 1826 the Van Buren Republicans of
New York, and an important part of the Clintonians with the great governor at their head, had
determined to support Jackson. Van Buren is
said to have concealed his attitude until after his
reëlection to the Senate in 1827. But this is a
complete error, except as to his public choice of
a candidate. His opposition to the Adams-Clay
administration, it has already appeared, had been
outspoken from 1825. The Jackson candidacy was
not indeed definitely announced in New York until
1827. The cry for " Old Hickory " then went
up with a sudden unanimity which seemed to the
Adams men a bit of devilish magic, but which was
the patient prearrangement of a skillful politician
appreciating his responsibility, and waiting, as the
greatest of living politicians [1] recently told Eng-

---

[1] This and several other references of mine to Gladstone were
written ten years and more before his death. These years of his
brief but extraordinary Home Rule victory, of his final defeat, —
for Lord Rosebery's defeat was Gladstone's defeat, — and of his

land a statesman ought to wait, until the time was really ripe, until the popular inclination was sufficiently formed to justify action by men in responsible public station.

The opposition to the reëlection of John Quincy Adams in 1828 was sincerely considered by him, and has been often described by others, as singularly causeless, unworthy, and even monstrous. But in truth it led to one of the most necessary, one of the truest, political revolutions which our country has known.  Both Adams and Clay were positive and able men.  They were resolute that the rather tepid democracy of Monroe should be succeeded by a highly national, a federally active administration.  Prior to the election of 1824 Clay had been as nearly in opposition as the era of good feeling permitted.  Early in Monroe's administration he had attacked the President's declaration that Congress had no right to construct roads and canals.  His criticism, Mr. Schurz tells us in his brilliant and impartial account of the time, " had a strong flavor of bitterness in it ; " it was in part made up of " oratorical flings," by which Clay unnecessarily sought to attack and humiliate Monroe. Adams's diary states Clay's opposition to have been " violent, systematic," his course to have been " angry, acrimonious."  Late in 1819 Monroe's

retirement, have not only added a mellow and almost sacred splendor to his noble career, but have still better demonstrated his superb political gifts.  What politician indeed, dead or living, is to be ranked above him ?

friends had even consulted over the wisdom of defeating Clay's reëlection to the speakership; and still later Clay had, as Mr. Schurz says, fiercely castigated the administration for truckling to foreigners. When Clay came into power, it would have been unreasonable for him to suppose that there must not arise vigorous parliamentary opposition on the part of those who consider themselves the true Republican successors of Monroe, seeking to stop the diversion into strange ways which Clay and Adams had now begun. Richard Rush of Pennsylvania, Adams's secretary of the treasury, and now the Adams candidate for vice-president, had, in one of his annual reports, declared it to be the duty of government " to augment the number and variety of occupations for its inhabitants; to hold out to every degree of labor, and to every modification of skill, its appropriate object and inducement; to organize the whole labor of a country; to entice into the widest ranges its mechanical and intellectual capacities, instead of suffering them to slumber; to call forth, wherever hidden, latent ingenuity, giving to effort activity and to emulation ardor; to create employment for the greater amount of numbers by adapting it to the diversified faculties, propensities, and situations of men, so that every particle of ability, every shade of genius, may come into requisition." Nor did this glowing picture of a useful and beneficent government go far beyond the utterances of Rush's senior associate on the presidential ticket. It is certain that it was highly agreeable to Clay.

Surely there could be no clearer political issue presented, on the one side by Van Buren's speeches in the Senate, and on the other by authoritative and solemn declarations of the three chief persons of the administration. Whatever the better side of the issue may have been, no issue was ever a more legitimate subject of a political campaign. It is true that the accusations were unfounded, which were directed against Adams for treachery to the Republican principles he professed after, on adhering to Jefferson, he had resigned his seat in the Senate. He had joined Jefferson on questions of foreign policy and domestic defense, and had, until his election to the presidency, been chiefly concerned with diplomacy. But though the accusations were false, it is true enough that Adams himself had made the issue of the campaign. Nor was it creditable to him that he saw in the opposition something merely personal to himself. If he were wrong upon the issue, as Van Buren and a majority of the people thought, his long public service, his utter integrity, his exalted sense of the obligations of office, ought not to have saved him from the battle or from defeat. How true and deep was this political contest of 1828 one sees in the fact that from it, almost as much as from the triumph of Jefferson, flow the traditions of one of the great American parties, traditions which survived the corruptions of slavery, and are still powerful in party administration.[1] If John Quincy

[1] This was written nine years before the lamentable surrender

Adams had been elected, and if, as might naturally have been the case, there had followed, at this commencement of railway building, a firm establishment of the doctrine that the national government could properly build roads within the States, it is more than mere speculation to say that the later history of the United States would, whether for the better or the worse, have been very different from what it has been. The dangers to which American institutions would be exposed, if the federal government had become a great power levying taxes upon the whole country to be used in constructing railways, or, what was worse, purchasing stock in railway corporations, and doing this, as it would inevitably have done, according to the amount of pressure here or there, — such dangers, it is easy to understand, seem, whether rightly or wrongly, appalling to a large class of political thinkers. To realize this sense of danger dissipates the aspect of *doctrinaire* extravagance in the speeches of Adams's opponents against latitudinarian construction.

In the canvass of 1828 there was on both sides more wicked and despicable exhibition of slander than had been known since Jefferson and John Adams were pitted against each other. Jackson was a military butcher and utterly illiterate; the

of the organization of Van Buren's party at Chicago in 1896. It is safe to say that these traditions, even if fallen sadly out of sight, still make a deep and powerful force, which must in due time assert itself.

chastity of his wife was doubtful. Adams had corruptly bargained away offices; his accounts of public moneys received by him needed serious scrutiny ; and, that the charges might be precisely balanced, he had when minister at St. Petersburg acted as procurer to the Czar of Russia. These lies doubtless defeated themselves; but in each election since 1828 there have been politicians low enough and silly enough to imitate them. To nothing of this kind did Van Buren descend. Nor does it seem that even then he used the cry of a corrupt bargain between Adams and Clay, in which Jackson believed as long as he lived. The coalition of 1825, defeating, as it had, a candidate chosen by a larger number of voters than any other, was the most used, and probably the most successfully used, of any of the campaign issues. Nor was this clearly illegitimate, although Adams and many for him have hotly condemned its immorality. Every political coalition between men lately in opposition political and personal, by which both get office, is fairly open to criticism. In experience it has always been full of political danger, although since the prejudice of the times has worn away, the defense of Adams and Clay is seen to be amply sufficient. Whatever had been their mutual dislikes political or personal, each of them was politically and in his practical statesmanship far nearer to the other than to any other of the competitors. But we have yet to see a political campaign against a coalition whose members have been rewarded with office, in which this form of attack is not made by men very intelligent and most honest. Nor is there any reason to hold the followers of Jackson to a higher standard. In our own time we have seen two coalitions whose parties wisely recognized this danger. The chief leaders of the Republican revolt in 1884 neither sought nor took office from the former adversaries with whom for once they then acted. The Dissenting Liberals in England did not take office in the Conservative ministry formed in 1886; and the odium which, in the change later made in it, followed Mr. Goschen into its second place, illustrated very well the truth that, however honorable the course may be, it is inevitably dangerous.[1]

Nor can moral condemnation be passed upon the use in 1828 of the defeat in 1824, of the candidate having the largest popular vote. We see pretty clearly in a constitutionally governed country that when power is lawfully lodged with a public man, he must act upon his own judgment; and that, if he be influenced by others, then he ought to be influenced by the wishes and interests of those who

[1] After the Dissenting Liberals had acted with the Conservatives, not only in the first Home Rule campaign in 1886, but during the Salisbury administration from 1886 to 1892, and in the campaigns of 1892 and 1895, the coalition was ended and a new and single party formed, of which the Duke of Devonshire and Mr. Chamberlain were leaders as really as Lord Salisbury or Mr. Balfour. The accession of the former to the Unionist ministry of 1895 was in no sense a reward for bringing over some of the enemy.

supported him, and not of those who opposed him,
even though far more numerous than his supporters. Repeatedly have we seen a state legislature, which the arrangement of districts has caused
to be elected from a party in minority in the whole
State, choose a federal senator who it was known
would have been defeated upon a popular vote; and
this without criticism of the conduct of the legislators, but only of the defective district division. In
Connecticut it has happened more than once that,
neither candidate for governor having a majority
vote, the legislature has chosen a candidate having
one of the smaller minorities; and here again without criticism of the legislature's morality. But still
the general rule of American elections is, that the
candidate shall be chosen who is preferred by more
votes than any other. To assent to a constitutional
defeat of such a preference, but afterwards and
under the law to make strong appeal to right the
wrong which the law has wrought, seems a highly
defensible course, and to deserve little of the criticism visited upon the Jackson canvass of 1828. If
party divisions be justifiable, if chief public officers
are to be chosen for their views on great questions
of state, if the cold appeals of political reasoning
are ever rightly strengthened by appeals to popular
feelings, the campaign which Van Buren and his
associates began in 1825 or 1826 was perfectly
justifiable. Nor in its result can any one deny,
whether it were for better or worse, that their success in the battle worked a change in the principles

of administration, and not a mere vulgar driving from office of one body of men that another might take their places.

The death of De Witt Clinton left Van Buren easily the largest figure in public life, as he had for several years been the most powerful politician, in New York State. The gossip that the most important place in Jackson's cabinet was really allotted to him before the election of 1828 is probably true. But, whether true or not, there was, apart from a natural desire to administer the first office in his State, obvious advantage to his political prestige in passing successfully through a popular election. The most cynical of managing politicians recognize the enormous strength of a man for whom the people have actually shown that they like to vote. Van Buren may have counted besides upon the advantage which Jackson's personal popularity brought to those in his open alliance, although Adams was known still to have, as the election showed he had, considerable Democratic strength. Van Buren took therefore the Bucktail nomination for governor of New York. The National Republicans, as the Adams men were called, nominated Smith Thompson, a judge of the federal Supreme Court. Van Buren got 136,794 and Thompson 106,444 votes. But in spite of so large a plurality Van Buren did not quite have a majority of the popular vote. Solomon Southwick, the anti-Masonic candidate, received 33,345 votes. It was the first election after this extraordinary movement. The abduction of Morgan and his probable murder to prevent his revelation of Masonic secrets had occurred in the fall of 1826. The criminal trials consequent upon it had caused intense excitement; and a political issue was easily made, for many distinguished men of both parties were members of that secret order. How powerful for a time may be a popular cry, though based upon an utterly absurd issue, became more obvious still later when electoral votes for president were cast for William Wirt, the anti-Masonic candidate; and when John Quincy Adams, after graduating from the widest experience in public affairs of any American of his generation, was, as he himself records, willing to accept, and when William H. Seward was willing to tender him, a presidential nomination of the anti-Masonic party. As Southwick's preposterous vote was in 1828 drawn from both parties, Van Buren's prestige, although he had but a plurality vote, was increased by his victory at the polls. Jackson very truly said in February, 1832, that it was now "the general wish and expectation of the Republican party throughout the Union" that Van Buren should take the place next to the President in the national administration. Jackson was himself elected by a very great popular and electoral majority. In New York, where on this single occasion the electors were chosen in districts, and where the anti-Masonic vote was cast against Jackson who held high rank in the Masonic order, Adams secured 16 votes to

Jackson's 18 ; but to the latter were added the two electors chosen by the thirty-four district electors.

Van Buren's career as governor was very brief. He was inaugurated on January 1, 1829, and at once resigned his seat in the federal Senate.  On March 12th of the same year he resigned the governor's seat.  His inaugural message is said by Hammond, the political historian of New York, by no means too friendly to Van Buren, to have been " the best executive message ever communicated to the legislature ; "  and after nearly sixty years, it seems, in the leather-covered tome containing it, a remarkably clear, wise, and courageous paper.  The excitement over internal improvements in communication was then at its height.  He declared that, whatever difference there might be as to whether such improvements ought to be undertaken by the federal government or by the States, none seriously doubted that it was wise to apply portions of the means of New York to such improvements.  The investment of the State in the Delaware and Hudson canal, then just completed, had, he thought, been " crowned with the most cheering success." Splendid, too, as had been the success of the Erie and Champlain canals, it was still clear that all had not been equally benefited.  The friends of the state road and of the Chemung and Chenango canals had urged him to recommend for them a legislative support.  But it was a time, he said, for " the utmost prudence and circumspection " upon that " delicate and vitally interesting subject."

The banking question, he told the legislature, would make the important business of its session. It turned out besides to be one of the important businesses of Van Buren's career. To meet the attacks upon him for having once been interested in a bank, he dexterously recited that, "having for many years ceased to have an interest in those institutions and declined any agency in their management," he was conscious of his imperfect information. But he could not ignore a matter of such magnitude to their constituents. The whole bank agitation at this time showed the difficulties and scandals caused by the absence of a free banking system, and by the long accustomed grants of exclusive banking charters. Of the forty banks in the State, all specially incorporated, the charters of thirty-one would expire within one, two, three, or four years. Their actual capital was $15,000,000; their outstanding loans, more than $30,000,000. Van Buren urged, therefore, the legislature now to make by general law final disposition of the whole subject. The abolition of banks had, he said, no advocate, and a dependence solely upon those established by federal authority deserved none; but he rejected the idea of a state bank. "Experience," he declared, "has shown that banking operations, to be successful, and consequently beneficial to the community, must be conducted by private men upon their own account." He condemned the practice by which the State accepted a money bonus for granting a bank charter, neces-

sarily involving some monopoly. The concern of
the State, he pointed out, should be to make its
banks and their circulation secure; and such security was impaired, not increased, by encouraging
banks in competition with one another, and "stimulated by the golden harvest in view," to make large
payments for their charters. He submitted for
legislative consideration the idea of the "safety
fund" communicated to him in an interesting and
intelligent paper by Joshua Forman. Under this
system all the banks of the State, whatever their
condition, were to contribute to a fund to be administered under state supervision, the fund to be
a security for all dishonored bank-notes. To this
extent all the banks were to insure or indorse the
circulation of each bank, thus saving the scandal
and loss arising from the occasional failure of
banks to redeem their notes, and making every
bank watchful of all its associates. In compelling
the banks to submit to some general scheme, the
representative of the people would indeed, he said,
enter into "conflict with the claims of the great
moneyed interest of the country; but what political
exhibition so truly gratifying as the return to his
constituents of the faithful public servant after
having turned away every approach and put far
from him every sinister consideration!"

Van Buren proposed a separation of state from
national elections; a question still discussed, and
upon each side of which much is to be said. He
attacked the use of money in elections, "the prac-

tice of employing persons to attend the polls for
compensation, of placing large sums in the hands
of others to entertain the electors," and other devices by which the most valuable of all our temporal
privileges "was brought into disrepute." If the
expenses of elections should increase as they had
lately done, the time would soon arrive "when a
man in middling circumstances, however virtuous,
will not be able to compete upon anything like
equal terms with a wealthy opponent." In long
advance of a modern agitation for reform which,
lately beginning with us, will, it is to be hoped,
not cease until the abuses are removed, he proposed
a law imposing "severe and enforcible penalties
upon the advance of money by individuals for any
purposes connected with the election except the
single one of printing."

Turning to the field of general politics, he again
declared the political faith to whose support he
wished to rally his party. That "a jealousy of
the exercise of delegated political power, a solicitude to keep public agents within the precise limits
of their authority, and an assiduous adherence to a
rigid and scrupulous economy, were indications of
a contracted spirit unbecoming the character of a
statesman," he pronounced to be a political heresy,
from which he himself had not been entirely free,
but which ought at once to be exploded. Official
discretion, as a general rule, could not be confided
to any one without danger of abuse. But he re-
proved the parsimony which disagreeably charac-

terized the democracy of the time, and which inadequately paid great public servants like the chancellor and judges. In the tendency of the federal government to encroach upon the States lay, he thought, the danger of the federal Constitution. But of the disposition and capacity of the American people to resist such encroachments as our political history recorded, there were, he said, without naming either Adams, "two prominent and illustrious instances." As long as that good spirit was preserved, the republic would be safe; and for that preservation every patriot ought to pray.

The reputation of the country had in some degree suffered, he said, from "the uncharitable and unrelenting scrutiny to which private as well as public character" had been subjected in the late election. But this injury had been "relieved, if not removed, by seeing how soon the overflowing waters of bitterness" had spent themselves, and "that already the current of public feeling had resumed its accustomed channels." These excesses were the price paid for the full enjoyment of the right of opinion. With an assertion of "perfect deference to that sacred privilege, and in the humble exercise of that portion of it" which belonged to him, and of a sincere desire not to offend the feelings of those who differed from him, he ended his message by congratulating the legislature upon the election of Jackson and Calhoun. This result, he said in words not altogether insincere or untrue, but full of the unfairness of partisan dispute, infused fresh vigor into the American political system, refuted the odious imputation that republics are ungrateful, dissipated the vain hope that our citizens could be influenced by aught save appeals to their understanding and love of country, and finally exhibited in "bold relief the omnipotence of public opinion, and the futility of all attempts to overawe it by the denunciation of power, or to reduce it by the allurements of patronage."

Among the Hoyt letters, afterwards published by Van Buren's rancorous enemy, Mackenzie, are two letters of his upon his patronage as governor. It is not unfair to suppose that he wrote many other letters like them, and they give a useful glimpse of the distribution of offices at Albany sixty years ago. These letters to Hoyt were of the most confidential character, and showed a strong but not uncontrolled desire to please party friends and to meet party expectations. But in none of them is there a suggestion of anything dishonorable. He asked, " When will the Republican party be made sensible of the indispensable necessity of nominating none but true and tried men, so that when they succeed they gain something?" He was unable to oblige his "good friend Coddington . . . in relation to the health appointments." Dr. Westervelt's claims were "decidedly the strongest; and much was due to the relations in which he stood to Governor Tompkins, especially from one who knew so well what the latter has done and suffered for this State." He wrote of Marcy, whom he appointed a judge of the supreme court, that he " was so situated that I must make him a judge or ruin him." All this is doubtless not unlike what the best of public officers have sometimes said and thought, though rarely written ; and, like most talk over patronage, it is not in very exalted tone. But if Van Buren admitted as one of Westervelt's claims to public office that he was of a Whig family and a Democrat "from his cradle," he found among his other claims that he was " a gentleman and a man of talent," and had been " three years in the hospital and five years deputy health officer, until he was cruelly removed." Dr. Manley he refused to remove from the health office, because "his extraordinary capacity is universally admitted ; " and pointed out that the removal "could only be placed on political grounds, and as he was a zealous Jackson man at the last election, that could not have been done without danger." "I should not," he said, however, " have given Manley the office originally, if I could have found a competent Republican to take it." William L. Marcy, whom he made judge, was already known as one of the ablest men in the State, and his appointment was admirable, though his salvation from ruin, if Van Buren was speaking seriously, was not a public end fit to be served by high judicial appointment. John C. Spencer, one of the best lawyers of New York, was appointed by Van Buren special counsel for the prosecution of Morgan's

murderers.  Hammond wondered " how so rigid a
party man as Mr. Van Buren was, came to appoint
a political opponent to so important an office," but
concluded that it was a fine specimen of his peculiar tact, because Spencer, though a man of talents
and great moral courage, might be defeated in the
prosecution, and thus be injured with the anti-
Masons ; while if he succeeded, his vigor and fidelity would draw upon him Masonic hostility.   But
the simpler explanation is the more probable.  Van
Buren desired to adhere in this, as he did in most
of his appointments, to a high standard.  Upon
this particular appointment his own motives might
be distrusted ; and he therefore went to the ranks
of his adversaries for one of their most distinguished and invulnerable leaders.  Van Buren was
long condemned as a " spoils " politician ; but he
was not accused of appointing either incompetent
or dishonest men to office.   In the great place of
governor he must have already begun to see how
difficult and dangerous was this power of patronage.  It must be fairly admitted that he pretty
carefully limited, by the integrity and efficiency of
the public service, the political use which he made
of his appointments, — a use made in varying degrees by every American holding important executive power from the first Adams to our own time.

On March 12, 1829, Governor Van Buren resigned his office with the hearty and unanimous
approval of his party friends, whom he gathered
together on receiving Jackson's invitation to Wash-

ington.  He was in their hands, he said, and should abide by their decision.  Both houses of the legislature passed congratulatory and even affectionate resolutions; and his brief and brilliant career in the executive chamber of the State ended happily, as does any career which ends that a seemingly greater one may begin.

## CHAPTER VI

SECRETARY OF STATE. — DEFINITE FORMATION OF
THE DEMOCRATIC CREED

VAN BUREN was appointed secretary of state on
March 5, 1829; but did not reach Washington
until the 22d, and did not act as secretary until
April 4. James A. Hamilton, a son of Alexander
Hamilton, but then an influential Jackson man,
was acting secretary in the meantime. The two
years of Van Buren's administration of this office
are perhaps the most picturesque years of American political history. The Eaton scandal; the
downfall of Calhoun's political power; the magical
success of Van Buren; the "kitchen cabinet;" the
odious removals from office, and the outcries of
the removed; the fiery passion of Jackson; the
horror both real and affected of the opposition, —
all these have been an inexhaustible quarry to historical writers. Until very recently the larger use
has been made of the material derived from hostile
sources; and it has seemed easy to paint pictures of
this really important time in the crudest and highest colors of dislike. The American democracy,
at last let loose, driven by Jackson with a sort of
demoniac energy and cunningly used by Van Buren

for his own selfish and even Mephistophelian ends, is supposed to have broken from every sound and conservative principle. Perhaps for no other period in our history has irresponsible and unverified campaign literature of the time so largely become authority to serious writers; and for no other period does truth more strongly require a judgment upon well established results rather than upon partisan rumor and gossip. During these years there was definitely and practically formed, under the auspices of Jackson's administration, a political creed, a body of principles or tendencies in politics which have ever since strongly held the American people. Some of them have become established by a universal acquiescence. During the same years there began an extension into federal politics of the "spoils system," which has been an evil second only to slavery, and from which we are only now recovering. To Van Buren more than to any man of his time must be awarded the credit of forming the creed of the Jacksonian Democracy. And in the shame of the abuse, which has so greatly tended to neutralize the soundest articles of political faith, Van Buren must participate with other and inferior men of his own time, and with the very greatest of the men who followed him. In this narrative it is impossible to ignore some of the petty and undignified details which characterized the time, — details from part of the discredit of which Van Buren cannot escape. But it would lead to gross error to let such details obscure the vital and lasting

political work of the highest order in which Van
Buren was a central and controlling power.

Besides Van Buren, Jackson's cabinet included
Ingham of Pennsylvania in the Treasury, Eaton
in the War Department, Branch in the Navy, Berrien of Georgia attorney-general, and Barry of
Kentucky in the Post-Office, succeeding McLean,
who after a short service was appointed to the
Supreme Court.    Eaton, Branch, and Berrien had
been federal senators, the first chiefly commended
by Jackson's strong personal liking for him.    Ingham, Branch, and Berrien represented, or were
supposed to represent, the Calhoun influence.    Van
Buren in ability and reputation easily stood head
and shoulders above his associates.    When he left
Albany for Washington he was believed to have
done more than any one else to secure the Republican triumph; and if Webster's recollections
twenty years later were correct, he did more to
prevent "Mr. Adams's reëlection in 1828, and to
obtain General Jackson's election, than any other
man — yes, than any ten other men — in the country."    He was the first politician in the party;
Calhoun and he were its most distinguished statesmen.    Already the succession after Jackson belonged to one of them, the only doubt being to
which; and in that doubt was stored up a long and
complicated feud.    The rivalry between these two
great men was inevitable; it was not dishonorable
to either.    Calhoun's fame was the older; he was
already one of the junior candidates for the presi-

dency, popular in Pennsylvania and even in New
England, when Van Buren was hardly known out
of New York. In 1829 he had been chosen vice-
president for the second time. He had shown talents of a very high order. But he had now suffered
some years from the presidential fever which dis-
torts the vision, and which, when popularity wanes,
becomes heavy with enervating melancholy. He
was an able doctrinaire, but narrow and dogmatic.
The jealous and ravenous temper of the rich slaveholders of South Carolina already possessed him.
He was a Southern man; and all the presidents
thus far, except the elder and younger Adams,
had been Southerners. In 1824 he had stood indifferent between Jackson and Adams, and in Jackson's final triumph had borne no decisive part.
Van Buren's wider, richer, and more constructive
mind, his superior political judgment, his mellower
personality, his practical skill in affairs, sufficiently
explain his victory over Calhoun, without resort to
the bitter rumors of tricks and magical manœuvres
spread by Calhoun's and Clay's friends, and which,
though without authentic corroboration, have to
our own day been widely accepted.

Before Jackson's inauguration, Calhoun sought
to prevent Van Buren's selection for the State Department. He told the general that Tazewell of
Virginia ought to be appointed. New York, he
said, would have been secured by Clinton if he
had lived; but now New York needed no appointment. Jackson listened coldly to the plainly

jealous appeal; and James A. Hamilton, who was at
the time on intimate terms with Jackson, supposed
it to be Calhoun's last interview with Jackson
about the cabinet. Van Buren had been Jackson's
choice a year ago; and to all the reasons which
had then existed were now added his great services
in the canvass, and the prestige of his popular
election as governor.

The episode of Mrs. Eaton, the wife of the new
secretary of war, was absurd enough in a constitutionally governed country; but this silly "court
scandal," which might very well have enlivened
the pages of a secretary of a privy council or an
ambassador from a petty German prince, did no
more than hasten the inevitable division. In the
hastening, however, Van Buren doubtless reaped
some profit in Jackson's greater friendship. Many
respectable people in Washington believed that
unchastity on the part of this lady had induced
her former husband, Timberlake, to cut his throat.
Her second marriage to Eaton had just taken
place in January, 1829, after Jackson, learning
of the scandal but disbelieving it, had said to
Eaton, "Your marrying her will disprove these
charges, and restore Peg's good name." The general treated with violent contempt the persons,
some of them clergymen, "whose morbid appetite,"
he wrote the Rev. Dr. Ely on March 23, 1829,
"delights in defamation and slander." Burning
with anger at those who had dared in the recent
canvass to malign his own wife now dead, he de-

fended with chivalrous resolution the lady whom his own wife "to the last moment of her life believed . . . to be an innocent and much-injured woman." Even Mrs. Madison, he said, "was assailed by these fiends in human shape." When protests were made against Eaton's appointment to the cabinet, Jackson savagely cried, "I will sink or swim with him, by God!" All this had happened before Van Buren reached Washington. There then followed the grave question, whether Mrs. Eaton should be adjudged guilty by society and sentenced to exclusion from its ceremonious enjoyments. The ladies generally were determined against her, even the ladies of Jackson's own household. Jackson proposed the task, impossible even to an emperor, of compelling recognition of this distressed and persecuted consort of a minister of state. The unfortunate married men in the cabinet were in embarrassment indeed. They would not if they could, so they said, — or at least they could not if they would, — induce their wives to visit or receive visits from the wife of their colleague. Jackson showed them very clearly that no other course would satisfy him. Calhoun in his matrimonial state was at the same disadvantage. Even foreign ministers and their wives met the President's displeasure for not properly treating the wife of the American secretary of war.

When Van Buren entered this farcical scene, his widowed condition, and the fortune of having sons rather than daughters, left him quite unembar-

rassed.   He politely called upon his associate's
wife, as he called upon the others ; he treated her
with entire deference of manner.   It is probable,
though by no means clear, for popular feeling
was supposed to run high in sacred defense of the
American home, that this was the more politic
course.   It is now, however, certain that by doing
so he gave to Jackson, and some who were personally very close to Jackson, more gratification than
he gave offense elsewhere; and this has been the
occasion of much aspersion of Van Buren's motives.
But whether his course were politic or not, it is
easy enough to see that any other course would
have been inexcusable.   It would have been dastardly in the extreme for Van Buren, reaching
Washington and finding a controversy raging
whether or not the wife of one of his associates
were virtuous, to pronounce her guilty, as he most
unmistakably would have done had he refused her
the attention which etiquette required him to pay
all ladies in her position.   Parton in his Life of
Jackson quotes from an anonymous Washington
correspondent, whose account he says was "exaggerated and prejudiced but not wholly incorrect,"
the story that Van Buren induced the British and
Russian ministers, both of whom to their immediate
peace of mind happened to be bachelors, to treat
Mrs. Eaton with distinction at their entertain-
ments.   But the supposition seems quite gratuitous.
Neither of those unmarried diplomats was likely to
do so absurdly indefensible a thing as to insult by

marked exclusion a cabinet minister's wife, whom
the President for any reason, good or bad, treated
with special distinction and respect. Van Buren's
common sense was a strong characteristic; and he
doubtless looked upon the whole affair with amused
contempt. As the cabinet officer who had most
to do with social ceremonies, he may well have
sought to calm the irritation and establish for Mrs.
Eaton, where he could, the usual forms of civility.
Like many other blessings of etiquette, these forms
permit one to hold unoffending neutrality upon the
moral deserts of persons whom he meets. It happened that Calhoun's friends had tried to prevent
Eaton's appointment to the War Department, and
afterwards sought to remove him from the cabinet.
The episode added, therefore, keen edge to the
growing hostility of Jackson and his near friends
to Calhoun, and thus tended to strengthen his
rival. But all this would have signified little but
for something deeper and broader. The preference
of Van Buren had been dictated by powerful causes
long before Mrs. Timberlake became Mrs. Eaton.
These causes now grew more and more powerful.

Calhoun was serving his second term as Vice-
President. A third term for that office was obnoxious to the rule already established for the
presidency. Calhoun therefore desired Jackson
to be content with one term; for if he took a
second, Calhoun feared, and with good reason, that
he himself, being then out of the vice-presidency,
and so no longer in sight on that conspicuous seat

of preparation, might fall dangerously out of mind.
So it was soon known that Calhoun's friends were
opposed to a second term for Jackson. At a Pennsylvania meeting on March 31, 1830, the opposition was openly made. Before this, and quite apart
from Jackson's natural hostility to the nullification
theory which had arisen in Calhoun's State, he had
conceived a strong dislike for Calhoun for a personal reason. With this Van Buren had nothing
whatever to do, so far as appears from any evidence better than the uncorroborated rumors which
ascribe to Van Buren's magic every incident which
injured Calhoun's standing with Jackson. Years
before, Monroe's cabinet had discussed the treatment due Jackson for his extreme measures in
the Seminole war. Calhoun, then secretary of
war, had favored a military trial of the victorious
general; but John Quincy Adams and Monroe
had defended him, as did also Crawford, the secretary of the treasury. For a long while Jackson had erroneously supposed that Calhoun was
the only member of the cabinet in his favor;
and Calhoun had not undeceived him. Some time
before Jackson's election, Hamilton had visited
Crawford to promote the desired reconciliation
between him and the general; and a letter was
written by Governor Forsyth of Georgia to Hamilton, quoting Crawford's explanation of the real
transactions in Monroe's cabinet. Jackson was
ignorant of all this until a dinner given by him in
honor of Monroe in November, 1829. Ringold, a

personal friend of Monroe's, in a complimentary
speech at seeing Jackson and Monroe seated together, said to William B. Lewis that Monroe had
been "the only one of his cabinet" friendly to
Jackson in the Seminole controversy; and after
dinner the remark, after being discussed between
Lewis and Eaton the secretary of war, was repeated
by the latter to Jackson, who said he must be
mistaken.  Lewis then told Jackson of Forsyth's
letter, which greatly excited him, already disliking
Calhoun as he did, and not unnaturally susceptible
about his reputation in a war which had been the
subject of violent and even savage attacks upon
him in the recent canvass.  Jackson sent at once
to New York for the letter.  But Hamilton was
unwilling to give it without Forsyth's permission;
and when Forsyth, on the assembling of Congress,
was consulted, he preferred that Crawford should
be directly asked for the information.  This was
done, and Crawford wrote an account which in
May, 1830, Jackson sent to Calhoun with a demand
for an explanation.  Calhoun admitted that he had,
after hearing of the seizure of the Spanish forts in
Florida and Jackson's execution of the Englishmen
Arbuthnot and Ambrister, expressed an opinion
against him, and proposed an investigation of his
conduct by a court of inquiry.  He further told
Jackson, with much dignity of manner, that the
latter was being used in a plot to effect Calhoun's
political extinction and the exaltation of his enemies.  The President received Calhoun's letter on

his way to church, and upon his return from religious meditation wrote to the Vice-President that
"motives are to be inferred from actions and
judged by our God;" that he had long repelled
the insinuations that it was Calhoun, and not
Crawford, who had secretly endeavored to destroy
his reputation; that he had never expected to say
to Calhoun, " *Et tu, Brute!* " and that there need
be no further communication on the subject.
Thus was finally established the breach between
Calhoun and Jackson, which this personal matter
had widened but had by no means begun. In none
of it did Van Buren have any part. When Jackson sent Lewis to him with Calhoun's letter and
asked his opinion, he refused to read it, saying
that an attempt would undoubtedly be made to
hold him responsible for the rupture, and he wished
to be able to say that he knew nothing of it. This
course was doubtless politic, and deserves no applause; but it was also simply right. On getting
this message Jackson said, " I reckon Van is right;
I dare say they will attempt to throw the whole
blame on him."

A few weeks before, on April 13, 1830, the
dinner to celebrate Jefferson's birthday was held
at Washington. It was attended by the President
and Vice-President, the cabinet officers, and many
other distinguished persons. There were reports
at the time that it was intended to use Jefferson's
name in support of the state-rights doctrines, and
against internal improvements and a protective

tariff. This shows how clearly were already recognized some of the great causes underlying the
political movements and personal differences of the
time. The splendid parliamentary encounter between Hayne and Webster had taken place but
two or three months before. In his speech Hayne,
who was understood, as Benton tells us, to give
voice to the sentiments of Calhoun, had plainly
enough stated the doctrine of nullification. Jackson at the dinner robustly confronted the extrem-
ists with his famous toast, "Our federal Union: it
must be preserved." Calhoun, already conscious
of his leadership in a sectional controversy, followed with the sentiment, true indeed, but said in
words very sinister at that time: "The Union:
next to our liberty the most dear. May we all remember that it can only be preserved by respecting
the rights of the States, and distributing equally
the benefit and burden of the Union." The secretary of state next rose with a toast with little ring
or inspiration in it, but plainly, though in conciliatory phrase, declaring for the Union. He asked
the company to drink, "Mutual forbearance and
reciprocal concessions: through their agency the
Union was established. The patriotic spirit from
which they emanated will forever sustain it."

Van Buren was now definitely a candidate for
the succession. His Northern birth and residence,
his able leadership in Congress of the opposition
to the Adams administration, his almost supreme
political power in the first State of the Union, his

clear and systematic exposition of an intelligible
and timely political creed, the support his friends
gave to Jackson's reëlection, — all these advantages
were now reënforced by the tendency to disunion
clear in the utterances from South Carolina, by
Calhoun's efforts to exclude Van Buren and Eaton
from the cabinet, by the hostility to Mrs. Eaton of
the ladies in the households of Calhoun and of his
friends in the cabinet, and now by Jackson's discovery that, at a critical moment of his career ten
years before, Calhoun had sought his destruction.
Here was a singular union of really sound reasons
why Van Buren should be preferred by his party
and by the country for the succession over Calhoun, with the strongest reasons why Jackson, and
those close to him, should be in most eager personal sympathy with the preference. In December, 1829, Jackson had explicitly pronounced in
favor of Van Buren. This was in the letter to
Judge Overton of Tennessee, which Lewis is doubtless correct in saying he asked Jackson to write
lest the latter should die before his successor was
chosen. Jackson himself drafted the letter, which
Lewis copied with some verbal alteration ; and the
letter sincerely expressed his own strong opinions
After alluding to the harmony between Van Buren
and his associates in the War and Post-Office Departments, he said : " I have found him everything
that I could desire him to be, and believe him not
only deserving my confidence, but the confidence
of the nation. Instead of his being selfish and

intriguing, as has been represented by some of his opponents, I have ever found him frank, open, candid, and manly. As a counselor, he is able and prudent, republican in his principles, and one of the most pleasant men to do business with I ever knew. He, my dear friend, is well qualified to fill the highest office in the gift of the people, who in him will find a true friend and safe depositary of their rights and liberty. I wish I could say as much for Mr. Calhoun and some of his friends." He criticised Calhoun for his silence on the bank question, for his encouragement of the resolution in the South Carolina legislature relative to the tariff, and for his objection to the apportionment of the surplus revenues after the national debt should be paid. Jackson had not yet definitely learned from Forsyth's letter about Calhoun's attitude in Monroe's cabinet; but his well-aroused suspicion doubtless influenced his expression. His strong personal liking for the secretary of state had been evident from the beginning of the administration. In a letter to Jesse Hoyt of April 13, 1829, the latter wrote that he had found the President affectionate, confidential, and kind to the last degree, and that he believed there was no degree of good feeling or confidence which the president did not entertain for him. In July he wrote to Hamilton: "The general grows upon me every day. I can fairly say that I have become quite enamored with him."

The break between Calhoun and Jackson was

kept from the public until early in 1831. In the preceding winter, Duff Green, the editor of the " Telegraph," until then the administration newspaper, but still entirely committed to Calhoun, sought to have the publication of the Calhoun-Jackson correspondence accompanied by a general outburst from Republican newspapers against Jackson. The storm, Benton tells us, was to seem so universal, and the indignation against Van Buren so great, that even Jackson's popularity would not save the prime minister. Jackson's friends, Barry and Kendall, learning of this, called to Washington an unknown Kentuckian to be editor of a new and loyal administration paper. Francis P. Blair was a singularly astute man, whose name, and the name of whose family, afterwards became famous in American politics. He belonged to the race of advisers of great men, found by experience to be almost as important in a democracy as in a monarchy. In February, 1831, Calhoun openly declared war on Jackson by publishing the Seminole correspondence. Green having now been safely reëlected printer to Congress, the " Telegraph," according to the plan, strongly supported Calhoun. The " Globe," Blair's paper, attacked Calhoun and upheld the President. The importance in that day ascribed by politicians to the control of a single newspaper seems curious. In 1823, Van Buren, while a federal senator, was interested in the " Albany Argus," almost steadily from that time until the present the ably managed

organ of the Albany Regency;[1] and he then confidentially wrote to Hoyt: "Without a paper thus
edited at Albany we may hang our harps on the
willows. With it, the party can survive a thousand
such convulsions as those which now agitate and
probably alarm most of those around you." This
seems an astonishingly high estimate of the power
of a paper which, though relatively conspicuous in
the State, could have then had but a small circulation. It was, however, the judgment of a most
sagacious politician. In 1822 he complained to
Hoyt that his expenses of this description were too
heavy. In 1833 James Gordon Bennett, then a
young journalist of Philadelphia, wrote Hoyt a
plain intimation that money was necessary to enable
him to continue his journalistic warfare in Van
Buren's behalf. Anguish, disappointment, despair,
he said, brooded over him, while Van Buren chose
to sit still and sacrifice those who had supported
him in every weather. Van Buren replied that he
could not directly or indirectly afford pecuniary
aid to Bennett's press, and more particularly as he
was then situated; that if Bennett could not continue friendly to him on public grounds and with
perfect independence, he could only regret it, but
he desired no other support. He added, however,

[1] This was written in 1887. The Albany Regency, after a life
of sixty years, ended with the death of Daniel Manning, in Mr.
Cleveland's first presidency, and with it ended the characteristic
influence of its organ. The Democratic management at Albany
has since proceeded upon very different lines and has engaged
the ability of very different men.

not to burn his ships behind him, that he had supposed there would be no difficulty in obtaining money in New York, if their "friends in Philadelphia could not all together make out to sustain one press." Thus was invited a powerful animosity, vindictively shown even when Van Buren was within three years of his death.

Soon after his arrival Blair entered the famous Kitchen Cabinet, a singularly talented body, fond enough indeed of "wire-pulling," but with clear and steady political convictions. William B. Lewis had long been a close personal friend of Jackson and manager of his political interests, and had but recently earned his gratitude by rushing successfully to the defense of Mrs. Jackson's reputation. Kendall and Hill were adroit, industrious, skillful men; the former afterwards postmaster-general, and the latter to become a senator from New Hampshire. Blair entered this company full of zeal against nullification and the United States Bank. Jackson himself was so strong-willed a man, so shrewd in management, so skillful in reading the public temper, that the story of the complete domination of this junto over him is quite absurd. The really great abilities of these men and their entire devotion to his interests gained a profound and justifiable influence with him, which occasional petty or unworthy uses made of it did not destroy. No one can doubt that Jackson was confirmed by them in the judgment to which Van Buren urged him upon great political issues. The secretary of state refused to give the new paper of Blair any of the printing of his department, lest its origin should be attributed to him, and because he wished to be able to say truly that he had nothing to do with it. Kendall, who lived through the civil war, strongly loyal to the Union and to Jackson's memory, to die a wealthy philanthropist, declared in his autobiography, and doubtless correctly, that the "Globe" was not established by Van Buren or his friends, but by friends of Jackson who desired his reëlection for another four years. Nevertheless Van Buren was held responsible for the paper; and its establishment was soon followed by the dissolution of the cabinet.

This explosion, it is now clear, was of vast advantage to the cause of the Union. It took place in April, 1831, and in part at least was Van Buren's work. On the 9th of that month he wrote to Edward Livingston, then a senator from Louisiana spending the summer at his seat on the Hudson River, asking him to start for Washington the day after he received the letter, and to avoid speculation "by giving out that" he was "going to Philadelphia." Livingston wrote back from Washington to his wife that Van Buren had taken the high and popular ground that, as a candidate for the presidency, he ought not to remain in the cabinet when its public measures would be attributed to his intrigue, and thus made to injure the President; and that Van Buren's place was pressed upon him "with all the warmth of friendship and every appeal to my love of country."

Van Buren, with courageous skill, put his resignation to the public distinctly on the ground of his own political aspiration. On April 11, 1831, he wrote to the President a letter for publication, saying that from the moment he had entered the cabinet it had been his " anxious wish and zealous endeavor to prevent a premature agitation of the question " of the succession, " and at all events to discountenance, and if possible repress, the disposition, at an early day manifested," to connect his name " with that disturbing topic." Of " the sincerity and constancy of his disposition" he appealed to the President to judge. But he had not succeeded, and circumstances beyond his control had given the subject a turn which could not then " be remedied except by a self-disfranchisement, which, even if dictated by" his " individual wishes, could hardly be reconcilable with propriety or self-respect." In the situation existing at the time, " diversities of ulterior preference among the friends of the administration " were unavoidable, and he added : " Even if the respective advocates of those thus placed in rivalship be patriotic enough to resist the temptation of creating obstacles to the advancement of him to whose elevation they are opposed, by embarrassing the branch of public service committed to his charge, they are nevertheless, by their position, exposed to the suspicion of entertaining and encouraging such views, — a suspicion which can seldom fail, in the end, to aggravate into present alienation and hostility the

prospective differences which first gave rise to it."
The public service, he said, required him to remove
such " obstructions " from " the successful prosecution of public affairs; " and he intimated, with the
affectation of self-depreciation which was disagreeably fashionable among great men of the day, that
the example he set would, " notwithstanding the
humility of its origin," be found worthy of respect
and observance. When four years later he accepted the presidential nomination he repeated the
sentiment of this letter, but more explicitly, saying
that his " name was first associated with the question of General Jackson's successor more through
the ill-will of opponents than the partiality of
friends." This seemed very true. For every movement which had tended to commit the administration or its chief against Calhoun or his doctrines,
he had been held responsible as a device to advance
himself. His adversaries had proclaimed him not
so much a public officer as a self-seeking candidate.
It was a rare and true stroke of political genius to
admit his aspiration to the presidency; to deny his
present candidacy and his self-seeking ; but, lest
the clamor of his enemies should, if he longer
held his office, throw doubt upon his sincerity, to
withdraw from that station, and to prevent the
continued pretense that he was using official opportunities, however legitimately, to increase his
public reputation or his political power. Thus
would the candidacy be thrust on him by his enemies. In his letter he announced that Jackson had

consented to stand for reëlection; and that, "without a total disregard of the lights of experience," he could not shut his eyes to the unfavorable influence which his continuance in the cabinet might have upon Jackson's own canvass in 1832.

In accepting the resignation Jackson declared the reasons which the letter had presented too strong to be disregarded, thus practically assenting to Van Buren's candidacy to succeed him. Jackson looked with sorrow, he said, upon the state of things Van Buren had described. But it was "but an instance of one of the evils to which free governments must ever be liable," an evil whose remedy lay "in the intelligence and public spirit of" their "common constituents," who would correct it; and in that belief he found "abundant consolation." He added that, with the best opportunities for observing and judging, he had seen in Van Buren no other desire than "to move quietly on in the path of" his duties, and "to promote the harmonious conduct of public affairs." "If on this point," he apostrophized the departing premier, "you have had to encounter detraction, it is but another proof of the utter insufficiency of innocence and worth to shield from such assaults."

Never was a presidential candidate more adroitly or less dishonorably presented to his party and to the country. For the adroitness lay in the frank avowal of a willingness or desire to be president and a resolution to be a candidate, — for which,

so far as their conduct went, his adversaries were
really responsible, — and in seizing an undoubted
opportunity to serve the public.   Quite apart from
the sound reason that the secretary of state should
not, if possible, be exposed in dealing with public
questions to aspersions upon his motives, as Van
Buren was quite right in saying that he would be,
it was also clear that the cabinet was inharmoni-
ous ; and that its lack of harmony, whatever the
facts or wherever the fault, seriously interfered
with the public business.   The administration and
the country, it was obvious, were now approaching
the question of nullification, and upon that question it was but patriotic to desire that its members
should firmly share the union principles of their
chief.   Within a few weeks after the dissolution of
the cabinet, Jackson seized the opportunity afforded
him by an invitation from the city of Charleston to
visit it on the 4th of July, to sound in the ears of
nullification a ringing blast for the Union.   If he
could go, he said, he trusted to find in South Carolina " all the men of talent, exalted patriotism,
and private worth," however divided they might
have been before, " united before the altar of their
country on the day set apart for the solemn celebration of its independence, — independence which
cannot exist without union, and with it is eternal."
The disunion sentiments ascribed to distinguished
citizens of the State were, he hoped, if indeed they
were accurately reported, " the effect of momentary
excitement, not deliberate design."   For all the

work then performed in defense of the Union, Jackson and his advisers of the time must share with Webster and Clay the gratitude of our own and all later generations. The burst of loyalty in April, 1861, had no less of its genesis in the intrepid front and the political success of the national administration from 1831 to 1833, than in the pathetic and glorious appeals and aspirations of the great orators.

Jackson now called to the work Edward Livingston, privileged to perform in it that service of his which deserves a splendid immortality. He became secretary of state on May 24, 1831. Eaton, the secretary of war, voluntarily resigned to become governor of Florida; and Barry, the postmaster-general, who was friendly to the reorganization, was soon appointed minister to Spain, in which post Eaton later succeeded him. Ingham, Branch, and Berrien, the Calhoun members, were required to resign. The new cabinet, apart from the state department, was on the whole far abler than the old; indeed, it was one of the ablest of American cabinets. Below Livingston at the council table sat McLane of Delaware, recalled from the British mission to take the treasury, Governor Cass of Michigan, and Senator Woodbury of New Hampshire, secretaries of war and navy. Amos Kendall brought to the post-office his extraordinary astuteness and diligence in administration; and Taney, later the chief justice, was attorney-general. The executive talents of this body of men, loyal as they were to the plans of Jackson and Van Buren, promised, and they afterwards brought, success in the struggle for the principles now adopted by the party, as well as for the control of the government. Van Buren stood as truly for a policy of state as ever stood any candidate before the American people. One finds it agreeable now to escape for a moment from the Washington atmosphere of personal controversy and ambition. It is not to be forgotten, however, that a like atmosphere has surrounded even those political struggles in America, only three or four in number, which have been greater and deeper than that in which Jackson and Van Buren were the chief figures. From this temper of personal controversy and ambition the greatest political benefactors of history have not been free, so inevitable is the mingling with large affairs of the varied personal motives, conscious and unconscious, of those who transact them.

When Van Buren left the first place in Jackson's cabinet, the latter, too, at last stood for the definite policy which he had but imperfectly adopted when he was elected, and which, as a practical and immediate political plan, it is reasonably safe to assert, was most largely the creation of the sagacious mind of his chief associate. Before Van Buren left Albany he had written to Hamilton on February 21, 1829, with reference to Jackson's inaugural: "I hope the general will not find it necessary to avow any opinion upon constitutional questions at war with the doctrines of the Jefferson school. Whatever his views may be, there can be no necessity of doing so in an inaugural address." This shows the doubt, which had been caused by some of Jackson's utterances and votes, of his intelligent and systematic adherence to the political creed preached by Van Buren. Jackson's inaugural was colorless and safe enough. Upon strict construction he said that he should "keep steadily in view the limitations as well as the extent of the executive power;" that he would be "animated by a proper respect for those sovereign members of our Union, taking care not to confound the powers they have reserved to themselves with those they have granted to the confederacy." The bank he did not mention. And upon the living and really great question, to which Van Buren had given so much study, Jackson said, himself probably having a grim sense of humor at the absurd emptiness of the sentence: "Internal improvement and the diffusion of knowledge, so far as they can be promoted by the constitutional acts of the federal government, are of high importance."

Very different was the situation when two years later Van Buren left the cabinet. In several state papers of great dignity and ability and yet popular and interesting in style, Jackson had formulated a political creed closely consistent with that advocated by Van Buren in the Senate. Upon internal improvements, Jackson, on May 27, 1830, sent to the House his famous Maysville Road veto. That road was exclusively within the State of Ohio, and not connected with any existing system of improvements. Jackson very well said that if it could be considered national, no further distinction between the appropriate duties of the general and state governments need be attempted. He pointed out the tendency of such appropriations, little by little, to distort the meaning of the Constitution; and found in former legislation "an admonitory proof of the force of implication, and that necessity of guarding the Constitution with sleepless vigilance against the authority of precedents which have not the sanction of its most plainly defined powers." In his annual message of December, 1830, he referred to the system of federal subscriptions to private corporate enterprises, saying: " The power which the general government would acquire within the several States by becoming the principal stockholder in corporations, controlling every canal and each sixty or hundred miles of every important road, and giving a proportionate vote to all their elections, is almost inconceivable, and in my view dangerous to the liberties of the people." With these utterances ended the very critical struggle to give the federal government a power which even in those days would have been great, and which, as has already been said, had it continued with the growth of railways, would have enormously and radically changed our system of government.

Before he left the Senate Van Buren had pronounced against the Bank of the United States; but Jackson did not mention it in his inaugural. In

his first annual message, however, Jackson warned
Congress that the charter of the bank would
expire in 1836, and that deliberation upon its renewal ought to commence at once. "Both the
constitutionality and the expediency of the law
creating this bank," he said, "are well questioned
. . .; and it must be admitted by all that it has
failed in the great end of establishing a uniform
and sound currency." This was plain enough for
a first utterance. A year later he told Congress
that nothing had occurred to lessen in any degree
the dangers which many citizens apprehended from
that institution as then organized, though he out-
lined an institution which should be not a corporation, but a branch of the Treasury Department,
and not, as he thought, obnoxious to constitutional
objections.

The removal of the Cherokee Indians from
within the State of Georgia he defended by considerations which were practically unanswerable. It
was dangerously inconsistent with our political system to maintain within the limits of a State Indian
tribes, free from the obligations of state laws,
having a tribal independence, and bound only by
treaty relations with the United States. It was
harsh to remove the Indians; but it would have
been harsher to them and to the white people of
the State to have supported by federal arms an
Indian sovereignty within its limits. Jackson, with
true Democratic jealousy, refused in his political
and executive policy to defer to the merely moral

weight of the opinion of the Supreme Court. For in that tribunal political and social exigencies could have but limited force in answering a question which, as the court itself decided, called for a political remedy, which the President and not the court could apply.

The tariff might, Jackson declared, be constitutionally used for protective purposes ; but the deliberate policy of his party was now plainly intimated. In his first message he " regretted that the complicated restrictions which now embarrass the intercourse of nations could not by common consent be abolished." In the Maysville veto he said that, " as long as the encouragement of domestic manufactures " was " directed to national ends," . . . it should receive from him " a temperate but steady support." But this is to be read with the expression in the same paper that the people had a right to demand " the reduction of every tax to as low a point as the wise observance of the necessity to protect that portion of our manufactures and labor, whose prosperity is essential to our national safety and independence, will allow." This encouragement was, he said in his inaugural, to be given to those products which might be found " essential to our national independence." In his second message he declared " the obligations upon all the trustees of political power to exempt those for whom they act from all unnecessary burdens ; " that " the resources of the nation beyond those required for the immediate and necessary purposes of government can nowhere be so well deposited as in the pockets of the people;" that "objects of national importance alone ought to be protected;" and that "of those the productions of our soil, our mines, and our workshops, essential to national defense, occupy the first rank." Other domestic industries, having a national importance, and which might, after temporary protection, compete with foreign labor on equal terms, merited, he said, the same attention in a subordinate degree. The economic light here was not very clear or strong, but perhaps as strong as it often is in a political paper. Jackson's conclusion was that the tariff then existing taxed some of the comforts of life too highly; protected interests too local and minute to justify a general exaction; and forced some manufactures for which the country was not ripe.

All this practical and striking growth in political science had taken place during the two years of Jackson's and Van Buren's almost daily intercourse at Washington. It is impossible from materials yet made public to point out with precision the latter's handiwork in each of these papers. James A. Hamilton describes his own long nights at the White House on the messages of 1829 and 1830; and his were not the only nights of the kind spent by Jackson's friends. Jackson, like other strong men, and like some whose opportunities of education had been far ampler than his, freely used literary assistance, although, with all his inaccuracies, he himself wrote in a vigorous, lucid, and interesting style. But with little doubt the political positions taken in these papers, and which made a definite and lasting creed, were more immediately the work of the secretary of state. The consultations with Van Buren, of which Hamilton tells, are only glimpses of what must continually have gone on. At the time of Jackson's inauguration Hamilton wrote that the latter's confidence was reposed in men in no way equal to him in natural parts, but who had been useful to him in covering " his very lamentable defects of education," and whom, through his reluctance to expose these defects to others, he was compelled to keep about him. He added that Van Buren could never reach the same relation which Lewis held with the general, because the latter would " not yield himself so readily to superior as to inferior minds." This was a mistake. Van Buren's personal loyalty to Jackson, his remarkable tact and delicacy, had promptly aroused in Jackson that extraordinary liking for him which lasted until Jackson died. With this advantage, Van Buren's clear-cut theories of political conduct were easily lodged in Jackson's naturally wise mind, to whose prepossessions and prejudices they were agreeable, and received there the deference due to the practical sagacity in which Van Buren's obvious political success had proved him to be a master. Van Buren was doubtless greatly aided by the kitchen cabinet. He was careful to keep on good terms with those who had so familiar an access to Jackson. Kendall's singular and useful ability he soon discovered. It was at the latter's instance that Kendall was invited to dinner at the White House, where Van Buren paid him special attention. The influence of the members of the kitchen cabinet with their master has been much exaggerated. Soon after Lewis was appointed, and in spite of his personal intimacy and of his rumored influence with the President, he was, as he wrote to Hamilton, in some anxiety whether he might not be removed; the President had at least, he said, entertained a proposition to remove him, and was therefore, in view of Jackson's great debt to him, no longer entitled to his "friendship or future support."

Very soon after Van Buren's withdrawal from the cabinet, he was accused of primarily and chiefly causing the official proscription of men for political opinions which began in the federal service under Jackson. From that time to the present the accusation has been carelessly repeated from one writer to another, with little original examination of the facts. It is clear that Van Buren neither began nor caused this demoralizing and disastrous abuse. When he reached Washington in 1829, the removals were in full and lamentable progress. In the very first days of the administration, McLean was removed from the office of postmaster-general to a seat in the Supreme Court, because, so Adams after an interview with him wrote in his diary on March 14, 1829, " he refused to be made the instrument of the sweeping proscription of postmasters which is to be one of the samples of the promised reform." This was a week or two before Van Buren reached Washington. On the same day Samuel Swartwout wrote to Hoyt from Washington: "No damned rascal who made use of his office or its profits for the purpose of keeping Mr. Adams in, and General Jackson out of power, is entitled to the least lenity or mercy, save that of hanging. . . . Whether or not I shall get anything in the general scramble for plunder remains to be proven; but I rather guess I shall. . . . I know Mr. Ingham slightly, and would recommend you to push like a devil, if you expect anything from that quarter. . . . If I can only keep my own legs, I shall do well; but I'm darned if I can carry any weight with me." This man, against Van Buren's earnest protest and to his great disturbance, had some of the devil's luck in pushing. He was appointed collector of customs at New York, — one of the principal financial officers in the country. It is not altogether unsatisfactory to read of the scandalous defalcation of which he was afterwards guilty, and of the serious injury it dealt his party. The temper which he exposed so ingenuously, filled Washington at the time. Nor did it come only or chiefly from one quarter of the country. Kendall, then fresh from Kentucky, who had been appointed fourth auditor, wrote to his wife, with interestingly mingled sentiments: "I turned out six clerks on Saturday. Several of them have families and are poor. It was the most painful thing I ever did;

but I could not well get along without it. Among them is a poor old man with a young wife and several children. I shall help to raise a contribution to get him back to Ohio. . . . I shall have a private carriage to go out with me and bring my whole brood of little ones. Bless their sweet faces."

Van Buren confidentially wrote to Hamilton from Albany in March, 1829: " If the general makes one removal at this moment he must go on. Would it not be better to get the streets of Washington clear of office-seekers first in the way I proposed ? . . . As to the publication in the newspapers I have more to say. So far as depends on me, my course will be to restore by a single order every one who has been turned out by Mr. Clay for political reasons, unless circumstances of a personal character have since arisen which would make the reappointment in any case improper. To ascertain that will take a little time. There I would pause." Among the Mackenzie letters is one from Lorenzo Hoyt, describing an interview with Van Buren while governor, and then complaining that the latter would " not lend the utmost weight of his influence to displace from office such men as John Duer," Adams's appointee as United States attorney at New York. If they had been struggling for political success for the benefit of their opponents, he angrily wrote, he wished to know it. He added, however, that, from the behavior of the President thus far, he thought Jackson

would " go the whole hog." This was before Van
Buren reached Washington. In answer to an
insolent letter of Jesse Hoyt urging a removal,
and telling the secretary of state that there was a
" charm attending bold measures extremely fascinating " which had given Jackson all his glory,
Van Buren wrote back : " Here I am engaged in
the most intricate and important affairs, which are
new to me, and upon the successful conduct of
which my reputation as well as the interests of the
country depend, and which keep me occupied from
early in the morning until late at night. And can
you think it kind or just to harass me under such
circumstances with letters which no man of common
sensibility can read without pain ? . . . I must be
plain with you. . . . The terms upon which you
have seen fit to place our intercourse are inad-
missible." Ingham, Jackson's secretary of the
treasury, the next day wrote to this typical office-
seeker that the rage for office in New York was
such that an enemy menacing the city with desolation would not cause more excitement. He added,
speaking of his own legitimate work : " These
duties cannot be postponed ; and I do assure you
that I am compelled daily to file away long lists of
recommendations, etc., without reading them, although I work 18 hours out of the 24 with all
diligence. The appointments can be postponed ;
other matters cannot ; and it was one of the prominent errors of the late administration that they
suffered many important public interests to be

neglected, while they were cruising about to secure or buy up partisans.   This we must not do."

Benton, friendly as he was to Jackson, condemned the system of removals; and his fairness may well be trusted.   He said that in Jackson's first year (in which De Tocqueville, whom he was answering, said that Jackson had removed every removable functionary) there were removed but 690 officers through the whole United States for all causes, of whom 491 were postmasters: the entire number of postmasters being at the time nearly 8000.   Kendall, reviewing the first three years of Jackson's administration near their expiration, said that in the city of Washington there had been removed but one officer out of seven, and "most of them for bad conduct and character," a statement some of the significance of which doubtless depends upon what was "bad character," but which still fairly limits the epithet "wholesale" customarily applied to these removals.   In the Post-Office Department, he said, the removals had been only one out of sixteen, and in the whole government but one out of eleven.   Kendall was speaking for party purposes; but he was cautious and precise; and his statements, made near the time, show how far behind the sudden "clean sweep" of 1861 was this earlier essay in "spoils," and how much exaggeration there has been on the subject.   Benton says that in the departments at Washington a majority of the employees were opposed to Jackson throughout his administration.   Of the officers having a judicial function, such as land and claims commissioners, territorial judges, justices in the District of Columbia, none were removed. The readiness to remove was stimulated by the discovery of the frauds of Tobias Watkins, made just after his removal from the fourth auditor's place, to which Kendall was appointed. Watkins had been Adams's warm personal friend, so the latter states in his diary, and " an over active partisan against Jackson at the last presidential election." Unreasonable as was a general inference from one of the instances of dishonesty which occur under the best administrations, and a flagrant instance of which was soon to occur under his own administration, it justified Jackson in his own eyes for many really shameful removals. There had doubtless been among office-holders under Adams a good deal of the " offensive partisanship " of our day, many expressions of horror by subordinate officers at the picture of Jackson as president. All this had angered Jackson, whose imperial temper readily classed his subordinates as servants of Andrew Jackson, rather than as ministers of the public service. Moreover, his accession, as Benton not unfairly pointed out, was the first great party change since Jefferson had succeeded the elder Adams. Offices had greatly increased in number. In the profound democratic change that had been actively operating for a quarter of a century, the force of old traditions had been broken in many useful as in many useless things. Great numbers of inferior offices had now become political, not only in New York, but in Pennsylvania, Georgia, and other States. Adams's administration, except in the change of policy upon large questions, had been a continuation of Monroe's. He went from the first place in Monroe's cabinet to the presidency. His secretaries of the treasury and the navy and his postmaster-general and attorney-general had held office under Monroe, the latter three in the very same places. But Jackson thrust out of the presidency his rival, who had naturally enough been earnestly sustained by large numbers of his subordinates; and Adams's appointees were doubtless in general followers of himself and of Clay.

Jackson's first message contained a serious defense of the removals. Men long in office, he said, acquired the "habit of looking with indifference upon the public interests," and office became considered "a species of property." "The duties of all public officers," he declared, with an ignorance then very common among Americans, could be "made so plain and simple that men of intelligence may readily qualify themselves for their performance." Further, he pointed out that no one man had "any more intrinsic right" to office than another; and therefore "no individual wrong" was done by removal. The officer removed, he concluded, with almost a demagogic touch, had the same means of earning a living as "the millions who never held office." In spite of individual distress he wished "rotation in office" to become "a leading principle in the Republican creed." Unfounded as most of this is now clearly seen to be, it is certain that the reasoning was convincing to a very large part of the American people.

In his own department Van Buren practiced little of the proscription which was active elsewhere. Of seventeen foreign representatives, but four were removed in the first year. Doubtless he was fortunate in having an office without the amount of patronage of the Post-Office or the Treasury. Nothing in his career, however, showed a personal liking for removals. The distribution of offices was not distasteful to him; but his temper was neither proscriptive nor unfriendly. At times even his partisan loyalty was doubted for his reluctance in this, which was soon deemed an appropriate and even necessary party work.

But Van Buren did not oppose the ruinous and demoralizing system. Powerful as he was with Jackson, wise and far-seeing as he was, he must receive for his acquiescence, or even for his silence, a part of the condemnation which the American people, as time goes on, will more and more visit upon one of the great political offenses committed against their political integrity and welfare. But it must in justice be remembered, not only that Van Buren did not begin or actively conduct the distribution of spoils; not only that his acquiescence was in a practice which in his own State he had found well established; but that the practice in which he thus joined was one which it is probable he could not have fully resisted without his own political destruction, and perhaps the temporary prostration of the political causes to which he was devoted. Though these be palliations and not defenses, the biographer ought not to apply to human nature a rule of unprecedented austerity. In Van Buren's politic yielding there was little, if any, more timidity or time-serving than in the like yielding by every man holding great office in the United States since Jackson's inauguration; and the worst, the most corrupting, and the most demoralizing official proscription in America took place thirty-two years afterwards, and under a president who, in wise and exalted patriotism, was one of the greatest statesmen, as he has been perhaps the best loved, of Americans, and to whom blame ought to be assigned all the larger by reason of the extraordinary power and prestige he enjoyed, and the moral fervor of the nation behind him, which rendered less necessary this unworthy aid of inferior patronage.

So crowded and interesting were the two years of Van Buren's life in the cabinet with matters apart from the special duties of his office, that it is only at the last, and briefly, that an account can be given of his career as secretary of state. His conduct of foreign affairs was firm, adroit, dignified, and highly successful. It utterly broke the ideal of turbulent and menacing incompetence which the Whigs set up for Jackson's presidency.

He had to solve no difficulty of the very first order; for the United States were in profound peace with the whole world. He performed, however, with skill and success two diplomatic services of real importance, services which brought deserved and most valuable strength to Jackson's administration. The American claims for French spoliations upon American ships during the operation of Napoleon's Berlin and Milan decrees had been under discussion for many years. They were now resolutely pressed. In his message of December, 1829, Jackson, doubtless under Van Buren's advice, paid some compliments to "France, our ancient ally;" but then said very plainly that these claims, unless satisfied, would continue "a subject of unpleasant discussion and possible collision between the two governments." He politely referred to "the known integrity of the French monarch," Charles X., as an assurance that the claims would be paid. A few months afterwards this Bourbon was tumbled off the French throne; and in December, 1830, Jackson with increased courtliness, and with a flattering allusion to Lafayette, conspicuous in this milder revolution as he had been in 1789, rejoiced in "the high voucher we possess for the enlarged views and pure integrity" of Louis Philippe. The new American vigor, doubtless aided by the liberal change in France, brought a treaty on July 4, 1831, under which $5,000,000 was to be paid by France, a result which Jackson, with pardonable boasting, said in his message of December, 1831, was an encouragement "for perseverance in the demands of justice," and would admonish other powers, if any, inclined to evade those demands, that they would never be abandoned. The French treaty came so soon after Van Buren's retirement from the state department, and followed so naturally upon the methods of his negotiation, and his instructions to William C. Rives, our minister at Paris, that much of its credit belonged to him. In March, 1830, a treaty was made with Denmark requiring the payment of $650,000 for Danish spoliations on American commerce. The effective pressing of these claims was justly one of the most popular performances of the administration. Commercial treaties were concluded with Austria in August, 1829; with Turkey in May, 1830; and with Mexico in April, 1831.

But the chief transaction of Van Buren's foreign administration was the opening of trade in American vessels between the United States and the British West Indian colonies. This commerce was then relatively much more important to the United States than in later times; and it was chiefly by American shipping that American commerce was carried on with foreign countries. The absurd and odious restrictions upon intercourse so highly natural and advantageous to the people of our seaboard and of the British West Indian islands had led to smuggling on a large scale, and were fruitful of international irritations. Retaliatory acts of Con-

gress and Parliament, prohibitive proclamations of
our presidents, and British orders in council, had
at different times, since the close of the second
British war in 1815, oppressed or prevented honest
and profitable trade between neighbors who ought
to have been friendly traders. Van Buren found
the immediate position to be as follows. In July,
1825, an act of Parliament had allowed foreign
vessels to trade to the British colonies upon conditions. To secure for American vessels the benefit
of this act, it was necessary that within one year
American ports should be open to British vessels
bringing the same kind of British or colonial produce as could be imported in American vessels ;
that British and American vessels in the trade
should pay the same government charges ; that
alien duties on British vessels and cargoes, that is,
duties not imposed on the like vessels and cargoes
owned by Americans, should be suspended ; and
that the provision of an American law of 1823
limiting the privileges of the colonial trade to British vessels carrying colonial produce to American
ports directly from the colonies exporting it, and
without stopping at intermediate ports, should be
repealed. John Quincy Adams's administration
had failed within the year to comply with the conditions imposed by the British law of 1825. In
1826, therefore, Great Britain forbade this trade
and intercourse in American vessels. Adams retorted with a counter prohibition in March, 1827.
And in this unfortunate position Van Buren found

our commercial relations with the West Indian,
Bahama, and South American colonies of England.
The situation was aggravated by a claim made by
the American government in 1823 that American
goods should pay in the colonial ports no higher
duties than British goods, a protest against British
protection to British industry in the British colonies coming with little grace from a country itself
maintaining the protective system. Adams had
sent Gallatin to England to remedy the difficulty,
but without success.

Van Buren adopted a different method of negotiation. A more conciliatory bearing was assumed
towards our traditional adversary. Jackson, in
language sounding strangely from his imperious
mouth, was made to say in his first message that
"with Great Britain, alike distinguished in peace
and war, we may look forward to years of peaceful,
honorable, and elevated competition; that it is
their policy to preserve the most cordial relations."
These, he said, were his own views; and such were
"the prevailing sentiments of our constituents."
In his instructions to McLane, the minister at
London, Van Buren, departing widely from conventional diplomacy, expressly conceded that the
American government had been wrong in its claim
that England should admit to its colonies American
goods on as favorable terms as British goods; that
it had been wrong in requiring British ships bringing colonial produce to come and go directly from
and to the producing colonies; and that it had

been wrong in refusing the privileges offered by
the British law of 1825. This frank surrender of
untenable positions showed the highest skill in negotiation, a business for which Van Buren was
perhaps better equipped than any American of his
time. In these points we were "assailable;" we
had "too long and too tenaciously" resisted British rights. After these admissions, it would, he
said, be improper for Great Britain to suffer "any
feelings that find their origin in the past pretensions of this government to have an adverse influence upon the present conduct of Great Britain."
McLane was to tell the Earl of Aberdeen that "to
set up the act of the late administration as the
cause of forfeiture of privileges which would otherwise be extended to the people of the United States
would, under existing circumstances, be unjust in
itself, and could not fail to excite their deepest
sensibility." McLane was also to allude to the
parts taken by the members of Jackson's administration in the former treatment of the question
under discussion. And here Van Buren used the
objectionable sentence which led to his subsequent
rejection by the Senate as minister to England,
and which through that, such are the curious ca-
prices of politics, led, or at least helped to lead,
him to the presidency. He said, "Their views
upon that point have been submitted to the people
of the United States; and the counsels by which
your conduct is now directed are the result of the
judgment expressed by the only earthly tribunal

to which the late administration was amenable for its acts."

In Van Buren's sagacious desire to emphasize the abandonment of claims preventing the negotiation, he here introduced to a foreign nation the American people as a judge that had condemned the assertion of such claims by Jackson's predecessor. The statement was at least an exaggeration. There was little reason to suppose that Adams's failure in the negotiation over colonial trade had much, if at all, influenced the election of 1828. Nor was it dignified to officially expose our party contests to foreign eyes. But Van Buren was intent upon success in the negotiation. He could succeed where others had failed, only by a strong assertion of a change in American policy. His fault was at most one of taste in the manner of an assertion right enough and wise enough in itself. Nor were these celebrated instructions lacking in firmness or dignity. Great Britain was clearly warned that she must then decide for all time whether the hardships from which her West Indian planters suffered should continue; and that the United States would not " in expiation of supposed past encroachments " repeal their laws, leaving themselves " wholly dependent upon the indulgence of Great Britain," and not knowing in advance what course she would follow. In his speech in the Senate in February, 1827, Van Buren had clearly stated the general positions which he took in this famous dispatch. It is rather curious, how-

ever, that he found occasion then to say upon this
very subject what he seemed afterwards to forget,
that " in the collisions which may arise between
the United States and a foreign power, it is our
duty to present an unbroken front; domestic differences, if they tend to give encouragement to
unjust pretensions, should be extinguished or deferred ; and the cause of our government must be
considered as the cause of our country." So easy
it is to advise other men to be bold and firm.

McLane's long and very able letter to the British
foreign secretary closely followed his instructions.
Lord Aberdeen was frankly told that the United
States had committed " mistakes " in the past ; and
that the " American pretensions " which had prevented a former arrangement would not be revived.
The negotiation was entirely successful. In October, 1830, the President, with the authorization of
Congress, declared American ports open to British
vessels and their cargoes coming from the colonies,
and that they should be subject to the same charges
as American vessels coming from the same colonies.
In November a British order in council gave to
American vessels corresponding privileges. On
January 3, 1831, Jackson sent to the Senate the
papers, including Van Buren's letter of instructions. No criticism was made upon their tenor ;
and the public, heedless of the phrases used in
reaching the end, rejoiced in a most beneficent
opening of commerce.

# CHAPTER VII

MINISTER TO ENGLAND. — VICE-PRESIDENT. —
ELECTION TO THE PRESIDENCY

In the summer of 1831 Van Buren knew very
well the strong hold he had upon his party, the
entire and almost affectionate confidence which he
enjoyed from Jackson, and the prestige which his
political and official success had brought him. But
to the country, as he was well aware, he seemed
also to be, as he was, a politician, obviously skilled
in the art, and an avowed candidate for the presidency. His conciliatory bearing, his abstinence
from personal abuse, his freedom from personal
animosities, all were widely declared to be the
mere incidents of constant duplicity and intrigue.
The absence of proof, and his own explicit denial
and appeal to those who knew the facts, did not
protect him from the belief of his adversaries — a
belief which, without examination, has since been
widely adopted — that to prostrate a dangerous
rival he had promoted the quarrel between Jackson
and Calhoun. McLane, the minister at London,
wished to come home, and was to be the new secretary of the treasury. Van Buren gladly seized the
opportunity. He would leave the field of political

management. Three thousand miles in distance and a month in time away from Washington or New York, there could, he thought, be little pretense of personal manœuvres on his part. He would thus plainly submit his candidacy to popular judgment upon his public career, without interference from himself. He would escape the many embarrassments of every politician upon whom demands are continually made, — demands whose rejection or allowance alike brings offense. The English mission was prominently in the public service, but out of its difficulties; and it was made particularly grateful to him by his success in the recent negotiation over colonial trade. He therefore accepted the post, for which in almost every respect he had extraordinary equipment. He finally left the State Department in June, 1831; and on his departure from Washington Jackson conspicuously rode with him out of the city. On August 1, he was formally appointed minister to Great Britain; and in September he arrived in London, accompanied by his son John.

Van Buren found Washington Irving presiding over the London legation in McLane's absence as *chargé d'affaires*. Irving's appointment to be secretary of legation under McLane had been one of Van Buren's early acts, — a proof, Irving wrote, " of the odd way in which this mad world is governed, when a secretary of state of a stern republic gives away offices of the kind at the recommendation of a jovial little man of the seas like Jack

Nicholson." But this was jocose. When the appointment was suggested, it was particularly pleasant to Van Buren that this graceful and gentle bit of patronage should be given by so grim a figure as Jackson. Irving had come on from Spain, his "Columbus" just finished, and his "Alhambra Tales" ready for writing. His extraordinary popularity in England and his old familiarity with its life made him highly useful to the American minister, as Van Buren himself soon found. It was not the last time that Englishmen respected the republic of the west the more because the respect carried with it an homage to the republic of letters. Irving's was an early one of the appointments which established the agreeable tradition of the American diplomatic and consular service, that literary men should always hold some of its places of honor and profit. When Van Buren arrived, Irving was already weary of his post and had resigned. He remained, however, with the new minister until he too surrendered his office. The two men became warm and lifelong friends. The day after Van Buren's arrival Irving wrote: "I have just seen Mr. Van Buren, and do not wonder you should all be so fond of him. His manners are most amiable and ingratiating; and I have no doubt he will become a favorite at this court." After an intimacy of several months he wrote: "The more I see of Mr. Van Buren, the more I feel confirmed in a strong personal regard for him. He is one of the gentlest and most amiable men I have ever met with; with an affectionate disposition that attaches itself to those around him, and wins their kindness in return."

After a few months of the charming life which an American of distinction finds open to him in London, a life for whose duties and whose pleasures Van Buren was happily fitted,[1] there came to him an extraordinary and enviable delight. He posted through England in an open carriage with the author of the "Sketch Book" and "Bracebridge Hall." From those daintiest sources he had years before got an idea of English country life, and of the festivities of an old-fashioned English Christmas; and now in an exquisite companionship the idea became more nearly clothed with reality than happens with most literary enchantments. After Oxford and Blenheim; after quartering in Stratford at the little inn of the Red Horse, where they "found the same obliging little landlady that kept it at the time of the visit recorded in the 'Sketch Book';" after Warwick Castle and Kenilworth and Lichfield and Newstead Abbey and Hardwick Castle; after a fortnight at Christmas in Barlborough Hall, — "a complete scene of old English hospitality," with many of the ancient games and customs then obsolete in other parts of England;

[1] A month or two after his arrival Van Buren wrote Hamilton that his place was decidedly the most agreeable he had ever held, but added: "Money — money is the thing." His house was splendid and in a delightful situation; but it cost him £500. His carriage cost him £310, and his servants with their board $2,600.

after seeing there the "mummers and morris dancers and glee singers;" after "great feasting with the boar's-head crowned with holly, the wassail bowl, the yule-log, snapdragon, etc.;" — after all these delights, inimitably told by his companion, Van Buren returned to London, but not for long. He there enjoyed the halcyon days which the brilliant society of London knew, when George IV. had just left the throne to his undignified but good-hearted and jovial brother; when Louis Philippe had found a bourgeois crown in France and the condescending approval of England; when Wellington was the first of Englishmen; when Prince Talleyrand, his early republicanism and sacrileges not at all forgotten, but forgiven to the prestige of his abilities and the splendid fascinations of his society, was the chief person in diplomatic life; when the Wizard of the North, though broken, and on his last and vain trip to the Mediterranean for health, still lingered in London, one of its grand figures, and sadly recalled to Irving the times when they "went over the Eildon hills together;" when Rogers was playing Mæcenas and Catullus at breakfast-tables of poets and bankers and noblemen. It was amid this serene, shining, and magical translation from the politics at home that Van Buren received the rude and humiliating news of his rejection by the Senate; for his appointment had been made in recess, and he had left without a confirmation.

One evening in February, 1832, before attending

a party at Talleyrand's, Van Buren learned of the rejection, as had all London which knew there was an American minister. He was half ill when the news came; but he seemed imperturbable. Without shrinking he mixed in the splendid throng, gracious and easy, as if he did not know that his official heart would soon cease to beat. Lord Auckland, then president of the board of trade and afterwards governor-general of India, said to him very truly, and more prophetically than he fancied: "It is an advantage to a public man to be the subject of an outrage." Levees and drawing-rooms and state dinners were being held in honor of the queen's birthday. After a doubt as to the more decorous course, he kept the tenor of diplomatic life until he ceased to be a minister; and Irving said that, "to the credit of John Bull," he "was universally received with the most marked attention," and "treated with more respect and attention than before by the royal family, by the members of the present and the old cabinet, and the different persons of the diplomatic corps." On March 22, 1832, he had his audience of leave; two days later he dined with the king at Windsor; and about April 1 left for Holland and a continental trip, this being, so he wrote a committee appointed at an indignation meeting in Tammany Hall, "the only opportunity" he should probably ever have for the visit.

Van Buren's dispatches from England, now preserved in the archives of the State Department, are not numerous. They were evidently written by a minister who was not very busy in official duties apart from the social and ceremonial life of a diplomat. Some of them are in his own handwriting, whose straggling carelessness is quite out of keeping with the obvious pains which he bestowed upon every subject he touched, even those of seemingly slight consequence. Interspersed with allusions to the northeastern boundary question, and with accounts of his protests against abuses practiced upon American ships in British ports, and of the spread of the cholera, he gave English political news and even gossip. He discussed the chances of the reform bill, rumors of what the ministry would do, and whether the Duke of Wellington would yield. Van Buren participated in no important dispute, although before surrendering his post he presented one of the hateful claims which American administrations of both parties had to make in those days. This was the demand for slaves who escaped from the American brig "Comet," wrecked in the Bahamas, on her way from the Potomac to New Orleans, and who were declared free by the colonial authorities.

It is safe to believe that Secretary Livingston read the more interesting of these letters at the White House. Van Buren discreetly lightened up some of the diplomatic pages with passages very agreeable to Jackson. In describing his presentation to William IV., he told Livingston that the king had formed the highest estimate of Jackson's character, and repeated the royal remark "that detraction and misrepresentation were the common lot of all public men." Of the President's message of December, 1831, he wrote that few in England refused to recognize its ability or the "distinguished talents of the executive by whose advice and labors" the affairs "of our highly favored country" had been "conducted to such happy results."

On July 5, 1832, Van Buren arrived at New York, having several weeks before been nominated for the vice-presidency. He declined a public reception, he said, because, afflicted as New York was with the cholera, festivities would be discordant with the feelings of his friends; and a few days later he was in Washington. Congress was in session, debating the tariff bill; and he quickly enough found it true, as he had already believed, that his rejection had been a capital blunder of his enemies. The rejection occurred on January 25, 1832. Jackson's nomination had gone to the Senate early in December, but the opposition had hesitated at the responsibility for the affront. The debate took place in secret session, but the speeches were promptly made public for their effect on the country. Clay and Webster, the great leaders of the Whigs, and Hayne, the eloquent representative of the Calhoun Democracy, and others, spoke against Van Buren. Clay and Webster based their rejection upon his language in the dispatch to McLane, already quoted. Webster said that he would pardon almost anything where he saw true patriotism and sound American feeling; but he could not forgive the sacrifice of these to party. Van Buren, with sensible and skillful foresight, had frankly admitted that we had been wrong in some of our claims; and Gallatin, it was afterwards shown from his original dispatch to Clay, had expressly said the same thing. But in a bit of buncombe Webster insisted that no American minister must ever admit that his country had been wrong. "In the presence of foreign courts," he solemnly said, "amidst the monarchies of Europe, he is to stand up for his country and his whole country; that no jot nor tittle of her honor is to suffer in his hands; that he is not to allow others to reproach either his government or his country, and far less is he himself to reproach either; that he is to have no objects in his eye but American objects, and no heart in his bosom but an American heart." To say all this, Webster declared, was a duty whose performance he wished might be heard "by every independent freeman in the United States, by the British minister and the British king, and every minister and every crowned head in Europe." Van Buren's language, Clay said, had been that of an humble vassal to a proud and haughty lord, prostrating and degrading the American eagle before the British lion. These cheap appeals fell perfectly flat. If Van Buren had been open to criticism for the manner in which he pointed out a party change in American administration, the error

was, at the worst, committed to preclude a British
refusal from finding justification in the offensive
attitude previously taken by Adams.   In admitting
our mistaken "pretensions," Van Buren had been
entirely right, barring a slight fault in the word,
which did not, however, then seem to import the
consciousness of wrong which it carries to later
ears.   Webster and Clay ought to have known
that Van Buren's success where all before had
failed would make the American people loath to
find fault with his phrases.   Nor were they at
all ready to believe that Jackson's administration
toadied to foreign courts.   They knew better; they
were convinced that no American president had
been more resolute towards other nations.

It was also said that Van Buren had introduced
the system of driving men from office for political
opinions; that he was a New York politician who
had brought his art to Washington.   Marcy, one
of the New York senators, defended his State with
these words, which afterwards he must have wished
to recall: "It may be, sir, that the politicians of
New York are not so fastidious as some gentlemen are as to disclosing the principles on which
they act.   They boldly preach what they practice.
When they are contending for victory they avow
their intention of enjoying the fruits of it.   If they
are defeated, they expect to retire from office; if
they are successful, they claim, as a matter of
right, the advantages of success.   They see nothing
wrong in the rule that to the victor belong the

spoils of the enemy." To this celebrated and exe-
crable defense Van Buren owes much of the later
and unjust belief that he was an inveterate "spoils-
man." It has already been shown how little foundation there is for the charge that he introduced
the system of official proscription. Benton truly
said that Van Buren's temper and judgment were
both against it, and that he gave ample proofs of
his forbearance. Webster did not touch upon this
objection. Clay made it very subordinate to the
secretary's abasement before the British lion.

The attack of the Calhoun men was based upon
Van Buren's supposed intrigue against their chief,
and his breaking up of the cabinet. But people
saw then, better indeed than some historians have
since seen, that between Calhoun and Van Buren
there had been great and radical political diver-
gence far deeper than personal jealousy. To surrender the highest cabinet office, to leave Washington and all the places of political management, in
order to take a lower office in remote exile from
the sources of political power, — these were not believed to be acts of mere trickery, but rather to be
parts of a courageous and self-respecting appeal for
justice. It seemed a piece of political animosity
wantonly to punish a rival with such exquisite
humiliation in the eyes of foreigners.

There was a clear majority against confirming
Van Buren. But to make his destruction the more
signal, and as Calhoun had no opportunity to
speak, enough of the majority refrained from vot-

ing to enable the Democratic vice-president to give the casting vote for the rejection of this Democratic nominee. Calhoun's motive was obvious enough from his boast in Benton's hearing: " It will kill him, sir, kill him dead. He will never kick, sir, never kick." This bit of unaffected nature was refreshing after all the solemnly insincere declarations of grief which had fallen from the opposition senators in performing their duty.

The folly of the rejection was quickly apparent. Benton very well said to Moore, a senator from Alabama who had voted against Van Buren, " You have broken a minister and elected a vice-president. The people will see nothing in it but a combination of rivals against a competitor." The popular verdict was promptly given. Van Buren had already become a candidate to succeed Jackson five years later; he was only a possible candidate for vice-president at the next election. When the rejection was widely known, it was known almost equally well and soon that Van Buren would be the Jacksonian candidate for vice-president. Meetings were held ; addresses were voted ; the issue was eagerly seized. The Democratic members of the New York legislature early in February, 1832, under an inspiration from Washington, addressed to Jackson an expression of their indignation in the stately words which our fathers loved, even when they went dangerously near to bathos. They had freely, they said, surrendered to his call their most distinguished fellow-citizen ; when Van Buren had withdrawn from the cabinet they had beheld in Jackson's continual confidence in him irrefragable proof that no combination could close Jackson's eyes to the cause of his country; New York would indeed avenge the indignity thus offered to her favorite son; but they would be unmindful of their duty if they failed to console Jackson with their sympathy in this degradation of the country he loved so well. On February 28, Jackson replied with no less dignity and with skill and force. He was, he said, — and the whole country believed him, — incapable of tarnishing the pride or dignity of that country whose glory it had been his object to elevate; Van Buren's instructions to McLane had been his instructions; American pretensions which Adams's administration had admitted to be untenable had been resigned; if just American claims were resisted upon the ground of the unjust position taken by his predecessor, then and then only was McLane to point out that there had been a change in the policy and counsels of the government with the change of its officers. Jackson said that he owed it to the late secretary of state and to the American people to declare that Van Buren had no participation whatever in the occurrences between Calhoun and himself; and that there was no ground for imputing to Van Buren advice to make the removals from office. He had called Van Buren to the state department not more for his acknowledged talents and public services than to meet the general wish and expectation of the Republican party; his signal ability and success in office had fully justified the selection; his own respect for Van Buren's great public and private worth, and his full confidence in his integrity were undiminished. This blast from the unquestioned head of the party prodigiously helped the general movement. The only question was how best to avenge the wrong.

It was suggested that Van Buren should return directly and take a seat in the Senate, which Dudley would willingly surrender to him, and should there meet his slanderers face to face. Some thought that he should have a triumphal entry into New York, without an idea of going into the "senatorial cock-pit" unless he were not to receive the vice-presidency. Others thought that he should be made governor of New York, an idea shadowed forth in the Albany address to Jackson. As a candidate for that place, he would escape the jealousies of Pennsylvania and perhaps Virginia, and augment the local strength of the party in New York. To this it was replied from Washington that they might better cut his throat at once; that if the Republican party could not, under existing circumstances, make Van Buren vice-president, they need never look to the presidency for him. This was declared to be the unanimous opinion of the cabinet. New York Republicans were begged not to "lose so glorious an opportunity of strengthening and consolidating the party." The people at Albany, it was said, were "mad, . . .

as if New York can make amends for an insult offered by fourteen States of the Union."

In this temper the Republican or Democratic convention met at Baltimore on May 21, 1832. It was the first national gathering of the party; and was summoned simply to nominate a vice-president. Jackson's renomination was already made by the sovereign people, which might be justly affronted by the assembling of a body in apparent doubt whether to obey the popular decree. National conventions were inevitable upon the failure of the congressional caucus in 1824. The system of separate nominations in different States at irregular times was too inconvenient, too inconsistent with unity of action and a central survey of the whole situation. In 1824 its inconvenience had been obvious enough. In 1828 circumstances had designated both the candidates with perfect certainty; and isolated nominations in different parts of the country were then in no danger of clashing. It has been recently said that the convention of 1832 was assembled to force Van Buren's nomination for vice-president. But it is evident from the letter which Parton prints, written by Lewis to Kendall on May 25, 1831, when the latter was visiting Isaac Hill, the Jacksonian leader in New Hampshire, that the convention was even then proposed by "the most judicious" friends of the administration. It was suggested as a plan "of putting a stop to partial nominations" and of "harmonizing" the party. Barbour, Dickinson, and McLane were the candidates discussed in this letter; Van Buren was not named. He was about sailing for England; and although an open candidate for the presidential succession after Jackson, he was not then a candidate for the second office. The ascription of the convention to management in his behalf seems purely gratuitous. Upon this early invitation, the New Hampshire Democrats called the convention. One of them opened its session by a brief speech alluding to the favor with which the idea of the convention had met, " although opposed by the enemies of the Democratic party," as the Republican party headed by Jackson was now perhaps first definitely called. He said that " the coming together of representatives of the people from the extremity of the Union would have a tendency to soothe, if not to unite, the jarring interests ; " and that the people, after seeing its good effects in conciliating the different and distant sections of the country, would continue the mode of nomination. This natural and sensible motive to strengthen and solidify the party is ample explanation of the convention, without resorting to the rather worn charge brought against so many political movements of the time, that they arose from Jackson's dictatorial desire to throttle the sentiment of his party. In making nominations the convention resolved that each State should have as many votes as it would be entitled to in the electoral college. To assure what was deemed a reasonable approach to unanimity, two thirds of the

whole number of votes was required for a choice,
— a precedent sad enough to Van Buren twelve
years later. On the first ballot Van Buren had
208 of the 283 votes. Virginia, South Carolina,
Indiana, and Kentucky, with a few votes from
North Carolina, Alabama, and Illinois, were for
Philip P. Barbour of Virginia or Richard M.
Johnson of Kentucky. The motion, nowadays immediately made, that the nomination be unanimous
was not offered; but after an adjournment a resolution was adopted that inasmuch as Van Buren
had received the votes of two thirds of the delegates, the convention unanimously concur " in re-
commending him to the people of the United States
for their support."

No platform was adopted. A committee was
appointed after the nomination to draft an address;
but after a night's work they reported that, although " agreeing fully in the principles and sentiments which they believe ought to be embodied in
an address of this description, if such an address
were to be made," it still seemed better to them
that the convention recommend the several delegations " to make such explanations by address, report, or otherwise to their respective constituents
of the objects, proceedings, and result of the meeting as they may deem expedient." This was a
franker intimation than those to which we are now
used, that the battle was to be fought in each State
upon the issue best suited to its local sentiments;
and was entitled to quite as much respect as mean-

ingless platitudes adopted lest one State or another be offended at something explicit. Jackson's firm and successful foreign policy, his opposition to internal improvements by the federal government, his strong stand against nullification, his opposition to the United States Bank, — for from the battle over the re-charter, precipitated by Clay early in 1832 to embarrass Jackson, the latter had not shrunk, — and above all Jackson himself, these were the real planks of the platform. But the party wanted the votes of Pennsylvania Jacksonians who believed in the Bank and of western Jacksonians who wished federal aid for roads and canals. The great tariff debate was then going on in Congress; and the subject seemed full of danger. The election was like the usual English canvass on a parliamentary dissolution. The country was merely asked without specifications: Do you on the whole like Jackson's administration?

There is no real ground for the supposition that intrigue or coercion was necessary to procure Van Buren's nomination. It was dictated by the simplest and plainest political considerations. Calhoun was in opposition. After Jackson, Van Buren was clearly the most distinguished and the ablest member of the administration party; he had rendered it services of the highest order; he was very popular in the most important State of New York; he was abroad, suffering from what Irving at the time truly called "a very short-sighted and mean-spirited act of hostility." The affront had

aroused a general feeling which would enable Van
Buren to strengthen the ticket.    In his department
had been performed the most shining achievements
of the administration.    To the politicians about
Jackson, and very shrewd men they were, Van
Buren's succession to Jackson promised a firmer,
abler continuance of the administration than that
of any other public man.    Could he indeed have
stayed minister to England, he would have continued a figure of the first distinction, free from
local and temporary animosities and embarrassments.    From that post he might perhaps, as did
a later Democratic statesman, most easily have
ascended to the presidency; the vice-presidency
would have been unnecessary to the final promotion.    But after the tremendous affront dealt him
by Calhoun and Clay, his tame return to private
life would seem fatal.    He must reënter public
life.    And no reëntry, it was plain, could be so
striking as a popular election to the second station
in the land, nominal though it was, and in taking
it to displace the very enemy who had been finally
responsible for the wrong done him.

A month after his return Van Buren formally
accepted the nomination.    The committee of the
convention had assured him that if the great Republican party continued faithful to its principles,
there was every reason to congratulate him and
their illustrious president that there was in reserve
for his wounded feelings a just and certain reparation.    Van Buren said in reply that previous to

his departure from the United States his name
had been frequently mentioned for the vice-presidency; but that he had uniformly declared himself
altogether unwilling to be considered a candidate,
and that to his friends, when opportunity offered,
he had given the grounds of his unwillingness.
All this was strictly true. He had become a candidate for the presidential succession; and honorable absence as minister to England secured a
better preparation than presence as vice-president
amidst the difficulties and suspicions of Washington. But his position, he added, had since that
period been essentially changed by the circum-
stance to which the committee had referred, and
to which, with some excess of modesty he said,
rather than to any superior fitness on his part, he
was bound to ascribe his nomination. He gratefully received this spontaneous expression of confidence and friendship from the delegated democracy
of the Union. He declared it to be fortunate for
the country that its public affairs were under the
direction of one who had an early and inflexible
devotion to republican principles and a moral courage which distinguished him from all others. In
the conviction, he said, that on a faithful adherence
to these principles depended the stability and value
of our confederated system, he humbly hoped lay
his motive, rather than any other, for accepting
the nomination. This rather clumsy affectation of
humility would have been more disagreeable had
it not been closely associated with firm and manly

expressions, and because it was so common a formality in the political vernacular of the day. In treating the people as the sovereign, there were adopted the sort of rhetorical extravagances used by attendants upon monarchs.

On October 4, 1832, Van Buren, upon an interrogation by a committee of a meeting at Shocco Springs, North Carolina, wrote a letter upon the tariff. He said that he believed " the establishment of commercial regulations with a view to the encouragement of domestic products to be within the constitutional power of Congress." But as to what should be the character of the tariff he indulged in the generalities of a man who has opinions which he does not think it wise or timely to exhibit. He did not wish to see the power of Congress exercised with " oppressive inequality " or " for the advantage of one section of the Union at the expense of another." The approaching extinguishment of the national debt presented an opportunity for a " more equitable adjustment of the tariff," an opportunity already embraced in the tariff of 1832, whose spirit as " a conciliatory measure " he trusted would be cherished by all who preferred public to private interests. These vague expressions would have fitted either a revenue reformer or an extreme protectionist. Both disbelieved, or said they did, in oppression and inequality. With a bit of irony, perhaps unconscious, he added that he had been thus " explicit " in the statement of his sentiments that there might not be room for misapprehension of his views. He did, however, in the letter approve " a reduction of the revenue to the wants of the government," and " a preference in encouragement given to such manufactures as are essential to the national defense, and its extension to others in proportion as they are adapted to our country and of which the raw material is produced by ourselves." The last phrase probably hinted at Van Buren's position. He believed in strictly limiting protective duties, although he had voted for the tariff of 1828. But he told Benton that he cast this vote in obedience to the " *demos krateo* " principle, that is, because his State required it. He again spoke strongly against the policy of internal improvements, and the " scrambles and combinations in Congress" unavoidably resulting from them. He was " unreservedly opposed " to a renewal of the charter of the Bank, and equally opposed to nullification, which involved, he believed, the " certain destruction of the confederacy."

A few days later he wrote to a committee of " democratic-republican young men " in New York of the peculiar hatred and contumely visited upon him. Invectives against other men, he said, were at times suspended ; but he had never enjoyed a moment's respite since his first entrance into public life. Many distinguished public men had, he added, been seriously injured by favors from the press ; but there was scarcely an instance in which the objects of its obloquy had not been raised in

public estimation in exact proportion to the intensity and duration of the abuse.

Both the letter from the Baltimore convention
and Van Buren's reply alluded to "diversity of
sentiments and interests," disagreements "as to
measures and men" among the Republicans. The
secession of Calhoun and the bitter hostility of his
friends seriously weakened the party. But against
this was to be set the Anti-Masonic movement
which drew far more largely from Jackson's opponents than from his supporters, for Jackson was a
Mason of a high degree. This strange agitation
had now spread beyond New York, and secured the
support of really able men. Judge McLean of the
Supreme Court desired the Anti-Masonic nomination; William Wirt, the famous and accomplished
Virginian, accepted it. John Quincy Adams would
probably have accepted it, had it been tendered
him. He wrote in his diary: "The dissolution of
the Masonic institution in the United States I believe to be really more important to us and our
posterity than the question whether Mr. Clay or
General Jackson shall be the president." In New
York the National Republicans or Whigs, with the
eager and silly leaning of minority parties to political absurdities or vagaries, united with the Anti-
Masons, among whom William H. Seward and
Thurlow Weed had become influential. In 1830
they had supported Francis Granger, the Anti-
Masonic candidate for governor. In 1832 the
Anti-Masons in New York nominated an electoral

ticket headed by Chancellor Kent, whose bitter, narrow, and unintelligent politics were in singular contrast with his extraordinary legal equipment and his professional and literary accomplishments, and by John C. Spencer, lately in charge of the prosecution of Morgan's abductors. If the ticket were successful, its votes were to go to Wirt or Clay, whichever they might serve to elect. Amos Ellmaker of Pennsylvania was the Anti-Masonic candidate for vice-president. In December, 1831, Clay had been nominated for president with the loud enthusiasm which politicians often mistake for widespread conviction. John Sergeant of Pennsylvania was the candidate for vice-president. The Whig Convention made the Bank re-charter the issue. The very ably conducted Young Men's National Republican Convention, held at Washington in May, 1832, gave Clay a noble greeting, made pilgrimage to the tomb of Washington there to seal their solemn promises, and adopted a clear and brief platform for protection, for internal improvements by the federal government, for the binding force upon the coördinate branches of the government of the Supreme Court's opinions as to constitutional questions, not only in special cases formally adjudged, but upon general principles, and against the manner in which the West Indian trade had been recovered. They declared that "indiscriminate removal of public officers for a mere difference of political opinion is a gross abuse of power, corrupting the morals and dangerous to the liberties of the people of this country."

Even more clearly than in the campaign of 1828 was the campaign of 1832 a legitimate political battle upon plain issues. The tariff bill of 1832, supported by both parties and approved by Jackson, prevented the question of protection from being an issue, however ready the Whigs might be, and however unready the Democrats, to give commercial restrictions a theoretical approval. Except on the "spoils" question, the later opinion of the United States has sustained the attitude of Jackson's party and the popular verdict of 1832. The verdict was clear enough. In spite of the Anti-Masonic fury, the numerous secessions from the Jacksonian ranks, and some alarming journalistic defections, especially of the New York "Courier and Enquirer" of James Watson Webb and Mordecai M. Noah, the people of the United States continued to believe in Jackson and the principles for which he stood. Upon the popular vote Jackson and Van Buren received 687,502 votes against 530,189 votes for Clay and Wirt combined, a popular majority over both of 157,313. In 1828 Jackson had had 647,276 votes and Adams 508,064, a popular majority of 139,212. The increase in Jackson's popular majority over two candidates instead of one was particularly significant in the north and east. The majority in New York rose from 5350 to 13,601. In Maine a minority of 6806 became a majority of 6087. In New Hampshire a minority of 3212 became a majority of 6476. In Massachusetts a minority of 23,860

was reduced to 18,458.   In Rhode Island and Connecticut the minorities were reduced.   In New Jersey a minority of 1813 became a majority of 463.
The electoral vote was even more heavily against
Clay.   He had but 49 votes to Jackson's 219.
Wirt had the 7 votes of Vermont, while South
Carolina, beginning to step out of the Union, gave
its 11 votes to John Floyd of Virginia.   Clay carried only Massachusetts, Rhode Island, Connecticut, Delaware, a part of Maryland, and his own
affectionate Kentucky.   Van Buren received for
vice-president the same electoral vote as Jackson,
except that the 30 votes of Pennsylvania went to
Wilkins, a Pennsylvanian.   Sergeant had the same
49 votes as Clay, Ellmaker the 7 votes of Vermont,
and Henry Lee of Massachusetts the 11 votes of
South Carolina.[1]

This popular triumph brought great glory to
Jackson's second inauguration.   The glory was
soon afterwards made greater and almost universal
by his bold attack upon nullification, and by the
vigorous and ringing yet dignified and even pathetic proclamation of January, 1833, drafted by

[1] In estimating the popular vote in 1828, Delaware and South
Carolina are excluded, their electors having been chosen by the
legislature.   In Georgia in that year there was no opposition to
Jackson.   In 1832 no popular vote is included for South Carolina
or for Alabama.   In Mississippi and Missouri there was no opposition to Jackson.   In 1829, upon Van Buren's recommendation
when governor, the system in New York of choosing electors by
districts, which had been in force in the election of 1838, was
abolished; and there was adopted the present system of choosing
all the electors by the popular vote of the whole State.

Edw Livingston

Edward Livingston, in which the President commanded obedience to the law and entreated for loyalty to the Union. It could not be overlooked that the treasonable attitude of South Carolina had been taken by the portion of the Democratic party hostile to Van Buren. In a peculiar way therefore he shared in Jackson's prestige.

The election seemed to clarify some of the views of the administration. They now dared to speak more explicitly. On his way to the inauguration, Van Buren, declining a dinner at Philadelphia, recited with approval what he called Jackson's repeated and earnest recommendations of " a reduction of duties to the revenue standard." In his second inaugural Jackson said that there should be exercised " by the general government those powers only that are clearly delegated." In his message of December, 1833, he again spoke of " the importance of abstaining from all appropriations which are not absolutely required for the public interests, and authorized by the powers clearly delegated to the United States ; " and this he said with the more emphasis because under the compromise tariff of 1833 a large decrease in revenue was anticipated.

In September, 1833, was announced Jackson's refusal longer to deposit the moneys of the government with the Bank of the United States. It is plain that the dangers of the proposed deposits of the moneys in the state banks were not appreciated. Van Buren at first opposed this so-called

"removal of the deposits." Kendall tells of an
interview with the Vice-President not long after
his inauguration, and while he was a guest at the
White House. Van Buren then warmly remonstrated against the continued agitation of the subject, after the resolution of the lower House at the
last session that the government deposits were safe
with the banks. Kendall replied that so certain to
his mind was the success of the Whig party at the
next presidential election and the consequent re-
charter of the Bank, unless it were now stripped
of the power which the charge of the public moneys
gave it, that if the Bank were to retain the deposits
he should consider further opposition useless and
would lay down his pen, leaving to others this question and all other politics. "I can live," he said
to the Vice-President, "under a corrupt despotism
as well as any other man by keeping out of its way,
which I shall certainly do." They parted in excitement. A few weeks later Van Buren confessed to
Kendall, "I had never thought seriously upon the
deposit question until after my conversation with
you; I am now satisfied that you were right and I
was wrong." Kendall was sent to ascertain whether
suitable state banks would accept the deposits, and
on what terms. While in New York Van Buren,
with McLane lately transferred from the Treasury
to the State Department, called on him and proposed that the order for the change in the government depositories should take effect on the coming
first of January. The date being a month after

the meeting of Congress, the executive action would seem less defiant; and in the mean time the friends of the administration could be more effectually united in support of the measure. Kendall yielded to the proposition though against his judgment, and wrote to the President in its favor. But Jackson would not yield. Whether or not its first inspiration came from Francis P. Blair or Kendall, the removal of the deposits was peculiarly Jackson's own deed. The government moneys should not be left in the hands of the chief enemy of his administration, to be loaned in its discretion, that it might secure doubtful votes in Congress and the support of presses pecuniarily weak. As the Bank's charter would expire within three years, it was pointed out that the government ought to prepare for it by withholding further deposits and gradually drawing out the moneys then on deposit. Van Buren's assent was given, but probably with no enthusiasm. He disliked the Bank heartily enough. The corrupting danger of intrusting government moneys to a single private corporation to loan in its discretion was clear. But a system of "pet banks" through the States was too slight an improvement, if an improvement at all. And any change would at least offend and alarm the richer classes. It is impossible to say what effect upon the re-charter of the Bank and the election of 1836 its continued possession of the deposits would have had. Its tremendous power over credits doubtless gave it many votes of administration congressmen. Pos-

sibly, as Jackson and Blair feared, it might have
secured enough to pass a re-charter over a veto.  If
it had been thus re-chartered, it may be doubtful
whether the blow to the prestige of the administration might not have been serious enough to elect a
Whig in 1836.  But it is not doubtful that Van
Buren, and not Jackson, was compelled to face the
political results of this heroic and imperfect measure.

Some financial disturbance took place in the
winter of 1833–1834, which was ascribed by the
Whigs to the gradual transfer of the government
moneys from the United States Bank and its numerous branches to the state banks.  For political
effect, this disturbance was greatly exaggerated.
Deputations visited Washington to bait Jackson.
Memorial after memorial enabled congressmen to
make friends by complimenting the enterprise and
beauty of various towns, and to depict the utter
misery to which all their industries had been
brought, solely by a gradual transference throughout the United States of $10,000,000, from one
set of depositories to another.  The removal, Webster said, had produced a degree of evil that could
not be borne.  "A tottering state of credit, cramped
means, loss of property and loss of employment,
doubts of the condition of others, doubts of their
own condition, constant fear of failures and new
explosions, and awful dread of the future" — all
these evils, "without hope of improvement or
change," had resulted from the removal.  Clay

was more precise in his absurdity. The property of the country had been reduced, he declared, four hundred millions in value. Addressing Van Buren in the Vice-President's chair, he begged him in a burst of bathos to repair to the executive mansion and place before the chief magistrate the naked and undisguised truth. "Go to him," he cried, "and tell him without exaggeration, but in the language of truth and sincerity, the actual condition of this bleeding country, . . . of the tears of helpless widows no longer able to earn their bread, and of unclad and unfed orphans." Van Buren, in the story often quoted from Benton, while thus apostrophized, looked respectfully and innocently at Clay, as if treasuring up every word to be faithfully borne to the President; and when Clay had finished, he called a senator to the chair, went up to the eloquent and languishing Kentuckian, asked him for a pinch of his fine maccoboy snuff, and walked away. But this frivolity was not fancied everywhere. At a meeting in Philadelphia it was resolved "that Martin Van Buren deserves and will receive the execrations of all good men, should he shrink from the responsibility of conveying to Andrew Jackson the message sent by the Honorable Henry Clay." The whole agitation was hollow enough. Jackson was not far wrong in saying in his letter to Hamilton of January 2, 1834: "There is no real general distress. It is only with those who live by borrowing, trade or loans, and the gamblers in stocks." The business of the country was not injured by refusing to let Nicholas Biddle and his subordinates, rather than other men, lend for gain ten millions of government money. But business was soon to be injured by permitting the state banks to do the same thing. The change did not, as Jackson thought, " leave all to trade on their own credit and capital without any interference by the general government except using its powers by giving through its mint a specie currency."

Van Buren took a permanent residence in Washington after his inauguration as vice-president. He now held a rank accorded to no other vice-president before or since. He was openly adopted by the American Augustus, and seemed already to wear the title of Cæsar. As no other vice-president has been, he was the chief adviser of the President, and as much the second officer of the government in power as in the dignity of his station. His only chance of promotion did not lie in the President's death. That the President should live until after the election of 1836 was safely over, Van Buren had every selfish motive as well as many generous motives to desire. His ambition was nowise disagreeable to his chief. To see that ambition satisfied would gratify both patriotic and personal wishes of the tempestuous but not erratic old man in the White House. For there was the utmost intimacy and confidence between the two men. Van Buren had every reason, personal, political, and patriotic, to desire the entire success of the administration. He was not only the second member of it; but in his jealous and anxious watch over it he was preserving his own patrimony. His ability and experience were far greater than those of any other of its members. After Taney had been transferred from the attorney-general's office to the Treasury, in September, 1833, to make the transfer of the deposits, Jackson appointed Benjamin F. Butler, Van Buren's intimate friend, his former pupil and partner, to Taney's place. Louis McLane, Van Buren's predecessor in the mission to England, and his successor, after Edward Livingston, in the State Department, resigned the latter office in the summer of 1834. He had disapproved Jackson's removal of the deposits; he believed it would be unpopular, and the presidential bee was buzzing in his bonnet. John Forsyth of Georgia, an admirer of Van Buren, and one of his defenders in the senatorial debate at the time of his rejection, then took the first place in the cabinet. Van Buren accompanied Jackson during part of the latter's visit to the Northeast in the summer of 1833, when as the adversary of nullification his popularity was at its highest, so high indeed that Harvard College, to Adams's disgust, made him a Doctor of Laws. But the exciting events of Jackson's second term hardly belong, with the information we yet have, to Van Buren's biography. They have been often and admirably told in the lives of Jackson and Clay, the seeming chiefs on the two sides of the long encounter.

Van Buren's nomination for the presidency, bitter as the opposition to it still was, came as matter
of course.   The large and serious secession of Calhoun and his followers from the Jacksonian party
was followed by the later and more serious defection of the Democrats who made a rival Democratic candidate of Hugh L. White, a senator
from Tennessee, and formerly a warm friend and
adherent of Jackson.   It was in White's behalf
that Davy Crockett wrote, in 1835, his entertaining though scurrilous life of Van Buren.   Jackson's friendship for Van Buren, Crockett said, had
arisen from his hatred to Calhoun, of which Van
Buren, who was " secret, sly, selfish, cold, calculat-
ing, distrustful, treacherous," had taken advantage.
Jackson was now about to give up " an old, long-
tried, faithful friend, Judge White, who stuck to
him through all his tribulations, helped to raise
his fortunes from the beginning ; adventurers together in a new country, friends in youth and in
old age, fought together in the same battles, risked
the same dangers, starved together in the same
deserts, merely to gratify this revengeful feeling."
Van Buren was " as opposite to General Jackson
as dung is to a diamond."

It is difficult to find any justification for White's
candidacy.   He was a modest, dignified senator
whose popularity in the Democratic Southwest rendered him available to Van Buren's enemies.   But
neither his abilities nor his services to the public or his party would have suggested him for

the presidency. Doubtless in him as with other
modest, dignified men in history, there burned ambition whose fire never burst into flame, and which
perhaps for its suppression was the more troublesome. He consented, apparently only for personal
reasons, to head the Southern schism from Jackson
and Van Buren; and in his political destruction
he paid the penalty usually and justly visited upon
statesmen who, through personal hatred or jealousy
or ambition, break party ties without a real difference of principle. Benton said that White consented to run " because in his advanced age he did
the act which, with all old men, is an experiment,
and with most of them an unlucky one. He married again; and this new wife having made an
immense stride from the head of a boarding-house
table to the head of a senator's table, could see no
reason why she should not take one step more, and
that comparatively short, and arrive at the head of
the presidential table."

The Democratic-Republican Convention met at
Baltimore on May 20, 1835, nearly eighteen months
before the election. There were over five hundred
delegates from twenty-three States. South Carolina, Alabama, and Illinois were not represented.
Party organization was still very imperfect. The
modern system of precise and proportional repre-
sentations was not yet known. The States which
approved the convention sent delegates in such
number as suited their convenience. Maryland,
the convention being held in its chief city, sent

183 delegates; Virginia, close at hand, sent 102; New York, although the home of the proposed candidate, sent but 42, the precise number of its electoral votes. Tennessee sent but one; Mississippi and Missouri, only two each. In making the nominations, the delegates from each State, however numerous or few, cast a number of votes equal to its representation in the electoral college. The 183 delegates from Maryland cast therefore but ten votes; while the single delegate from Tennessee, much courted man that he must have been, cast 15.

It was the second national convention of the party. The members assembled at the "place of worship of the Fourth Presbyterian Church." Instead of the firm and now long-recognized opening by the chairman of the national committee provided by the well-geared machinery of our later politics, George Kremer of Pennsylvania first "stated the objects of the meeting." Andrew Stevenson of Virginia, the president, felt it necessary in his opening speech to defend the still novel party institution. Efforts, he said, would be made at the approaching election to divide the Republican party and possibly to defeat an election by the people in their primary colleges. Their venerable president had advised, but in vain, constitutional amendments securing this election to the people, and preventing its falling to the House of Representatives. A national convention was the best means of concentrating the popular will, the only defense against a minority party. It was recommended by prudence, sanctioned by the precedent of 1832, and had proved effectual by experience. They must guard against local jealousies. "What, gentlemen," he said, "would you think of the sagacity and prudence of that individual who would propose the expedient of cutting up the noble ship that each man might seize his own plank and steer for himself?" The inquiries must be: Who can best preserve the unity of the Democratic party? Who best understands the principles and motives of our government? Who will carry out the principles of the Jeffersonian era and General Jackson's administration? These demands clearly enough pointed out Van Buren. Prayers were then offered up "in a fervent, feeling manner." The rule requiring two thirds of the whole number of votes for a nomination was again adopted, because "it would have a more imposing effect," though nearly half the convention, 210 to 231, thought a majority was more "according to Democratic principles." Niles records that the formal motion to proceed to the nomination caused a smile among the members, so well settled was it that Van Buren was to be the nominee. He received the unanimous vote of the convention. A strong fight was made for the vice-presidency between the friends of Richard M. Johnson of Kentucky and William C. Rives of Virginia. The former received barely the two-thirds vote. The Virginia delegation upon the defeat of the latter did what would now be a sacrilegious laying of violent hands on the ark. Party regularity was not yet so chief a deity in the political temple. The Virginians had, they said, an unpleasant duty to perform; but they would not shrink from it. They would not support Johnson for the vice-presidency; they had no confidence in his principles or his character; they had come to the convention to support principles, not men; they had already gone as far as possible in supporting Mr. Van Buren, and they would not go further. Not long afterwards Rives left the party. No platform was adopted; but a committee was appointed to prepare an address to the people.

The Whigs nominated General William Henry Harrison for the presidency and Francis Granger for the vice-presidency. They had but a forlorn hope of direct success. But the secession from the Democratic party of the nullifiers, and the more serious secession in the Southwest headed by White, made it seem possible to throw the election into the House. John Tyler of Virginia was the nominee of the bolting Democrats, for vice-president upon the ticket with White. The Whigs of Massachusetts preferred their unequaled orator; for they then and afterwards failed to see, as the admirers of some other famous Americans have failed to see, that other qualities make a truer equipment for the first office of the land than this noble art of oratory. South Carolina would vote against Calhoun's victorious adversary; but she would not, in the first instance at least, vote with the Whig heretics.

It was a disorderly campaign, lasting a year and a half, and never reaching the supreme excitement of 1840 or 1844. The opposition did not deserve success. It had neither political principle nor discipline. Calhoun described the Van Buren men as "a powerful faction (party it cannot be called) held together by the hopes of public plunder and marching under a banner whereon is written 'to the victors belong the spoils.'" There was in the rhetorical exaggeration enough truth perhaps to make an issue. But the political removals under Jackson were only incidentally touched in the canvass. Amos Kendall, then postmaster-general, towards the close of the canvass wrote a letter which, coming from perhaps the worst of Jackson's "spoilsmen," shows how far public sentiment was even then from justifying the political interference of federal officers in elections. Samuel McKean, senator from Pennsylvania, had written to Kendall complaining that three employees of the post-office had used the time and influence of their official stations to affect elections, by written communications and personal importunities. This, he said, was "a loathsome public nuisance," though admitting that since Kendall became postmaster-general he had given no cause of complaint. Kendall replied on September 27, 1836, that though it was difficult to draw the line between the rights of the citizen and the assumptions of the officeholder, he thought it dangerous to our institutions that government employees should "assume to direct public

opinion and control the results of elections in the
general or state government." His advice to members of his department was to keep as clear from
political strife as possible, "to shun mere political
meetings, or, if present, to avoid taking any part
in their proceedings, to decline acting as members
of political committees or conventions." In making
appointments he would prefer political friends; but
he "would not remove a good postmaster and honest man for a mere difference of political opinion."
The complaints were for offenses committed under
his predecessor; one of the three offenders had
left the service; the other two had been free from
criticism for seventeen months. There can be little
doubt that the standard thus set up in public was
higher than the general practice of Kendall or his
subordinates; but the letter showed that public
sentiment had not yet grown callous to this odious
abuse.

Jackson did not permit the presidential office to
restrain him from most vigorous and direct advocacy
of Van Buren's claims. He begged Tennessee not
to throw herself "into the embraces of the Federalists, the Nullifiers, or the new-born Whigs." They
were living, he said, in evil times, when political
apostasy had become frequent, when public men
(referring to White, John Tyler, and others who
had gone with them) were abandoning principle
and their party attachment for selfish ends. To
this it was replied that the president's memory was
treacherous; that he had forgotten his early friends,

and listened only " to the voice of flattery and the siren voice of sycophancy." The dissenting Republicans affected to support administration measures, but protested against Jackson's dictating the succession. They were then, they said, "what they were in 1828, — Jacksonians following the creed of that apostle of liberty, Thomas Jefferson."

Without principle as was this formidable secession, it is impossible to feel much more respect for the declaration of principles made for the Whig candidates. Clay, the chief spokesman, complained that Jackson had killed with the pocket veto the land bill, which proposed to distribute the proceeds of the sales of public lands among the States according to their federal population (which in the South included three fifths of the slaves), to be used for internal improvements, education, or other purposes. He pointed out, with "mixed feelings of pity and ridicule," that the few votes in the Senate against the "deposit bill," which was to distribute the surplus among the States, had been cast by administration senators, since deserted by their numerous followers who demanded distribution. He rejoiced that Kentucky was to get a million and a half from the federal treasury. He denounced Jackson's "tampering with the currency" by the treasury order requiring public lands to be paid for in specie and not in bank-notes. Jackson's treatment of the Cherokees seemed the only point of attack apart from his financial policy.

The real party platforms this year were curiously

found in letters of the candidates to Sherrod Williams, an individual by no means distinguished.
On April 7, 1836, he addressed a circular letter to
Harrison, Van Buren, and White, asking each of
them his opinions on five points: Did he approve
a distribution of the surplus revenue among the
States according to their federal population, for
such uses as they might appoint? Did he approve
a like distribution of the proceeds of the sales of
public lands? Did he approve federal appropriations to improve navigable streams above ports of
entry? Did he approve another bank charter, if it
should become necessary to preserve the revenue
and finances of the nation? Did he believe it constitutional to expunge from the records of a house
of Congress any of its proceedings? The last
question referred to Benton's agitation for a resolution expunging from the records of the Senate
the resolution of 1834, condemning Jackson's removal of the deposits as a violation of the Constitution.  Harrison, for whose benefit the questions
were put, returned what was supposed to be the
popular affirmative to the first three inquiries.
The fourth he answered in the affirmative, and the
fifth in the negative. Van Buren promptly pointed
out to Williams that he doubted the right of an
elector, who had already determined to oppose him,
to put inquiries " with the sole view of exposing,
at his own time and the mode he may select, the
opinions of the candidate to unfriendly criticism,"
but nevertheless promised a reply after Congress

had risen. This delay he deemed proper, because during the session he might, as president of the Senate, have to vote upon some of the questions. Williams replied that the excuse for delay was "wholly and entirely unsatisfactory." Van Buren curtly said that he should wait as he had stated. On August 8, not far from the time nowadays selected by presidential candidates for their letters of acceptance, Van Buren addressed a letter to Williams, the prolixity of which seems a fault, but which, when newspapers were fewer and shorter, and reading was less multifarious, secured perhaps, from its length, a more ample and deliberate study from the masses of the people.

For clearness and explicitness, and for cogency of argument, this letter has few equals among those written by presidential candidates. This most conspicuous of Van Buren's preëlection utterances has been curiously ignored by those who have accused him of "non-committalism." Congress, he said, does not possess the power under the Constitution to raise money for distribution among the States. If a distinction were justifiable, and of this he was not satisfied, between raising money for such a purpose and the distribution of an unexpected surplus, then the distribution ought not to be attempted without previous amendment of the Constitution. Any system of distribution must introduce vices into both the state and federal governments. It would be a great misfortune if the distribution bill already passed should be deemed a pledge of like legislation in the future. So much of the letter has since largely had the approval of American sentiment, and was only too soon emphasized by the miserable results of the bill thus condemned. The utterance was clear and wise; and it was far more. It was a singularly bold attitude to assume, not only against the views of the opposition, but against a measure passed by Van Buren's own party friends and signed by Jackson, a measure having a vast and cheap popularity throughout the States which were supposed, and with too much truth, not to see that for what they took out of the federal treasury they would simply have to put so much more in. " I hope and believe," said Van Buren, " that the public voice will demand that this species of legislation shall terminate with the emergency that produced it." To the inquiry whether he would approve a distribution among the States of the proceeds of selling the public lands, Van Buren plainly said that if he were elected he would not favor the policy. These moneys, he declared, should be applied " to the general wants of the treasury." To the inquiry whether he would approve appropriations to improve rivers above ports of entry, he quoted with approval Jackson's declaration in the negative. He would not go beyond expenditures for lighthouses, buoys, beacons, piers, and the removal of obstructions in rivers and harbors below such ports.

Upon the bank question, too, he left his interrogator in no doubt. If the people wished a national bank as a permanent branch of their institutions, or if they desired a chief magistrate who as to that would consider it his duty to watch the course of events and give or withhold his assent according to the supposed necessity, then another than himself must be chosen. And he added : "If, on the other hand, with this seasonable, explicit, and published avowal before them, a majority of the people of the United States shall nevertheless bestow upon me their suffrages for the office of president, skepticism itself must cease to doubt, and admit their will to be that there shall not be any Bank of the United States until the people, in the exercise of their sovereign authority, see fit to give to Congress the right to establish one." It was high time "that the federal government confine itself to the creation of coin, and that the States afford it a fair chance for circulation." With the power of either house of Congress to expunge from its records, he pointed out that the President could have no concern. But rather than avoid an answer, he said that he regarded the passage of Colonel Benton's resolution as "an act of justice to a faithful and greatly injured public servant, not only constitutional in itself, but imperiously demanded by a proper respect for the well-known will of the people."

This justly famous letter made up for the rather jejune and conventional letter of acceptance written a year before. Not concealing his sensitiveness to the charge of intrigue and management, Van Buren had then appealed to the members of the Democratic convention, to the "editors and politicians throughout the Union" who had preferred him, to his "private correspondents and intimate friends," and to those, once his "friends and associates, whom the fluctuations of political life" had "converted into opponents." No man, he declared, could truly say that he had solicited political support, or entered or sought to enter into any arrangement to procure him the nomination he had now received, or to elevate him to the chief magistracy. There was no public question of interest upon which his opinions had not been made known by his official acts, his own public avowals, and the authorized explanations of his friends. The last was a touch of the frankness which Van Buren used in vain to stop his enemies' accusations of indirectness. Instead of shielding himself, as public men usually and naturally do, behind Butler, the attorney-general, and others who had spoken for him, he directly assumed responsibility for their "explanations." He considered himself selected to carry out the principles and policy of Jackson's administration, "happy," he said, "if I shall be able to perfect the work which he has so gloriously begun." He closed with the theoretical declaration which consistently ran through his chief utterances, that, though he would "exercise the powers which of right belong to the general government in a spirit of moderation and brotherly love," he would on the other hand " religiously abstain from the assumption of such as have not been delegated by the Constitution."

Upon still another question Van Buren explicitly declared himself before the election. In 1835, the year of his nomination, appeared the cloud like a man's hand which was not to leave the sky until out of it had come a terrific, complete, and beneficent convulsion. Then openly and seriously began the work of the extreme anti-slavery men. Clay pointed out in his speech on colonization in 1836 that " this fanatical class " of abolitionists " were none of your old-fashioned gradual emancipationists, such as Franklin, Rush, and the other wise and benevolent Pennsylvanians who framed the scheme for the gradual removal of slavery." He was right. Many of the new abolitionists were on the verge, or beyond it, of quiet respectability. Educated, intelligent, and even wealthy as some of them were, the abolitionists did not belong to the always popular class of well-to-do folks content with the institutions of society. Most virtuous and religious people saw in them only wicked disturbers of the peace. All the comfortable, philosophical opponents of slavery believed that such wild and reckless agitators would, if encouraged, prostrate the pillars of civilization, and bring on anarchy, bloodshed, and servile wars worse even to the slaves than the wrongs of their slavery. But to the members of the abolition societies which now rose, this was no abstract or economical question. They were undaunted by the examples of Washington and Jefferson and Patrick Henry, who, whatever they said or hoped against slavery, nevertheless held human beings in bondage; or of Adams and other Northern adherents of the Constitution, who for a season at least had joined in a pact to protect the infamous slave traffic. To them, talk of the sacred Union, or of the great advance which negroes had made in slavery and would not have made in freedom, was idle. With unquenched vision they saw the horrid picture of the individual slave life, not the general features of slavery; they saw the chain, the lash, the brutalizing and contrived ignorance; they saw the tearing apart of families, with their love and hope, precisely like those of white men and women, crushed out by detestable cruelty; they saw the beastly dissoluteness inevitable to the plantation system. Nor would they be still, whatever the calm preaching of political wisdom, whatever the sincere and weighty insolence of men of wisdom and uprightness and property. Northern men of 1888 must look with a real shame upon the behavior of their fathers and grandfathers towards the narrow, fiery, sometimes almost hateful, apostles of human rights; and with even greater shame upon the talk of the sacred right of white men to make brutes of black men, a right to be treated, as the best of Americans were so fond of saying, with a tender and affectionate regard for the feelings of the white slave-masters. About the same time began

the continual presentation to Congress of petitions
for the abolition of slavery, and the foolish but
Heaven-ordained attack of slaveholders on the right
of petition. The agitation rapidly flaming up was
far different from the practical and truly political
discussion over the Missouri Compromise fifteen
years before.

As yet, indeed, the matter was not politically
important, except in the attack upon Van Buren
made by the Southern members of his party. Sixteen years before, he had voted against admitting
more slave States. He had aided the reëlection of
Rufus King, a determined enemy of slavery. He
had strongly opposed Calhoun and the Southern
nullifiers. In the " Evening Post " and the " Plain-
dealer " of New York appeared from 1835 to 1837
the really noble series of editorials by William
Leggett, strongly proclaiming the right of free
discussion and the essential wrong of slavery; although sometimes he condemned the fanaticism
now aroused as "a species of insanity." The
" Post " strongly supported Van Buren, and was
declared at the South to be his chosen organ for
addressing the public. It denied, however, that
Van Buren had any "connection in any way or
shape with the doctrines or movements of the abolitionists." But such denials were widely disbelieved by the slaveholders. It was declared that
he had a deep agency in the Missouri question
which fixed upon him a support of abolition; his
denials were answered by the anti-slavery petitions

from twenty thousand memorialists in his own State of New York, and by the support brought him by the enemies of slavery. To all this the Whig "dough-faces" listened with entire satisfaction. They must succeed, if at all, through Southern distrust or dislike of Van Buren. In July, 1834, he had publicly written to Samuel Gwin of Mississippi that his opinions upon the power of Congress over slave property in the Southern States were so well understood by his friends that he was surprised that an attempt should be made to deceive the public about them; that slavery was in his judgment "exclusively under the control of the state governments;" that no "contrary opinion to an extent deserving consideration" was entertained in any part of the United States; and that, without a change of the Constitution, no interference with it in a State could be had "even at the instance of either or of all the slaveholding States." But, it was said, "Tappan, Garrison, and every other fanatic and abolitionist in the United States not entirely run mad, will grant that." And, indeed, Abraham Lincoln was nominated twenty-four years later upon a like declaration of "the right of each State to order and control its own domestic institutions according to its own judgment exclusively."

The District of Columbia, however, was one bit of territory in which Congress doubtless had the power to abolish slavery. In our better days it would seem to have been a natural enough impulse to seek to make free soil at least of the capital of the land of freedom. But the District lay between and was completely surrounded by two slave States. Washington had derived its laws and customs from Maryland. If the District were free while Virginia and Maryland were slave, it was feared with much reason that there would arise most dangerous collisions. Its perpetual slavery was an unforeseen part of the price Alexander Hamilton had paid to procure the federal assumption of the war debts of the States. In Van Buren's time there was almost complete acquiescence in the proposition that, though slavery had in the District no constitutional protection, it must still be deemed there a part of the institution in Virginia and Maryland. How clear was the understanding may be seen from language of undoubted authority. John Quincy Adams had hitherto labored for causes which have but cold and formal interest to posterity. But now, leaving the field of statesmanship, where his glory had been meagre, and, fortunately for his reputation, with the shackles of its responsibility no longer upon him, the generous and exalted love of humanity began to touch his later years with the abiding splendor of heroic and far-seeing courage. He became the first of the great anti-slavery leaders. He entered for all time the group of men, Garrison, Lovejoy, Giddings, Phillips, Sumner, and Beecher, to whom so largely we owe the second and nobler salvation of our land. But Adams was emphatically opposed to the abolition of slavery in the District. In December, 1831, the first month of his service in the House, on presenting a petition for such abolition, he declared that he should not support it. In February, 1837, a few days before Van Buren's inauguration, there occurred the scene when Adams, with grim and dauntless irony, brought to the House the petition of some slaves against abolition. In his speech then he said: "From the day I entered this House down to the present moment, I have invariably here, and invariably elsewhere, declared my opinions to be adverse to the prayer of petitions which call for the abolition of slavery in the District of Columbia."

It is a curious but inevitable impeachment of the impartiality of history that for a declaration precisely the same as that made by a great and recognized apostle of anti-slavery, and made by that apostle in a later year, Van Buren has been denounced as a truckler to the South, a "Northern man with Southern principles." Van Buren's declaration was made, not like Adams's in the easy freedom of an independent member of Congress from an anti-slavery district, but under the constraint of a presidential nomination partially coming from the South. In the canvass before his election, Van Buren gave perfectly fair notice of his intention. "I must go," he said, "into the presidential chair the inflexible and uncompromising opponent of every attempt on the part of Congress to abolish slavery in the District of

Columbia against the wishes of the slaveholding States." This was the attitude, not only of Van Buren and Adams, but of every statesman North and South, and of the entire North itself with insignificant exceptions. The former's explicit declaration was doubtless aimed at the pro-slavery jealousy stirred up against himself in the South; it was intended to have political effect. But it was none the less the unambiguous expression of an opinion sincerely shared with the practically unanimous sense of the country.

A skillful effort was made to embarrass Van Buren with his Southern supporters over a more difficult question. The anti-slavery societies at the North sought to circulate their literature at the South. So strong an enemy of slavery as William Leggett condemned this as "fanatical obstinacy," obviously tending to stir up at the South insurrections, whose end no one could foresee, and as the fruit of desperation and extravagance. The Southern States by severe laws forbade the circulation of the literature. Its receipts from Southern post-offices led to great excitement and even violence. In August, 1835, Kendall, the postmaster-general, was appealed to by the postmaster at Charleston, South Carolina, for advice whether he should distribute papers "inflammatory, and incendiary, and insurrectionary in the highest degree," papers whose very custody endangered the mail. Kendall, in an extraordinary letter, said that he had no legal authority to prohibit the delivery of papers on account of their character, but that he was not prepared to direct the delivery at Charleston of papers such as were described. Gouverneur, the postmaster at New York, being then appealed to by his Charleston brother, declined to forward papers mailed by the American Anti-Slavery Society. This dangerous usurpation was defended upon the principle of *salus populi suprema lex*.

In December, 1835, Jackson called the attention of Congress to the circulation of "inflammatory appeals addressed to the passions of the slaves" (as they used to call the desire of black men to be free), "calculated to stimulate them to insurrection and produce all the horrors of a servile war." A bill was introduced making it unlawful for any postmaster knowingly to deliver any printed or pictorial paper touching the subject of slavery in States by whose laws their circulation was pro- hibited. Webster condemned the bill as a federal violation of the freedom of the press. Clay thought it unconstitutional, vague, indefinite, and unnecessary, as the States could lay hold of citi- zens taking such publications from post-offices within their borders. Benton and other senators, several of them Democrats, and seven from slave- holding States, voted against the bill, because they were, so Benton said, "tired of the eternal cry of dissolving the Union, did not believe in it, and would not give a repugnant vote to avoid the trial." The debate did not reach a very exalted

height. The question was by no means free from
doubt. Anti-slavery papers probably were, as the
Southerners said, "incendiary" to their States.
Slavery depended upon ignorance and fear. The
federal post-office no doubt was intended, as Kendall argued, to be a convenience to the various
States, and not an offense against their codes of
morality. There has been little opposition to the
present prohibition of the use of the post-office for
obscene literature, or, to take a better illustration,
for the circulars of lotteries which are lawful in
some States but not in others.

When the bill came to a vote in the Senate,
although there was really a substantial majority
against it, a tie was skillfully arranged to compel
Van Buren, as Vice-President, to give the casting
vote. White, the Southern Democratic candidate
so seriously menacing him, was in the Senate, and
voted for the bill. Van Buren must, it was supposed, offend the pro-slavery men by voting against
the bill, or offend the North and perhaps bruise
his conscience by voting for it. When the roll
was being called, Van Buren, so Benton tells us,
was out of the chair, walking behind the colonnade
at the rear of the vice-president's seat. Calhoun,
fearful lest he might escape the ordeal, eagerly
asked where he was, and told the sergeant-at-arms
to look for him. But Van Buren was ready, and
at once stepped to his chair and voted for the bill.
His close friend, Silas Wright of New York, also
voted for it. Benton says he deemed both the

votes to be political and given from policy. So they probably were. To Van Buren all the fire-eating measures of Calhoun and the pro-slavery men were most distasteful. He probably thought the bill would do more to increase than allay agitation at the North. Walter Scott, when the prince regent toasted him as the author of "Waverley," feeling that even royal highness had no right in a numerous company to tear away the long kept and valuable secrecy of "the great Unknown," rose and gravely said to his host: "Sire, I am not the author of 'Waverley.'" There were, he thought, questions which did not entitle the questioner to be told the truth. So Van Buren may have thought there were political interrogations which, being made for sheer party purposes, might rightfully be answered for like purposes. Since the necessity for his vote was contrived to injure him and not to help or hurt the bill, he probably felt justified so to vote as best to frustrate the design against him. This persuasive casuistry usually overcomes a candidate for great office in the stress of conflict. But lenient as may be the judgment of party supporters, and distressing as may seem the necessity, the untruth pretty surely returns to plague the statesman. Van Buren never deserved to be called a "Northern man with Southern principles." But this vote came nearer to an excuse for the epithet than did any other act of his career.

The election proved how large was the Southern defection. Georgia and Tennessee, which had been

almost unanimous for Jackson in 1836, now voted
for White. Mississippi, where in that year there
had been no opposition, and Louisiana, where
Jackson had eight votes to Clay's five, now gave
Van Buren majorities of but three hundred each.
In North Carolina Jackson had had 24,862 votes,
and Clay only 4563; White got 23,626 to 26,910
for Van Buren. In Virginia Jackson had three
times the vote of Clay; Van Buren had but one
fourth more votes than White. In Benton's own
State, so nearly unanimous for Jackson, White
had over 7000 to Van Buren's 11,000. But in
the Northeast Van Buren was very strong. Jackson's majority in Maine of 6087 became a majority
of 7751 for Van Buren. New Hampshire, the
home of Hill and Woodbury, had given Jackson
a majority of 6376; it gave Van Buren over
12,000. The Democratic majority in New York
rose from less than 14,000 to more than 28,000,
and this majority was rural and not urban. The
majority in New York city was but about 1000.
Of the fifty-six counties, Van Buren carried
forty-two, while nowadays his political successors
rarely carry more than twenty. Connecticut had
given a majority of 6000 for Clay; it gave Van
Buren over 500. Rhode Island had voted for
Clay; it now voted for Van Buren. Massachusetts was carried for Webster by 42,247 against
34,474 for Van Buren; Clay had had 33,003 to
only 14,545 for Jackson. But New Jersey shifted
from Jackson to Harrison, although a very close

State at both elections; and in Pennsylvania,
Ohio, Indiana, and Illinois, Van Buren fell far
behind Jackson. The popular vote, omitting South
Carolina, where the legislature chose the electors,
was as follows: —

|  | New England. | Middle States. | South. | West. | Total. |
|---|---|---|---|---|---|
| Van Buren . . | 112,480 | 310,203 | 141,942 | 198,053 | 762,678 |
| Harrison, White, and Webster . | 106,169 | 282,376 | 138,059 | 209,046 | 735,650 |

The electoral votes were thus divided:

|  | New England | Middle States. | South. | West. | Total. |
|---|---|---|---|---|---|
| Van Buren . . | 29 | 72 | 57 | 12 | 170 |
| Harrison . . . | 7 | 21 | — | 45 | 73 |
| Webster . . . | 14 | — | — | — | 14 |
| White . . . . | — | — | 26 | — | 26 |

Van Buren thus came to the presidency supported by the great Middle States and New England against the West, with the South divided.
Omitting the uncontested reëlection of Monroe in
1820, and the almost uncontested reëlection of
Jefferson in 1804, Van Buren was the first Democratic candidate for president who carried New
England. He had there a clear majority in both
the electoral and the popular vote. Nor has any
Democrat since Van Buren obtained a majority of
the popular vote in that strongly thinking and
strongly prejudiced community. Pierce, against
the feeble Whig candidacy of Scott, carried its
electoral vote in 1852, but by a minority of its

popular vote, and only because of the large Free
Soil vote for Hale.   No other Democrat since 1852
has had any electoral vote from New England outside of Connecticut.   Virginia refused its vote to
Johnson, who, in the failure of either candidate to
receive a majority of the electoral vote, was chosen
vice-president by the Senate.

When the electoral votes were formally counted
before the houses of Congress, the result, so con.
temporary record informs us, was "received with
perfect decorum by the House and galleries."
Enthusiasm was going out with Jackson, to come
back again with Harrison.   Van Buren's election
was the success of intellectual convictions, and not
the triumph of sentiment.   He had come to power,
as "the House and galleries" well knew, in " perfect decorum."   Not a single one of the generous
but sometimes cheap and fruitless rushes of feeling
occasionally so potent in politics had helped him
to the White House.   Not that he was ungenerous
or lacking in feeling.   Very far from it; few men
have inspired so steady and deep a political attachment among men of strong character and patriotic
aspirations.   But neither in his person nor in his
speech or conduct was there anything of the strong
picturesqueness which impresses masses of men,
who must be touched, if at all, by momentary
glimpses of great men or by vivid phrases which
become current about them.   His election was no
more than a triumph of disciplined good sense and
political wisdom.

# CHAPTER VIII

On March 4, 1837, Jackson and Van Buren rode together from the White House to the Capitol in a " beautiful phaëton " made from the timber of the old frigate Constitution, the gift to the general from the Democrats of New York city. He was the third and last president who has, after serving through his term, left office amid the same enthusiasm which attended him when he entered it, and to whom the surrender of place has not been full of those pangs which attend sudden loss of power, and of which the certain anticipation ought to moderate ambition in a country so rarely permitting a long and continuous public career. Washington, amid an almost unanimous love and reverence, left a station of which he was unaffectedly weary ; and he was greater out of office than in it. Jefferson and Jackson remained really powerful characters. Neither at Monticello nor at the Hermitage, after their masters had returned, was there any lack of the incense of sincere popular flattery or of the appeals for the exercise of admitted and enormous influence, in which lies much of the unspeakable fascination of a great public station.

Leaving the White House under a still and brilliant sky, the retiring and incoming rulers had such a popular and military attendance as without much order or splendor has usually gone up Capitol Hill with our presidents. Van Buren's inaugural speech was heard, it is said, by nearly twenty thousand persons; for he read it with remarkable distinctness and in a quiet air, from the historic eastern portico. He returned from the inauguration to his private residence; and with a fine deference insisted upon Jackson remaining in the White House until his departure, a few days later, for Tennessee. Van Buren in his own carriage took Jackson to the terminus of the new railway upon which the journey home was to begin. He bade the old man a most affectionate farewell, and promised to visit him at the Hermitage in the summer.

The new cabinet, with a single exception, was the same as Jackson's: John Forsyth of Georgia, secretary of state; Levi Woodbury of New Hampshire, secretary of the treasury; Mahlon Dickerson of New Jersey, secretary of the navy; Kendall, postmaster-general; and Butler, attorney-general. Joel R. Poinsett, a strong union man among the nullifiers of South Carolina, became secretary of war. Cass had left this place in 1836 to be minister to France, and Butler had since temporarily filled it, as well as his own post of attorney-general. The cabinet had indeed been largely Van Buren's, two years and more before he was president.

Van Buren's inaugural address began again with

the favorite touch of humility, but it now had an agreeable dignity.  He was, he said, the first president born after the Revolution; he belonged to a later age than his illustrious predecessors.  Nor ought he to expect his countrymen to weigh his actions with the same kind and partial hand which they had used towards worthies of Revolutionary times.  But he piously looked for the sustaining support of Providence, and the kindness of a people who had never yet deserted a public servant honestly laboring in their cause.  There was the usual congratulation upon American institutions and history.  We were, he said, — and the boast though not so delightful to the taste of a later time was perfectly true, — without a parallel throughout the world " in all the attributes of a great, happy, and flourishing people."  Though we restrained government to the " sole legitimate end of political institutions," we reached the Benthamite " greatest happiness of the greatest number," and presented "an aggregate of human prosperity surely not elsewhere to be found."  We must, by observing the limitations of government, perpetuate a condition of things so singularly happy.  Popular government, whose failure had fifty years ago been boldly predicted, had now been found " wanting in no element of endurance or strength."  His policy should be " a strict adherence to the letter and spirit of the constitution . . . viewing it as limited to national objects, regarding it as leaving to the people and the States all power not explicitly parted with." Upon one question he spoke precisely. For the first time slavery loomed up in the inaugural of an American president. It seemed, however, at once to disappear from politics in the practically unanimous condemnation of the abolition agitation, an agitation which, though carried on for the noblest purposes, seemed — for such is the march of human rights — insane and iniquitous to most patriotic and intelligent citizens. Van Buren quoted the explicit declaration made by him before the election against the abolition of slavery in the District of Columbia without the consent of the slave States, and against " the slightest interference with it in the States where it exists." Not a word was said of the extension of slavery in the Territories. That question still slept under the potion of the Missouri Compromise, to wake with the acquisition of Texas. In Van Buren's declaration there was nothing in the slightest degree inconsistent even with the Republican platforms of 1856 and 1860.

The inaugural concluded with a fine tribute to Jackson. " I know," Van Buren said, " that I cannot expect to perform the arduous task with equal ability and success. But united as I have been in his counsels, a daily witness of his exclusive and unsurpassed devotion to his country's welfare, agreeing with him in sentiments which his countrymen have warmly supported, and permitted to partake largely of his confidence, I may hope that somewhat of the same cheering approbation will be found to attend upon my path. For him

I but express, with my own, the wishes of all, that
he may yet long live to enjoy the brilliant evening
of his well-spent life."

The lucid optimism of the speech was in perfect
temper with this one of those shining and mellow
days, which even March now and then brings to
Washington. But there was latent in the atmosphere a storm, carrying with it a furious and
complete devastation. In the month before the
inauguration, Benton, upon whom Van Buren was
pressing a seat in the cabinet, told the President-
elect that they were on the eve of an explosion of
the paper-money system. But the latter offended
Benton by saying: "Your friends think you a little
exalted in the head on the subject." And doubtless the prophecies of the Bank opponents had been
somewhat discredited by the delay of the disaster
which was to justify their denunciations. The profoundly thrilling and hidden delight which comes
with the first taste of supreme power, even to the
experienced and battered man of affairs, had been
enjoyed by Van Buren only a few days, when the
air grew heavy about him, and then perturbed, and
then violently agitated, until in two months broke
fiercely and beyond all restraint the most terrific
of commercial convulsions in the United States.
Since Washington began the experiment of our
federal government amid the sullen doubts of extreme Federalists and extreme Democrats, no president, save only Abraham Lincoln, has had to face
at the outset of his presidency so appalling a political situation.

The causes of the panic of 1837 lay far deeper than in the complex processes of banking or in the faults of federal administration of the finances. But, as a man suddenly ill prefers to find for his ailment some recent and obvious cause, and is not convinced by even a long and dangerous sickness that its origin lay in old and continued habits of life, so the greater part of the American people and of their leaders believed this extraordinary crisis to be the result of financial blunders of Jackson's administration. They believed that Van Buren could with a few strokes of his pen repair, if he pleased, those blunders, and restore commercial confidence and prosperity. The panic of 1837 became, and has very largely remained, the subject of political and partisan differences, which obscure its real phenomena and causes. The far-seeing and patriotic intrepidity with which Van Buren met its almost overwhelming difficulties is really the crown of his political career. Fairly to appreciate the service he then rendered his country, the causes of this famous crisis must be attentively considered.

In 1819 the United States suffered from commercial and financial derangement, which may be assumed to have been the effect of the second war with Great Britain. The enormous waste of a great war carried on by a highly organized nation is apt not to become obvious in general business distress until some time after the war has ended. A buoyant extravagance in living and in commercial and manufacturing ventures will continue

after a peace has brought its extraordinary promises, upon the faith of which, and in joyful ignorance, the evil and inevitable day is postponed.
All this was seen later and on a vaster scale from
1865 to 1873. In 1821 the country had quite
recovered from its depression ; and from this time
on to near the end of Jackson's administration the
United States saw a material prosperity, doubtless
greater than any before known. The exuberant
outburst of John Quincy Adams's message of 1827,
— that the productions of our soil, the exchanges
of our commerce, the vivifying labors of human
industry, had combined "to mingle in our cup a
portion of enjoyment as large and liberal as the
indulgence of Heaven has perhaps ever granted to
the imperfect state of man upon earth," — was in
the usual tone of the public utterances of our presidents from 1821 to 1837. Our harvests were
always great. We were a chosen people delighting
in reminders from our rulers of our prosperity, and
not restless under their pious urgency of perennial
gratitude to Providence. In 1821 the national
debt had slightly increased, reaching upwards of
$90,000,000 ; but from that time its steady and
rapid payment went on until it was all discharged in
1834. Our cities grew. Our population stretched
eagerly out into the rich Mississippi valley. From
a population of ten millions in 1821, we reached
sixteen millions in 1837. New York from about
1,400,000 became 2,200,000 ; and Pennsylvania
from about 1,000,000 became 1,600,000. But the

amazing growth was at the West — Illinois from
60,000 to 400,000, Indiana from 170,000 to 600,-
000, Ohio from 600,000 to 1,400,000, Tennessee
from 450,000 to 800,000. Missouri had increased
her 70,000 five-fold; Mississippi her 80,000 four-
fold; Michigan her 10,000 twenty-fold. Iowa and
Wisconsin were entirely unsettled in 1821; in
1837 the fertile lands of the former maintained
nearly forty thousand and of the latter nearly
thirty thousand hardy citizens. New towns and
cities rose with magical rapidity. With much that
was unlovely there was also exhibited an amazing
energy and capacity for increase in wealth. The
mountain barriers once passed, not only by adventurous pioneers but by the pressing throngs of settlers, there were few obstacles to the rapid creation
of comfort and wealth. Nor in the Mississippi
valley and the lands of the Northwest were the
settlers met by the harsh soil, the hostilities and
reluctance of nature in whose conquest upon the
Atlantic seaboard the American people had gained
some of their strongest and most enduring characteristics. We hardly realize indeed how much better it was for after times that our first settlements
were difficult. In the easy opening and tillage of
the rich and sometimes rank lands at the West
there was an inferior, a less arduous discipline.
American temper there rushed often to speculation,
rather than to toil or venture. It did not seem
necessary to create wealth by labor; the treasures
lay ready for those first reaching the doors of the

treasure house. To make easy the routes to El
Dorado of prairies and river bottoms was the
quickest way to wealth.

Roads, canals, river improvements, preceded, attended, followed these sudden settlements, this vast
and jubilant movement of population. There was
an extraordinary growth of "internal improvements." In his message of 1831, Jackson rejoiced
at the high wages earned by laborers in the construction of these works, which he truly said were
"extending with unprecedented rapidity." The
constitutional power of the federal government to
promote the improvements within the States became a serious question, because the improvements
proposed were upon so vast a scale. No single interest had for fifteen years before 1837 held so
large a part of American attention as did the
making of canals and roads. The debates of Congress and legislatures, the messages of presidents
and governors, were full of it. If the Erie Canal,
finished in 1825, had rendered vast natural resources available, and had made its chief builder
famous, why should not like schemes prosper further west? The success of railroads was already
established; and there was indefinite promise in
the extensions of them already planned. In 1830
twenty-three miles had been constructed; in 1831
ninety-four miles; and in 1836 the total construction had risen to 1273 miles.

The Americans were then a far more homogene-
ous people than they are to-day. The great Irish,

German, and Scandinavian immigrations had not taken place. Our race diversities were, with exceptions, unimportant in extent or lost in the lapse of time, the diversities merely of British descendants. Nor were there the extremes of fortune or the diversities of occupation which have come with the growth of cities and manufacturing interests. The United States were still a nation of farmers. The compensations and balances, which in the varying habits and prejudices of a more varied population tend to restrain and neutralize vagaries, did not exist. One sentiment seized the whole nation far more readily than could happen in the complexity of our modern population and the diversity and rivalry of its strains. Not only did this homogeneity make Americans open to single impulses ; but there was little essential difference of environment. They all, since the later days of Monroe's presidency, had lived in the atmosphere of official delight and congratulation over the past, and of unrestrained promise for the future. All, whether in the grain fields at the North or the cotton fields at the South, had behind them the Atlantic with traditions or experiences of poverty and oppression beyond it. Every American had, in his own latitude, since the ampler opening of roads and waterways, and the peaceful conquest of the Appalachian mountain ranges, seen to the west of him fertility and promise and performance. And the fertility and promise had, since the second English war, been no longer in a land of hardship and adventure remote and almost foreign to the seaboard. Every American under Jackson's administration had before him, as the one universal experience of those who had taken lands at the West, an enormous and certain increase of value, full of enchantment to those lately tilling the flinty soil of New England or the overused fields of the South. If new lands at the West could be made accessible by internal improvements, the succession of seed time and harvest had for a dozen years seemed no more certain than that the value of those lands would at once increase prodigiously. So the American people with one consent gave themselves to an amazing extravagance of land speculation. The Eden which Martin Chuzzlewit saw in later malarial decay was to be found in the new country on almost every stream to the east of the Mississippi and on many streams west of it, where flatboats could be floated. Frauds there doubtless were; but they were incidental to the honest delusion of intelligent men inspired by the most extraordinary growth the world had seen. The often quoted illustration of Mobile, the valuation of whose real estate rose from $1,294,810 in 1831 to $27,482,961 in 1837, to sink again in 1846 to $8,638,250, not unfairly tells the story. In Pensacola, lots which to-day are worth $50 each were sold for as much as lots on Fifth Avenue in New York, which to-day are worth $100,000 apiece. Real estate in the latter city was assessed in 1836 at more than it was in the greatly larger and richer city of fifteen years later. From 1830 to 1837 the steamboat tonnage on the Western rivers rose from 63,053 to 253,661. From 1833 to 1837 the cotton crop of the newer slave States, Tennessee, Alabama, Mississippi, Louisiana, Arkansas and Florida, increased from 536,450 to 916,960 bales, while the price with fluctuations rose from ten to twenty cents a pound. Foreign capital naturally enough came to share in the splendid money-making. From 1821 to 1833 the annual import of specie from England had averaged about $100,000, in the last year being only $31,903; but in 1834 it became $5,716,253, in 1835 $914,958, and in 1836 $2,322,920, the entire export to England of specie for all these three years being but $51,807, while the average export from 1822 to 1830 had been about $400,000; and its amount in 1831 had been $2,089,766, and in 1832 $1,730,571. From 1830 to 1837, both years inclusive, although the imports from all countries of general merchandise exceeded the exports by $140,-700,000, there was no counter movement of specie. The imports of specie from all countries during these years exceeded the exports by the comparatively enormous sum of $44,700,000. The foreigners therefore took pay for their goods, not only in our raw materials, but also in our investments or rather our speculations, and sent these vast quantities of moneys besides. So our good fortune fired the imaginations of even the dull Europeans. They helped to feed and clothe us that we might experiment with Aladdin's lamp.

The price of public lands was fixed by law at $1.25 an acre; and they were open to any purchaser, without the wholesome limits of acreage and the restraint to actual settlers which were afterwards established. Here then was a commodity whose price to wholesale purchasers did not rise, and the very commodity by which so many fortunes had been made. In public lands, therefore, the fury of money-getting, the boastful confidence in the future of the country, reached their climax. From 1820 to 1829 the annual sales had averaged less than $1,300,000, in 1829 being $1,517,175. But in 1830 they exceeded $2,300,000, in 1831 $3,200,000, in 1832 $2,600,000, in 1833 $3,900,000, and in 1834 $4,800,000. In 1835 they suddenly mounted to $14,757,600, and in 1836 to $24,877,179. In his messages of 1829 and 1830 Jackson not unreasonably treated the moderate increase in the sales as a proof of increasing prosperity. In 1831 his congratulations were hushed; but in 1835 he again fancied, even in the abnormal sales of that year, only an ampler proof of ampler prosperity. In 1836 he at last saw that tremendous speculation was the true significance of the enormous increase. Prices of course went up. Everybody thought himself richer and his labor worth more. A week after Van Buren's inauguration a meeting was held in the City Hall Park in New York to protest against high rents and the high prices of provisions; and with much discernment the cry went up, " No rag money; give us gold and silver ! "

There is no longer dispute that the prostration of business in 1837, and for several years afterward, was the perfectly natural result of the speculation which had gone before. The absurd denunciations of Van Buren by the most eminent of the Whigs for not ending the crisis by governmental interference are no longer respected. But it is still fancied that the speculation itself was caused by one financial blunder, and the crisis immediately occasioned by another financial blunder, of Jackson. It is not improbable that the deposits of treasury moneys in fifty state banks [1] instead of in the United States Bank and its twenty and more branches, which began in the fall of 1833, aided the tendency to speculation. But this aid was at the most a slight matter. The impression has been sedulously created that these state banks, the "pet banks," were doubtful institutions. There seems little reason to doubt that in general they were perfectly sound and reputable institu-

[1] The Treasurer's statement for August, 1837, gave eighty-four deposit banks. But of these, nine had less than $5000 each on deposit, six from $5000 to $10,000, and eight from $10,000 to $20,000. Fourteen had from $50,000 to $100,000 each. Only twenty-nine had more than $100,000 each. It is not unfair to speak of the deposits as being substantially in fifty banks.

The enormous land sales at the Southwest had placed a most disproportionate amount of money in banks in that part of the country. John Quincy Adams seemed, but with little reason, to consider this an intentional discrimination against the North. It is quite probable that, if the deposits had been in one national bank, the peculiarly excessive strain at that point would have been modified. But this was no great factor in the crisis.

tions, with which the government moneys would be quite as safe as with the United States Bank. It is clear that if the latter Bank were not to be rechartered, the deposits should, without regard to the accusations of political meddling brought against it, have been removed some time in advance of its death in March, 1836. At best it is matter of doubtful speculation whether the United States Bank under Biddle's direction would, in 1834, 1835, and 1836, while the government deposits were enormously increasing, have behaved with much greater prudence and foresight than did the state deposit banks. So far as actual experience helps us, the doubt might well be solved in the negative. The United States Bank, when its federal charter lapsed, obtained a charter from Pennsylvania, continuing under the same management; and is said, and possibly with truth, to have entered upon its new career with a great surplus. But it proved no stronger than the state banks in 1837; it obstructed resumption in 1838; it suspended again in 1839, while the Eastern banks stood firm; and in 1841 it went to pieces in disgraceful and complete disaster.

The enormous extension of bank credits during the three years before the break-down in 1837 was rather the symptom than the cause of the disease. The fever of speculation was in the veins of the community before "kiting" began. Bank officers dwelt in the same atmosphere as did other Americans, and their sanguine extravagance in

turn stimulated the universal temper of speculation.

When the United States Bank lost the government deposits, late in 1833, they amounted to a
little less than $10,000,000. On January 1, 1835,
more than a year after the state banks took the
deposits, they had increased to a little more than
$10,000,000. But the public debt being then paid
and the outgo of money thus checked, the deposits
had by January 1, 1836, reached $25,000,000, and
by June 1, 1836, $41,500,000. This enormous ad-
vance represented the sudden increase in the sales
of public lands, which were paid for in bank paper,
which in turn formed the bulk of the government
deposits. The deposits were with only a small part
of the six hundred and more state banks then in
existence. But the increase in the sales of public
lands was the result of all the organic causes and
of all the long train of events which had seated
the fever of speculation so profoundly in the American character of the day. To those causes and
events must ultimately be ascribed the extension
of bank credits so far as it immediately arose out
of the increase of government deposits. Nor is
there any sufficient reason to suppose that if the
deposits, instead of being in fifty state banks,
had remained in the United States Bank and its
branches, the tendency to speculation would have
been less. The influences which surrounded that
Bank were the very influences most completely
subject to the popular mania.

But the increase of government deposits was only fuel added to the flames. The craze for banks and credits was unbounded before the removal of the deposits had taken place, and before their great increase could have had serious effect. Between 1830 and January 1, 1834, the banking capital of the United States had risen from $61,000,000 to about $200,000,000; the loans and discounts of the banks from $200,000,000 to $324,000,000; and their note circulation from $61,000,000 to $95,-000,000. The increase from January 1, 1834, to January 1, 1836, was even more rapid, the banking capital advancing in the two years to $251,000,000, the loans and discounts to $457,000,000, and the note circulation to $140,000,000. But there was certainty of disaster in the abnormal growth from 1830 to 1834. The insanity of speculation was in ample though unobserved control of the country while Nicholas Biddle still controlled the deposits, and was certain to reach a climax whether they stayed with him or went elsewhere.

It is difficult rightly to apportion among the statesmen and politicians of the time so much of blame for the mania of speculation as must go to that body of men. They had all drunk in the national intoxication over American success and growth. But if we pass from the greater and deeper causes to the lesser though more obvious ones, it is impossible not to visit the greater measure of blame upon the statesmen who resisted reduction of taxation, which would have left money in the pockets of those who earned it, and not collected it in one great bank with many branches or in fifty lesser banks; upon the statesmen who insisted that the government ought to aid commercial ventures by encouraging the loans to traders of its own moneys held in the deposit banks; upon the statesmen who promoted the dangerous scheme of distributing the surplus among the States instead of abolishing the surplus. As the condemnation of public men in the wrong must be proportioned somewhat to the distinction of their positions and the greatness of their natural gifts, this larger share of blame must go chiefly to Daniel Webster and Henry Clay. At the head of their associates, they had resisted the reduction of taxation. In his speech on the tariff bill of 1832 Clay said, with the exuberance so delightful to minds of easy discipline, that our resources should "not be hoarded and hugged with a miser's embrace, but liberally used." They insisted upon freely lending the public moneys. In his speech on the distribution of the surplus, Webster urged that the number of the deposit banks "be so far increased that each may regard that portion of the public treasure which it may receive as an increase of its effective deposits, to be used, like other moneys in deposit, as a basis of discount, to a just and proper extent." The public money was locked up, he declared, instead of aiding the general business of the country. Nor after this was he ashamed in 1838 to condemn Jackson's secretary of the trea-

sury for advising the new deposit banks, as he
had himself thus advised them, "to afford increased facilities to commerce." If, indeed, Congress would not take steps to keep a government
surplus out of the banks and in the pockets of
producers, the secretary ought not to have been
harshly judged for advising that the money go out
into commerce rather than lie in bank vaults.

The distribution of the surplus among the States
by the law of 1836 was the last and in some re-
spects the worst of the measures which aided and
exaggerated the tendency to speculation. By this
bill, all the money above $5,000,000 in the trea-
sury on January 1, 1837, was to be "deposited"
with the States in four quarterly installments com-
mencing on that day. According to the law the
"deposit" was but a loan to the States ; but, as
Clay declared, not "a single member of either
House imagined that a dollar would ever be recalled." It was in truth a mere gift. Clay's
triumphant ridicule of the opposition to this measure has already been mentioned. Webster in
sounding periods declared his "deep and earnest
conviction" of the propriety of the stupendous
folly. He did not, indeed, defend the general
system of making the federal government a tax-
gatherer for the States. But this one distribution
would, he said in his speech of May 31, 1836,
"remove that severe and almost unparalleled pressure for money which is now distressing and breaking down the industry, the enterprise, and even

the courage of the commercial community." The Whig press declared that a congressman who could for mere party reasons vote against a measure which would bring so much money into his State, must be "far gone in political hardihood as well as depravity;" and that "to the Republican-Whig party alone are the States indebted for the benefits arising from the distribution." William H. Seward, two years before and two years later the Whig candidate for governor of New York, said the proposal was "noble and just." The measure passed the Senate with six Democratic votes against it, among them the vote of Silas Wright, then probably closer than any other senator to Van Buren. Jackson yielded to the bill what in his message in December of the same year he called "a reluctant approval." He then gave at length very clear reasons for his reluctance, but none for his approval. He declared that "improvident expenditure of money is the parent of profligacy," and that no intelligent and virtuous community would consent to raise a surplus for the mere purpose of dividing it. In his first message, indeed, Jackson had called the distribution among the States "the most safe, just, and federal disposition" of the surplus. But his views upon this, as upon other subjects, had changed during the composition of the Democratic creed which went on during the early years of his administration. His second message rehearsed at length the objections to the distribution, though affecting to

meet them. In his third message he recommended
the abolition of unnecessary taxation, not the distribution of its proceeds ; and in 1832 he made his
explicit declaration that duties should be "reduced to the revenue standard." Benton says it
was understood that in 1836 some of Van Buren's
friends urged Jackson to approve the bill, lest a
veto of so popular a measure might bring a Democratic defeat. There must have been some reason
unrelated to the merit of the measure. But whatever the opinions of Van Buren's friends, he took
care before the election to make known unequivocally, in the Sherrod Williams letter already
quoted, his dislike of this piece of demagogy.
From the passage of the deposit bill in June,
1836, until the crash in 1837, this superb donation
of thirty-seven millions was before the enraptured
and deluded vision of the country. Over nine
millions a quarter to be poured into "improvements " or loaned to the needy, — what a delightful prospect to citizens harassed by the restraints
of prudent, fruitful industry ! The lesson is striking and wholesome, and ought not to be forgotten,
that it was when the land was in the very midst of
these largesses that the universal bankruptcy set
in.

During 1835 and 1836 there were omens of the
coming storm. Some perceived the rabid character of the speculative fever. William L. Marcy,
governor of New York, in his message of January,
1836, answering the dipsomaniac cry for more

banks, declared that an unregulated spirit of speculation had taken capital out of the State; but that the amount so transferred bore no comparison to the enormous speculations in stocks and in real property within the State. Lands near the cities and villages of the State had risen several hundred per cent. in value, and were sold, not to be occupied by the buyers, but to be sold again at higher prices. The passion for speculation prevailed to an extent before unknown, not only among capitalists, but among merchants, who abstracted capital from their business for land and stock speculations and then resorted to the banks. The warning was treated contemptuously; but before the year was out the federal administration also became anxious, and the increase in land sales no longer signified to Jackson an increasing prosperity. The master hand which drew the economic disquisition in his message of 1836 pointed to these sales as the effects of the extension of bank credit and of the over-issue of bank paper. The banks, it was declared, had lent their notes as " mere instruments to transfer to speculators the most valuable public land, and pay the government by a credit on the books of the banks." Each speculation had furnished means for another. No sooner had one purchaser paid his debt in the notes than they were lent to another for a like purpose. The banks had extended their business and their issues so largely as to alarm considerate men. The spirit of expansion and speculation had not been confined to deposit banks, but had pervaded the whole multitude of banks throughout the Union, and had given rise to new institutions to aggravate the evil. So Jackson proceeded with his sound defense of the famous specie circular, long and even still denounced as the *causa causans* of the crisis of 1837.

By this circular, issued on July 11, 1836, the secretary of the treasury had required payment for public lands to be made in specie, with an exception until December 15, 1836, in favor of actual settlers and actual residents of the State in which the lands were sold. The enormous sales of land in this year, and the large payments required for them under the circular, at once made the banks realize that there ought to be an actual physical basis for their paper transactions. Gold was called from the East to the banks at the West to make the land payments. Into the happy exaltation of unreal transactions was now plunged that harsh demand for real value which sooner or later must always come. The demand was passed on from one to another, and its magnitude and peremptoriness grew rapidly. The difference between paper and gold became plainer and plainer. Nature's vital and often hidden truth that value depends upon labor could no longer be kept secret by a few wise men. The suspicion soon arose that there was not real and available value to meet the demands of nominal value. The suspicion was soon bruited among the less as well as the more wary. Every man rushed to his bank or his debtor, crying, " Pay me in value, not in promises to pay ; there is, I at last see, a difference between them." But the banks and debtors had no available value, but only its paper semblances. Every man found that what he wanted, his neighbors did not have to give him, and what he had, his neighbors did not want.

This is hardly an appropriate place to attempt an analysis of the elements of a commercial crisis. But it is not possible rightly to estimate Van Buren's moral courage and keen-sighted wisdom in meeting the terrible pressure of 1837 without appreciating what it was which had really happened. The din of the disputes over the refusal to recharter the bank, over the removal of the deposits, over the refusal to pay the last installment of the distribution among the States, and over the specie circular, resounds even to our own time. To many the crisis seemed merely a financial or even a great banking episode. Many friends of the administration loudly cried that the disaster arose from the treachery of the banks in suspending. Many of its enemies saw only the normal fruit of administrative blunders, first in recklessness, and last in heartless indifference. To most Americans, whatever their differences, the explanation of this profound and lasting disturbance seemed to lie in the machinery of finance, rather than in the deeper facts of the physical wealth and power of the trading classes.

Speculation is sometimes said to be universal; and it was never nearer universality than from 1830 to 1837. But speculation affects after all but a small part of the community, — the part engaged in trade, venture, new settlement or new manufacture ; those classes of men the form of whose work is not established by tradition, but is changing and improving under the spur of ingenuity and invention, and with whom imagination is most powerful and fruitful. These men use the surplus resources of the vastly greater number who go on through periods of high prices and of low prices with their steady toil and unvaried production. In our country and in all industrial communities it is to the former comparatively small class that chiefly and characteristically belong " good times " and " bad times," panics and crises and depressions. It is this class which in newspapers and financial reviews becomes " the country." It chiefly supports the more influential of the clergy, the lawyers, the editors, and others of the professional classes. It deals with the new uses and the accumulations of wealth ; it almost monopolizes public attention ; it is chiefly and conspicuously identified with industrial and commercial changes and progress. But if great depressions were as nearly universal as the rhetoric of economists and historians would literally signify, our ancestors fifty years ago must have experienced a devastation such as Alaric is said to have brought to the fields of Lombardy. But this was not so. The processes of general production went on ; the land was tilled ; the farmer's work of the year brought about the same amount of comfort ; the ordinary mechanic was not much worse off. If some keen observer from another planet had in 1835 and again later in 1837 looked into the dining-rooms and kitchens and parlors of America, had seen its citizens with their families going to church of a Sunday morning, or watched the tea-parties of their wives, or if he had looked over the fields and into the shops, there would have seemed to him but slight difference between the two years in the occupations, the industry, or the comfort of the people. But if he had stopped looking and begun to listen, he would in 1837 at once have perceived a tremendous change. The great masses of producing men would have been mute, as they usually are. But the capitalists, the traders, the manufacturers, all whose skill, courage, imagination, and adventure made them the leaders of progress, and whose voices were the only loud, clear, intelligible voices, until there arose the modern organizations of laboring men, — all those who in 1835 were flushed and glorious with a royal money-getting, — he would now have heard crying in frenzy and desperation. It is not meant to disparage the importance of this smaller but louder body of men, or to underrate the disaster which they suffered. In proportion to their numbers, they were vastly the most important part of the community. If they were prostrated, there must not only suffer the body of clerks, operatives, and laborers immediately

engaged in their enterprises, and who may for economical purposes be ranked with them; but later
on, the masses of the community must to a real extent feel the interruption of progress which has
overtaken that section of the community to which
are committed the characteristic operations of material progress; and whether through the fault or
the misfortune of that section, the injury is alike
serious. A wise ruler, in touching the finances of
his country, will forget none of this. He will look
through all the agitation of bankers and traders
and manufacturers, the well-voiced leaders of the
richer classes of men, to the far vaster processes of
industry carried on by men who are silent, and
whose silent industry will go on whatever devices
of currency or banking may be adopted. This wisdom Van Buren now showed in an exalted degree.

The disaster which in 1837 overtook so large
and so important a part of the community was, in
its ultimate nature, not difficult to comprehend.

There had not been one equal and universal increase in nominal values. Such an increase would
not have produced the crisis. But while the great
mass of the national industry went on in channels
and with methods and rates substantially undis-
turbed, there took place an enormous and speculative advance of prices in the cities where were
carried on the operations of important traders and
the promoters of enterprises, and in the very new
country where these enterprises found their material. When a new canal or road was built, or a

new line of river steamers launched and an unsettled country made accessible, several things inevitably happened in the temper produced by the
jubilant observation of the past. There was not
only drawn from the ordinary industry of the country the wealth necessary to build the canal or road
or steamers ; but the country thus rendered accessible seemed suddenly to gain a value measured by
the best results of former settlements, however
exceptional, and by the most sanguine hopes for
the future. The owners of the prairies and woods
and river bottoms became suddenly rich, as a miner
in Idaho becomes rich when he strikes a true fis-
sure vein. The owners of the canal or road or
line of steamers found their real investment at
once multiplied in dollars by the value of the country whose trade they were to enjoy ; for, new as
that value was, it seemed assured. Like investments were made in banks, and in every implement
of direct or indirect use in the conduct of industries which seemed to belong as a necessity to the
new value of the land. The numerous sales of lands
and of stocks in roads or canals or banks at rapidly
advancing prices did not alter the nature, although
they vastly augmented the effect, of what was hap-
pening. The so-called " business classes " throughout the country, related as they quickly became,
under the great impetus of the national hopefulness
and vanity, to the new lands, to the new cities and
towns and farms, and to the means of reaching
them and of providing them with the necessities

and comforts of civilization, found their wealth
rapidly and largely increasing. Then naturally
enough followed the spending of money in personal luxury. This meant the withdrawal of labor
in the older part of the country from productive
work, for which the country was fitted, to work
which, whether suitable or not, was unproductive.
The unproductive labor was paid, as the employers
supposed, from the new value lately created at the
West. So capital, that is, accumulated labor, was
first spent in improvements in the new country,
and then, and probably in a far greater amount,
spent in more costly food, clothes, equipage, and
other luxuries in the older country. The succes-
sive sales at advancing prices simply increased the
sense of new wealth, and augmented more and
more this destructive consumption of the products
of labor, or the destructive diversion of labor from
productive to unproductive activity at the East by
the well-to-do classes.

On the eve of the panic the new wealth, whose
seeming possession apparently justified this destructive consumption or diversion to luxury of
physical value, was primarily represented by titles
to lands, stocks in land, canal, turnpike, railroad,
transportation, or banking companies, and the
notes issued by banks or traders or speculators.
The value of these stocks and notes depended upon
the fruitfulness of the lands or canals or roads or
steamboat lines. Prices of many commodities had,
indeed, been enhanced by speculation beyond all

proper relation to other commodities, measured by
the ultimate standard of the quantity and quality
of labor. But important as was this element, it
was subordinate to the apparent creation of wealth
at the West.

Before the panic broke, it began to appear that
mere surveys of wild tracts into lots made neither
towns nor cities ; that canals and roads and steam-
boats did not hew down trees or drain morasses or
open the glebe. The basis of the operations of
capitalists and promoters and venturers in new
fields, if those operations were to have real success, must lie in the masses of strong and skillful
arms of men of labor. The operations were fruitless until there came a population well sinewed and
gladly ready for arduous toil. In 1836 and 1837
the operators found that there was no longer a
population to give enduring life to their new operations. They had far outstripped all the immediate
or even the nearly promised movements of settlers.
Men, however hardy, preferred to work within an
easier reach of the physical and social advantages
of settlements already made, until they could see
the superior fruitfulness of labor further on. The
new cities and towns and farms and the means
of reaching them would be mere paper assets until
an army of settlers was ready to enter in and make
them sources of actual physical wealth. But the
army stopped far short of the new Edens and me-
tropolises. There was no creation among them of
the actual wealth, the return of physical labor, to

make good and real the popular semblances of wealth, upon the faith of which in the older part of the country had arisen new methods of business and habits of living. The withdrawal of actual wealth from the multifarious treasuries of capital and industry, to meet the expense of the improvements at the West and the increased luxury at the East, had reached a point where the pressure caused by the deficiency of physical wealth was too great for the hopefulness or credulity of those who had been surrendering that wealth upon the promises of successful and opulent settlements at the West. Nor was all this confined to ventures in the new States. Almost every Eastern city had a suburb where with slight differences all the phenomena of speculation were as real and obvious as in Illinois or Mississippi.

Jackson's specie circular toppled over the house of cards, which at best could have stood but little longer. In place of bank-notes, which symbolized the expectations and hopes of the owners of new towns and improvements, the United States after July, 1836, required from all but actual settlers gold and silver for lands. An insignificant part of the sales had been lately made to settlers. They were chiefly made to speculators. The public lands, which sold invariably at $1.25 an acre, were enormously magnified in nominal value the instant the speculators owned them. Paper money was freely issued upon these estimates of value, to be again paid to the government for more lands at

$1.25. But now gold and silver must be found; and nothing but actual labor could find gold and silver. A further stream of true wealth was summoned from the East, already denuded, as it was, of all the surplus it had ready to be invested upon mere expectation. Enormous rates were now paid for real money. But of the real money necessary to make good the paper bubble promises of the speculators not one-tenth part really existed. Banks could neither make their debtors pay in gold and silver, nor pay their own notes in gold and silver. So they suspended.

The great and long concealed devastation of physical wealth and of the accumulation of legitimate labor, by premature improvements and costly personal living, became now quickly apparent. Fancied wealth sank out of sight. Paper symbols of new cities and towns, canals and roads, were not only without value, but they were now plainly seen to be so. Rich men became poor men. The prices of articles in which there had been speculation sank in the reaction far below their true value. The industrious and the prudent, who had given their labor and their real wealth for paper promises issued upon the credit of seemingly assured fortunes, suffered at once with men whose fortunes had never been anything better than the delusions of their hope and imagination.

It is now plain enough that to recover from this crisis was a work of physical reparation to which must go time, industry, and frugality. There was

folly in every effort to retain and use as valuable
assets the investments in companies and banks
whose usefulness, if it had ever begun, was now
ended.   There was folly in every effort to conceal
from the world by words of hopefulness the fact
that the imagined values in new cities and garden
lands had disappeared in a rude disenchantment
as complete as that of Abou-Hassan in the Thousand and One Nights, or that of Sly, the tinker,
left untold in the Taming of the Shrew.   Their
sites were no more than wild lands, whose value
must wait the march of American progress, fast
enough indeed to the rest of the world, but slow as
the snail to the wild pacing of the speculators.
Every pretense of a politician, whether in or out
of the senate chamber, that the government could
by devices of financiering avoid this necessity of
long physical repair, was either folly or wickedness.
And of this folly or even wickedness there was no
lack in the anxious spring and summer of 1837.

There had already occurred in many quarters
that misery which is borne by the humbler producers of wealth not for their own consumption,
but simply for exchange, whose earnings are not
increased to meet the inflation of prices upon which
traders and speculators are accumulating apparent
fortunes and spending them as if they were real.
On February 14, 1837, several thousand people
met in front of the City Hall in New York under
a call of men whom the " Commercial Advertiser "
described as " Jackson Jacobins."   The call was

headed: "Bread, meat, rent, fuel! Their prices must come down!" It invited the presence of "all friends of humanity determined to resist monopolists and extortionists." A very respectable meeting about high prices had been held two or three weeks before at the Broadway Tabernacle. The meeting in the City Hall Park, with a mixture of wisdom and folly, urged the prohibition of bank-notes under $100, and called for gold and silver; and then denounced landlords and dealers in provisions. The excitement of the meeting was followed by a riot, in which a great flour warehouse was gutted. The rioters were chiefly foreigners and few in number; nor were the promoters of the meeting involved in the riot. The military were called out; and Eli Hart & Co., the unfortunate flour merchants, issued a card pointing out with grim truth "that the destruction of the article cannot have a tendency to reduce the price."

The distribution of the treasury surplus to the States precipitated the crash. The first quarter's payment of $9,367,000 was made on January 1, 1837. There was disturbance in taking this large sum of money from the deposit banks. Loans had to be called in, and the accommodation to business men lessened for the time. There was speculative disturbance in the receipt of the moneys by the state depositories. There was apprehension for the next payment on April 1, which was accomplished with still greater disturbance, and after the crisis had begun. The calls for gold and silver,

begun under the specie circular, and the disturbances caused by these distributions, were increased
by financial pressure in England, whose money
aids to America were but partly shown by the
shipments of gold and silver already mentioned.
The extravagance of living had been shown in foreign importations for consumption in luxury, to
meet which there had gone varied promises to pay,
and securities whose true value depended upon the
true and not the apparent creation of wealth in
America. Before the middle of March the money
excitement at Manchester was great; and to the
United States alone, it was then declared, attention
was directed for larger remittances and for specie.
The merchants of Liverpool about the same time
sent a memorial to the chancellor of the exchequer
saying " that the distress of the mercantile interest
is intense beyond example, and that it is rapidly
extending to all ranks and conditions of the community, so as to threaten irretrievable ruin in all
directions, involving the prudent with the impru-
dent." The " London Times " on April 10, 1837,
said that great distress and pressure had been produced in every branch of national industry, and
that the calamity had never been exceeded.

The cry was quickly reëchoed from America.
Commercial failures began in New York about
April 1. By April 8 nearly one hundred failures
had occurred in that city, — five of foreign and exchange brokers, thirty of dry-goods jobbers, sixteen
of commission houses, twenty-eight of real-estate

speculators, eight of stock brokers, and several others. Three days later the failures had reached one hundred and twenty-eight. Provisions, wages, rents, everything, as the "New York Herald" on that day announced, were coming down. Within a few days more the failures were too numerous to be specially noticed; and before the end of the month the rest of the country was in a like condition. The prostration in the newer cotton States was peculiarly complete. Their staple was now down to ten cents a pound; within a year it had been worth twenty. All other staples fell enormously in price.

Later in April the merchants of New York met. Instead of condemning their own folly, they resolved, in a silly fury, that the disaster was due to government interference with the business and commercial operations of the country by requiring land to be paid for in specie instead of paper, to its destruction of the Bank, and to its substitution of a metallic for a credit currency. A committee of fifty, including Thomas Denny, Henry Parish, Elisha Riggs, and many others whose names are still honored in New York, was appointed to remonstrate with the president. "What constitutional or legal justification," it was seriously demanded, "can Martin Van Buren offer to the people of the United States for having brought upon them all their present difficulties?" The continuance of the specie circular, they said, was more high-handed tyranny than that which had cost

Charles I. his crown and his head.  On May 3 the committee visited Washington and told the President that their real estate had depreciated forty millions, their stocks twenty millions, their immense amounts of merchandise in warehouses thirty per cent.  They piteously said to him, " The noble city which we represent lies prostrate in despair, its credit blighted, its industry paralyzed, and without a hope beaming through the darkness, unless " — and here we might suppose they would have added, " unless Americans at once stop spending money which has not been earned, and repair the ruin by years of sensible industry and strict economy."  But the conclusion of the merchants was that the darkness must continue unless relief came from Washington.  It was unjust, they said, to attribute the evils to excessive development of mercantile entérprise; they flowed instead from "that unwise system which aimed at the substitution of a metallic for a paper currency."  The error of their rulers " had produced a wider desolation than the pestilence which depopulated our streets, or the conflagration which laid them in ashes."  In the opinion of these sapient gentlemen of business, it was the requirement that the United States, in selling Western lands to speculators, should be paid in real and not in nominal money, which had prostrated in despair the metropolis of the country.  They asked for a withdrawal of the specie circular, for a suspension of government suits against importers on bonds given for duties, for

an extra session of Congress to pass Clay's bill
for the distribution of the land revenue among
the States, and for the re-chartering of the Bank.
Never did men out of their heads with fright propose more foolish attempts at relief than some of
these. But the folly, as will be seen, seized statesmen of the widest experience as well as frenzied
merchants. The President's answer was dignified,
but "brief and explicit." To the insolent suggestion that Jackson's financial measures had been
more destructive than fire or pestilence, he calmly
reminded them that he had made fully known,
before he was elected, his own approval of those
measures; that knowing this the people had deliberately chosen him; and that he would still adhere
to those measures. The specie circular should be
neither repealed nor modified. Such indulgence
in enforcing custom-house bonds would be allowed
as the law permitted. The emergency did not, he
thought, justify an extra session. Nicholas Biddle
called on Van Buren; and many were disgusted
that in the presence of this arch enemy the president remained "profoundly silent upon the great
and interesting topics of the day."

Van Buren's resolution to face the storm without either the aid or the embarrassment of the
early presence of Congress he was soon compelled
to abandon. Within a few days of the return of
the merchants to New York, that city sent the President an appalling reply. On May 10 its banks
suspended payment of their notes in coin. A few

days before some banks in lesser cities of the Southwest had stopped. On the day after the New York suspension, the banks of Philadelphia, Baltimore, Albany, Hartford, New Haven, and Providence followed. On the 12th the banks of Boston and Mobile, on the 13th those of New Orleans, and on the 17th those of Charleston and Cincinnati fell in the same crash. There was now simply a general bankruptcy. Men would no longer meet their promises to pay, because no longer could new paper promises pay off old ones. No longer would men surrender physical wealth safely in their hands for the expectation of wealth to be created by the future progress of the country. But men with perfectly real physical wealth in their storehouses, which they could not themselves use, were also in practical bankruptcy because of their commercial debts most prudently incurred. The natural exchange of their own goods for goods which they or their creditors might use was obstructed by the utter discredit of paper money, and by the almost complete disappearance of gold and silver. Extra sessions of state legislatures were called to devise relief. The banks' suspension of specie payment in New York was within a few days legalized by the legislature of that State. On May 12 the secretary of the treasury directed government collectors themselves to keep public moneys where the deposit banks had suspended.

For banks holding the public moneys sank with

the others. And it was this which compelled Van
Buren in one matter to yield to the storm. On
May 15 he issued a proclamation for an extra session of Congress to meet on the first Monday of
September. It would meet, the proclamation said,
to consider "great and weighty matters." No
scheme of relief was suggested. The locking up
of public moneys in suspended banks made necessary some relief to the government itself. It was,
perhaps, well enough that excited and terrified
people, casting about for a remedy, should, until
their wits were somewhat restored, be soothed by
assurance that the great council of the nation
would, at any rate, discuss the situation. Moreover, it was wise to secure time, that most potent
ally of the statesman. Within the three months
and a half to elapse, Van Buren, like a wise ruler,
thought the true nature of the calamity would become more apparent; proposals of remedies might
be scrutinized; and thoughtless or superficial men
might weary of their own absurd proposals, or
the people might fully perceive their absurdity.

During the summer popular excitement ran
very high against the administration. The Whig
papers declared it to be "the melancholy truth,
the awful truth," that the administration did
nothing to relieve, but everything to distress the
commercial community. Abbot Lawrence, one of
the richest and most influential citizens of Boston,
told a great meeting, on May 17, that there was
no other people on the face of God's earth that

were so abused, cheated, plundered, and trampled
on by their rulers ; that the government exacted
impossibilities. No overt act, he said, with almost
a sinister suggestion, ought to be committed until
the laws of self-preservation compelled a forcible
resistance ; but the time might come when the
crew must seize the ship. The friends of the administration sought, indeed, to stem the tide; and
a series of skillfully devised popular gatherings
was held, very probably inspired by Van Buren,
who highly estimated such organized appeals to
popular sentiment. In Philadelphia a great meeting denounced the bank suspensions and the issue
of small notes as devices in the interest of a foreign
conspiracy to throw silver coin out of circulation
and export it to Europe, to raise the prices of
necessaries, and recommence a course of gambling
under the name of speculation and trade, in which
the people must be the victims, and " the foreign
and home desperadoes " the gainers. The meeting
declared for a metallic currency. " We hereby
pledge our lives, if necessary," they said, " for the
support of the same." Later, on May 22, there
was in the same city a large gathering at Independence Square, which solemnly called upon the
administration " manfully, fearlessly, and at all
hazards to go on collecting the public revenues
and paying the public dues in gold and silver."
Their forefathers, who fought for their liberties,
the framers of our Constitution, the patriarchs
whose memory they revered, were, with a funny

mixture of truth and falsehood, declared to have been hard-money men. A week later, a great meeting in Baltimore approved the specie circular, and urged its fearless execution, " notwithstanding the senseless clamors of the British party ; " for the crisis, they said, was " a struggle of the virtuous and industrious portions of the community against bank advocates and the enemies to good morals and republicanism." Protests were elsewhere made against forcing small notes into circulation. Paper had, however, to be used, for there was nothing else. Barter must go on, even upon the most flimsy tokens. In New York one saw, as were seen twenty-four years later, bits of paper like this : " The bearer will be entitled to fifty cents' value in refreshments at the Auction Hotel, 123 and 125 Water Street. New York, May, 1837. Charles Redabock." In Tallahassee a committee of citizens was appointed to print bank tickets for purposes of change. In Easton the currency had a more specific basis. One of the tokens read : " This ticket will hold good for a sheep's tongue, two crackers, and a glass of red-eye."

When Congress assembled, the country had cried itself, if not to sleep, at least to seeming quiet. The sun had not ceased to rise and set. Although merchants and bankers were prostrate with anxiety or even in irremediable ruin ; although thousands of clerks and laborers were out of employment or earning absurdly low wages, — for near New York hundreds of laborers were rejected who applied for work at four dollars a month and board; although honest frontiersmen found themselves hopelessly isolated in a wilderness, — for the frontier had suddenly shrunk far behind them, — still the harvest had been good, the masses of men had been at work, and economy had prevailed. The desperation was over. But there was a profound melancholy, from which a recovery was to come only too soon to be lasting.

## CHAPTER IX

### PRESIDENT. — SUB-TREASURY BILL

VAN BUREN'S bearing in the crisis was admirable. Even those who have treated him with animosity or contempt do not here refuse him high praise. " In this one question," says Von Holst, " he really evinced courage, firmness, and statesmanlike insight. . . . Van Buren bore the storm bravely. He repelled all reproaches with decision, but with no bitterness. . . . Van Buren unquestionably merited well of the country, because he refused his coöperation, in accordance with the guardianship principle of the old absolutisms, to accustom the people of the Republic also to see the government enter as a saving *deus ex machina* in every calamity brought about by their own fault and folly. . . . Van Buren had won a brilliant victory and placed his countrymen under lasting obligations to him." [1]

[1] I cannot refrain from noticing here the curious fact that Dr. Von Holst, after a contemptuous picture of Van Buren as a mere verbose, coarse-grained politician given to scheming and duplicity, was not surprised at his meeting in so lofty a spirit this really great trial. For surely here, if anywhere, the essential fibre of the man would be discovered. I must also express my regret that this writer, to whom Americans owe very much, should have been

Van Buren met the extra session with a message
which marks the zenith of his political wisdom. It
is one of the greatest of American state papers.
With clear, unflinching, and unanswerable logic he
faced the crisis. There was no effort to evade the
questions put to him, or to divert public attention
from the true issue. The government could not,
he showed, help people earn their living; but it
could refuse to aid the deception that paper was
gold, and the delusion that value could arise without labor. The masterly argument seems long to a
sauntering reader; but it treated a difficult question which had to be answered by the multitudes
of a democracy many of whom were pinched and
excited by personal distresses and anxiety and who
were sure to read it. Few episodes in our political
history give one more exalted appreciation of the

content (although in this he has but joined some other historians of
American politics) to accept mere campaign or partisan rumors
which when directed against other men, have gone unnoticed, but
against Van Buren have become the basis for emphatic disparage-
ment and contumely. Even Mackenzie, the publisher of the pur-
loined letters, writing his pamphlet with the most obvious and
reckless venom, is quoted by this learned historian as respectable
authority. Van Buren had refused during nearly a year to pardon
Mackenzie from prison for his unlawful use of American territory
to prepare armed raids on Canada. Sir Francis B. Head's opinion
was doubtless somewhat colored; but he was not entirely without
justification in applying to Mackenzie the words: " He lies out of
every pore in his skin. Whether he be sleeping or waking, on foot
or on horseback, together with his neighbors or writing for a newspaper, a multitudinous swarm of lies, visible, palpable, and tan-
gible, are buzzing and settling about him like flies around a horse
in August." (Narrative of Sir F. B. Head, London, 1839.)

good sense of the American masses, than that, in this stress of national suffering, a skillful politician should have appealed to them, not even sweetening the truth, but resisting with direct and painful sobriety their angry and natural impulses; this, too, when most of the talented and popular leaders were promoting, rather than reducing or diverting the heated folly of the time.

Van Buren quietly began by saying that the law required the secretary of the treasury to deposit public moneys only in banks that paid their notes in specie. All the banks had stopped such payment. It was obvious therefore that some other custody of public moneys must be provided, and it was for this that he had summoned Congress. He then began what was really an address to the people. He pointed out that the government had not caused, and that it could not cure, the profound commercial distemper. Antecedent causes had been stimulated by the enormous inflations of bank currency and other credits, and among them the many millions of foreign loans, and the lavish accommodations extended "by foreign dealers to our merchants." Thence had come the spirit of reckless speculation, and from that a foreign debt of more than thirty millions; the extension to traders in the interior of credits for supplies greatly beyond the wants of the people; the investment of thirty-nine and a half millions in unproductive public lands; the creation of debts to an almost countless amount for real estate in existing or anticipated

cities and villages; the expenditure of immense
sums in improvements ruinously improvident; the
diversion to other pursuits of labor that should
have gone to agriculture, so that this first of agri-
cultural countries had imported two millions of
dollars worth of grain in the first six months of
1837; and the rapid growth of luxurious habits
founded too often on merely fancied wealth. These
evils had been aggravated by the great loss of
capital in the famous fire at New York in December, 1835, a loss whose effects, though real, were
not at once apparent because of the shifting and
postponement of the burdens through facilities of
credit, by the disturbance which the transfers of
public moneys in the distribution among the States
caused, and by necessities of foreign creditors which
made them seek to withdraw specie from the United
States. He pointed out the unprecedented expansion of credit in Great Britain at the same time,
and, with the redundancy of paper currency [1] there,
the rise of adventurous and unwholesome speculation.

To the demand for a reëstablishment of a national bank, he replied that quite a contrary thing
must be done; that the fiscal concerns of the government must be separated from those of individuals or corporations; that to create such a bank
would be to disregard the popular will twice
solemnly and unequivocally expressed; that the

---

[1] The reference was to commercial paper and not to bank-notes.
But both had been active characteristics of American speculation.

same motives would operate on the administrators of a national as on those of state banks ; that the Bank of the United States had not prevented former and similar embarrassments, and that the Bank of England had but lately failed in its own land to prevent serious abuses of credit. He knew indeed of loud and serious complaint because the government did not now aid commercial exchange. But this was no part of its duty. It was not the province of government to aid individuals in the transfer of their funds otherwise than through the facilities of the post-office. As justly might the government be asked to transport merchandise. These were operations of trade to be conducted by those who were interested in them. Throughout Europe domestic as well as foreign exchanges were carried on by private houses, and often, if not generally, without the assistance of banks. Our own exchanges ought to be carried on by private enterprise and competition, without legislative assistance, free from the influence of political agitation, and from the neglect, partiality, injustice, and oppression unavoidably attending the interference of government with the proper concerns of individuals. His own views, Van Buren declared, were unchanged. Before his election he had distinctly apprised the people that he would not aid in the reëstablishment of a national bank. His conviction had been strengthened that such a bank meant a concentrated money power hostile to the spirit and permanency of our republican institutions.

He then turned to those state banks which had held government deposits. At all times they had held some of the federal moneys, and since 1833 they had held the whole. Since that year the utmost security had been required from them for such moneys; but when lately called upon to pay the surplus to the States, they had, while curtailing their discounts and increasing the general distress, been with the other banks fatally involved in the revulsion. Under these circumstances it was a solemn duty to inquire whether the evils inherent in any connection between the government and banks of issue were not such as to require a divorce. Ought the moneys taken from the people for public uses longer to be deposited in banks and thence to be loaned for the profit of private persons? Ought not the collection, safe-keeping, transfer, and disbursement of public moneys to be managed by public officers? The public revenues must be limited to public expenses so that there should be no great surplus. The care of the moneys inevitably accumulated from time to time would involve expense; but this was a trifling consideration in so important a matter. Personally it would be agreeable to him to be free from concern in the custody and disbursement of the public revenue. Not indeed that he would shrink from a proper official responsibility, but because he firmly believed the capacity of the executive for usefulness was in no degree promoted by the possession of patronage not actually necessary. But he was clear that the connection of the executive with powerful moneyed institutions, capable of ministering to the interests of men in points where they were most accessible to corruption, was more liable to abuse than his constitutional agency in the appointment and control of the few public officers required by the proposed plan.

Thus was announced the independent treasury scheme, the divorce of bank and state, the famous achievement of Van Buren's presidency. He argued besides elaborately in favor of the specie circular. An individual could, if he pleased, accept payment in a paper promise or in any other way as he saw fit. But a public servant should in exchange for public domain take only what was universally deemed valuable. He ought not to have a discretion to measure the value of mere promises. The $9,367,200 in the treasury for deposit with the States in October, or rather for a permanent distribution to them, he desired to retain for federal necessities. This would doubtless inconvenience States which had relied on the federal donation; but as the United States needed the money to meet its own obligations, there was neither justice nor expediency in generously giving it away. Van Buren here left the defensive with a menace to the banks that a bankruptcy law for corporations suspending specie payment might impose a salutary check on the issues of paper money.

The President finally spoke in words which seem

golden to all who share his view of the ends of government. "Those who look to the action of this government," he said, "for specific aid to the citizen to relieve embarrassments arising from losses by revulsions in commerce and credit, lose sight of the ends for which it was created, and the powers with which it is clothed. It was established to give security to us all, in our lawful and honorable pursuits, under the lasting safeguard of republican institutions. It was not intended to confer special favors on individuals, or on any classes of them; to create systems of agriculture, manufactures, or trade; or to engage in them, either separately or in connection with individual citizens or organizations. . . . All communities are apt to look to government for too much . . . We are prone to do so especially at periods of sudden embarrassment and distress. . . . The less government interferes with private pursuits, the better for the general prosperity. It is not its legitimate object to make men rich, or to repair by direct grants of money or legislation in favor of particular pursuits, losses not incurred in the public service." To avoid unnecessary interference with such pursuits would be far more beneficial than efforts to assist limited interests, efforts eagerly, but perhaps naturally, sought for under temporary pressure. Congress and himself, Van Buren closed by saying, acted for a people to whom the truth, however unpromising, could always be spoken with safety, and who, in the phrase of which he was fond, were sure

never to desert a public functionary honestly laboring for the public good.

An angry and almost terrible outburst received
this plain, honest, and wise declaration that the
people must repair their own disasters without paternal help of government; and that, rather than to
promote the extension of credit with public moneys,
the crisis ought to afford means of departing forever from that policy. Most of the able men who
to this generation have seemed the larger statesmen of the day, joined with passionate declamation
in the furious gust of folly. It was a favorite
delusion that government was a separate entity
which could help the people, and not a mere agency,
simply using wealth and power which the people
must themselves create. Webster, in a speech at
Madison, Indiana, on June 1, 1837, professed his
conscientious convictions that all the disasters had
proceeded from " the measures of the general government in relation to the currency." He ridiculed
the idea that the people had helped cause them.
The people, he thought, had no lesson to learn.
"Over-trading, over-buying, over-selling, over-speculation, over-production," — these, he said, were
terms he "could not very well understand." In
his speech of December, 1836, on the specie circular, he had given a leonine laugh at the idea of
there being inflation. If he were asked, he said,
what kept up the value of money " in this vast and
sudden expansion and increase of it," he should
answer that it was kept up "by an equally vast

and sudden increase in the property of the country." That this amazing utterance upon the dynamics of national economy might be clear, he added that the vast and sudden increase was "in the value of that property intrinsic as well as marketable." No speculator of the day said a more foolish thing than did this towering statesman. There were, he admitted, "other minor causes," but they were "not worth enumerating." "The great and immediate origin of the evil" was "disturbances in the exchange . . . caused by the agency of the government itself." At the extra session Webster described the shock caused him by the President's "disregard for the public distress," by his "exclusive concern for the interest of government and revenue, by his refusal to prescribe for the sickness and disease of society," by the separation he would draw "between the interests of the government and the interests of the people." For his part he would be warm and generous in his statesmanship. He resisted the bill to suspend the "deposit" with the States; he would in the coming October pay out the last installment, stricken though the treasury was. He would again sweeten the popular palate with government manna, bitter as it had proved itself to the belly. It was the duty of the government, he said, to aid in exchanges by establishing a paper currency; he and those with him preferred the long-tried, well-approved practice of the government to letting Benton, as he said, "embrace us in his gold and silver arms and hug us to

his hard money breast." As if this were not a
time for soberness over its shameful abuses, credit,
and the banks and bank-notes which aided it were
almost apotheosized. At St. Louis in the summer,
Webster, in a speech which he did not include
in his collected works, said that help must come
" from the government of the United States, from
thence alone ; " adding, " Upon this I risk my political reputation, my honor, my all. . . . He who
expects to live to see all these twenty-six States
resuming specie payments in regular succession
once more, may expect to see the restoration of
the Jews. Never ! He will die without the sight."

John Quincy Adams had told his friends at
home that the distribution of the public moneys
among the state banks was the most pernicious
cause of the disaster, although, differing from
Webster, he admitted that "the abuse of credit,
especially by the agency of banks," and the unrestrained pursuit of individual wealth, were the
proximate causes of the disaster, for history had
testified

" Peace to corrupt, no less than war to waste."

He would punish suspension of specie payments
by a bank with a forfeiture of its charter and
the imprisonment of its president and officers.
A national bank, he said, was " the only practicable expedient for restoring and maintaining
specie payments." In the extra session he showed
that the deposit banks of the South already held

more money of the government than their States would receive, if the last installment of distribution should be paid, while the Northern banks held far less of that money than the Northern States were to receive. He denounced as a Southern measure the proposition to postpone this piece of recklessness. Should the Northern States hail with shouts of Hosanna " this evanescence of their funds from their treasuries," or be " humbugged out of their vested rights by a howl of frenzy against Nicholas Biddle," or be mystified out of their money and out of their senses by a Hark follow! against all banks, or by a summons to Doctors' Commons for a divorce of bank and state ?

That skillful political weathercock, Caleb Cushing, told his constituents at Lowell that private banking was the " shinplaster system; " and asked whether we wished to have men who, like the Rothschilds, make " peace or war as they choose, and wield at will the destiny of empires." The plan of the administration was like that of " a cowardly master of a sinking ship, to take possession of the long boat and provisions, cut off, and leave the ship's company and passengers to their fate." To the plausible cry of separating bank and state he would answer, " Why not separate court and state . . . or law and state . . . or custom-house and state." It was " the new nostrum of political quackery." Clay delivered a famous speech in the Senate on September 25, 1837. He was appalled at the heartlessness of the administra-

tion. "The people, the States, and their banks,"
he said in the favorite cant of the time, "are left
to shift for themselves," as if that were not the
very thing for them to do. We were all, he said,
— "people. States, Union, banks, . . . all entitled
to the protecting care of a parental government."
He cried out against "a selfish solicitude for the
government itself, but a cold and heartless insensi-
bility to the sufferings of a bleeding people." The
substitution of an exclusive metallic currency was
"forbidden by the principles of eternal justice."
For his part he saw no adequate remedy which did
"not comprehend a national bank as an essential
part of it." In banking corporations, indeed,
"the interests of the rich and poor are happily
blended;" nor should we encourage here private
bankers, Hopes and Barings and Rothschilds and
Hottinguers, "whose vast overgrown capitals, possessed by the rich exclusively of the poor, control
the destiny of nations."

The bill for the independent treasury was firmly
pressed by the administration. It did not deceive
the people with any pretense that banks and paper
money would stand in lieu of industry, economy,
and good sense. The summer elections, then far
more numerous than now, had, as Clay warningly
pointed out, gone heavily against Van Buren. The
bill passed the Senate, 26 to 20. In the House it
was defeated. Upon the election of speaker, the
administration candidate, James K. Polk, had had
116 votes to 103 for John Bell. But this very

moderate majority was insecure. A break in the administration ranks was promptly shown by the defeat, for printers to the House, of Francis P. Blair and his partner, who in their paper, the "Washington Globe," had firmly supported the hard money and anti-bank policy. They received only 107 votes, about fifteen Democrats uniting with the Whigs to defeat them. Van Buren was unable to educate all his party to his own firm, clear-sighted views. There was formed a small party of "conservatives," Democrats who took what seemed, and what for the time was, the popular course. The independent treasury bill was defeated in the House by 120 to 106.

Van Buren's proposal was carried, however, to postpone the "deposite," as it was called, the gift as it was, of the fourth installment of the surplus. On October 1, Webster and Clay led the seventeen senators who insisted upon the folly of the national treasury in its destitution playing the magnificent donor, and further debauching the States with streams of pretended wealth. Twenty-eight senators voted for the bill; and in the House it was carried by 118 to 105, John Quincy Adams heading the negative vote.

The administration further proposed the issue of $10,000,000 in treasury notes. It was a measure strictly of temporary relief. Gold and silver had disappeared; bank-notes were discredited. The government, whose gold and silver the banks would not pay out, was disabled from meeting its

current obligations; and the treasury notes were
proposed to meet the necessity. They were not to
be legal tender, but interest-bearing obligations in
denominations not less than $50, to be merely re-
ceivable for all public dues, and thus to gain a
credit which would secure their circulation. This
natural and moderate measure was assailed by
those who were lauding a paper currency to the
skies. The radical difference was ignored between
a general currency of small as well as large bills,
without intrinsic value, adopted for all time, and
a limited and perfectly secure government loan, to
be freely taken or rejected by the people, in bills
of large amounts, to meet a serious but brief embarrassment. " Who expected," said Webster in
the Senate, " that in the fifth year of the experiment for reforming the currency, and bringing
it to an absolute gold and silver circulation, the
Treasury Department would be found recommend-
ing to us a regular emission of paper money?"
He voted, however, for the bill, the only negative
votes in the Senate being given by Clay and four
others. In the House it was carried by 127 to 98.

Such was the substantial work of the extra session. To the experience of that crisis and the
wisdom with which it was met may not improbably be ascribed the hard-money leaven which,
thirty or forty years later, prevented the great
disaster of further paper inflation, and brought
the country to a currency which, if not the best, is
a currency of coin and of redeemable paper, whose

value, apart from the legal-tender notes left us by the war and the decision of the Supreme Court, depends upon the best of securities, coin or government bonds, deposited in the treasury, and a currency whose amount may therefore safely be left to the natural operations of trade.

Clay's appeal for a great banking institution, which should accomplish by magic the results of popular labor and saving, was met by a vote of the House, 123 to 91, that it was inexpedient to charter a national bank, many voting against a bank who had already voted against an independent treasury. The Senate also resolved against a national bank by 31 to 14, six senators who had voted against an independent treasury voting also against a bank. The temporary expedient adopted by the treasury on the suspension of the banks was therefore continued, and public moneys were kept in the hands of public officers.

Calhoun now rejoined the Democratic party. It was only the year before he had denounced it as " a powerful faction held together by the hopes of public plunder; " and early in this very year he had referred to the removal of the deposits as an act fit for " the days of Pompey or Cæsar," and had declared that even a Roman Senate would not have passed the expunging resolution " until the times of Caligula and Nero." But Van Buren, Calhoun now said, had been driven to his position; nor would he leave the position for that reason. He referred to the strict construction of the powers

of the government involved in the divorce of bank
and state. There was no suggestion that Van
Buren had become a convert to nullification. But
Calhoun could with consistency support Van
Buren. The independent treasury scheme was
plainly far different from the removal of the deposits from one great bank to many lesser ones.
The reasons for political exasperation had besides
disappeared. Van Buren was chief among the
*beati possidentes*, and could not for years be disturbed. His tact and skill left open no personal
feud; he had not yet conferred the title of Cæsar;
no successor to himself was yet named by any
clear designation. Calhoun joined Silas Wright
and the other administration senators; but he still
maintained a grim and independent front.

The extra session ended on October 16. Besides the issuance of $10,000,000 in treasury notes
and the postponement of the distribution among
the States, the only measure adopted for relief
was a law permitting indulgence of payment to
importers upon custom-house bonds. As those
payments were to be made in specie, and as specie
had left circulation, it was proper that the United
States as a creditor should exhibit the same leni-
ency which was wise and necessary on the part of
other creditors.

Commercial distress had now materially abated,
although many of its wounds were still deep and
unhealed. Before the regular session began in
December, substantial progress was made towards

specie payments.   The price of gold in New York, which had ruled at a premium of eight and seven eighths per cent., had fallen to five.  On October 20 the banks of New York, after waiting until Congress rose, to meet the wishes of the United States Bank and its associates in Philadelphia, now invited representatives from all the banks to meet in New York on November 27 to prepare for specie payment.  At this meeting the New York banks proposed resumption on March 1, 1838, but they were defeated ; and a resolution to resume on July 1 was defeated by the votes of Pennsylvania and all the New England States except Maine (which was divided), together with New Jersey, Delaware, Maryland, South Carolina, and Indiana. Virginia, Ohio, Georgia, North Carolina, Kentucky, and the District of Columbia, with New York, made the minority.  An adjournment was taken to the second Wednesday in April, the banks being urged meanwhile to prepare for specie payments.

The fall as well as the summer elections had been most disastrous for the Democrats.  New York, which the year before had given Van Buren nearly 30,000 plurality, was now overwhelmingly Whig.  The Van Buren party began to be called the Loco-focos, in derision of the fancied extravagance of their financial doctrines.  The Loco-foco or Equal Rights party proper was originally a division of the Democrats, strongly anti-monopolist in their opinions, and especially hostile to banks, —

not only government banks but all banks, — which enjoyed the privileges then long confirmed by special and exclusive charters. In the fall of 1835 some of the Democratic candidates in New York were especially obnoxious to the anti-monopolists of the party. When the meeting to regularly confirm the nominations made in committee was called at Tammany Hall, the anti-monopolist Democrats sought to capture the meeting by a rush up the main stairs. The regulars, however, showed themselves worthy of their regularity by reaching the room up the back stairs. In a general scrimmage the gas was put out. The anti-monopolists, perhaps used to the devices to prevent meetings which might be hostile, were ready with candles and loco-foco matches. The hall was quickly illuminated; and the anti-monopolists claimed that they had defeated the nominations. The regulars were successful, however, at the election; and they and the Whigs dubbed the anti-monopolists the Loco-foco men. The latter in 1836 organized the Equal Rights party, and declared it an imperative duty of the people "to recur to first principles." Their "declaration of rights" might well have been drawn a few years later by a student of Spencer's "Social Statics." The law, they said, ought to do no more than restrain each man from committing aggressions on the equal rights of other men; they declared "unqualified hostility to bank-notes and paper money as a circulating medium," and to all special grants by the legislature. A great cry was raised against them as dangerous and incendiary fanatics. The Democratic press, except the " Evening Post," edited by William Cullen Bryant, turned violently upon the seceders. There was the same horror of them as the English at almost the very time had of the Chartists, and which in our time is roused by the political movements of Henry George. But with time and familiarity Chartism and Loco-focoism alike lost their horrid aspect. Several of the cardinal propositions of the former have been adopted in acts of Parliament without a shudder. To the animosity of the Loco-focos against special legislation and special privileges Americans probably owe to-day some part of the beneficent movement in many of the States for constitutional requirements that legislatures shall act by general laws.

The Equal Rights party, though casting but a few votes, managed to give the city of New York to the Whigs, a result which convinced the Democrats that, dangerous as they were, they were less dangerous within than without the party. The hatred which Van Buren after his message of September, 1837, received from the banks commended him to the Loco-focos ; and in October, 1837, Tammany Hall witnessed their reconciliation with the regular Democrats upon the moderate declaration for equal rights. The Whigs had, indeed, been glad enough to have Loco-foco aid and even open alliance at the polls. But none the less they thought the Democratic welcome back of the

seceders an enormity. From this time the Democrats were, it was clear, no better than Loco-focos,
and ought to bear the name of those dangerous
iconoclasts.

Van Buren met Congress in December, 1837,
with still undaunted front. His first general review of the operations of the government was but
little longer than his message to the extra session
on the single topic of finance. He refused to consider the result of the elections as a popular disapproval of the divorce of bank and state. In only
one State, he pointed out, had a federal election
been held; and in the other elections, which had
been local, he intimated that the fear of a forfeiture of the state-bank charters for their suspension
of specie payments had determined the result. He
still emphatically opposed the connection between
the government and the banks which could offer
such strong inducements for political agitation.
He blew another blast against the United States
Bank, now a Pennsylvania corporation, for continuing to reissue its notes originally made before
its federal charter had expired and since returned.
He recommended a preëmption law for the benefit
of actual settlers on public lands, and a classification of lands under different rates, to encourage
the settlement of the poorer lands near the older
settlements. There was a conciliatory but firm
reference to the dispute with England over the
northeastern boundary. He announced his failure
to adjust the dispute with Mexico over the claims

which had been pressed by Jackson. The Texan cloud which six years later brought Van Buren's defeat was already threatening.

At this session the independent or sub-treasury bill was again introduced, and again a titanic battle was waged in the Senate. In this encounter Clay taunted Calhoun for going over to the enemy; and Calhoun, referring to the Adams-Clay coalition, retorted that Clay had on a memorable occasion gone over, and had not left it to time to disclose his motives. Here it was that, in the decorous fury of the times, both senators stamped accusations with scorn in the dust, and hurled back darts fallen harmless at their feet. The bill passed the Senate by 27 to 25; but Calhoun finally voted against it because there had been stricken out the provision that government dues should be paid in specie. The bill was again defeated in the House by 125 to 111. The latter vote was late in June, 1838. But while Congress refused a law for it, the independent treasury in fact existed. Under the circular issued upon the bank suspension, the collection, keeping, and payment of federal moneys continued to be done by federal officers. The absurdity of the declamation about one's blood curdling at Van Buren's recommendations, about this being the system in vogue where people were ground "to the very dust by the awful despotism of their rulers," was becoming apparent in the easy, natural operation of the system, dictated though it was by necessity rather than law. The

Whigs, in the sounding jeremiades of Webster and the perfervid eloquence of Clay, were joined by the Conservatives, former Democrats, with Tallmadge of New York and Rives of Virginia at their head. They had retired into the cave of superior wisdom, of which many men are fond when a popular storm seems rising against their party; they affected oppressive grief at Van Buren's reckless hatred of the popular welfare, and accused him of designing entire destruction of credit in the ordinary transactions of business. This silly charge was continually made, and gained color from the extreme doctrines of the Equal Rights movement and the fixing of the Loco-foco name upon the Democratic party.

The sub-treasury bill was again taken up at the long session of 1839–40 by the Congress elected in 1838. Again the wisdom of separating bank and state, again the wrong of using public moneys to aid private business and speculation, were stated with perfectly clear but uninspiring logic. Again came the antiphonal cry, warm and positive, against the cruelty of withdrawing the government from an affectionate care for the people, and from its duty generously to help every one to earn his living. In and out of Congress it was the debate of the time, and rightly; for it involved a profound and critical issue, which since the foundation of the government has been second in importance only to the questions of slavery and national existence and reconstruction. In 1840 the bill passed the Senate by

24 to 18 and the House by 124 to 107. This chief
monument of Van Buren's administration seemed
quickly demolished by the triumphant Whigs in
1841, but was finally set up again in 1846 without
the aid of its architect. From that time to our
own, in war and in peace, the independence of the
federal treasury has been a cardinal feature of
American finance. Nor was its theory lost even
in the system of national banks and public depositories created for the tremendous necessities of the
civil war.[1]

By the spring of 1838 business had revived
during the year of enforced industry and economy
among the people. In January, 1838, the premium
on gold at New York sank to three per cent. ; and
when the bank convention met on the adjourned
day in April, the premium was less than one per
cent. The United States Bank resisted resumption
with great affectation of public spirit, but for selfish reasons soon to be disclosed. The New York
banks, with an apology to their associates, resolved
to resume by May 10, five days before the date to
which the State had legalized the suspension. The
convention adopted a resolution for general resumption on January 1, 1839, without precluding
earlier resumption by any banks which deemed it
proper. In April it was learned that the Bank of

---

[1] The depositories now authorized for the proceeds of the internal revenue secured the government by a deposit of the bonds
of the latter, which the depositories must of course purchase and
own. (*U. S. Rev. Stats.* § 5153.)

England was shipping a million sterling to aid resumption by the banks. On July 10, Governor Ritner of Pennsylvania by proclamation required the banks of his State to resume by August 1. On the 13th of that month the banks of Massachusetts, Connecticut, Rhode Island, Delaware, Maryland, Virginia, Kentucky, Missouri, Ohio, Indiana, and Illinois yielded to the moral coercion of the New York banks, and to the resumption now enforced on the Bank of the United States. By the fall of 1838 resumption was general, although the banks at the Southwest did not follow until midwinter. Confidence was so much restored that " runs " on the banks did not occur. The crisis seemed at an end ; and Van Buren not unreasonably fancied that he saw before the country two years of steady and sound return to prosperity. Two such years would, in November, 1840, bring the reward of his sagacity and endurance. But a far deeper draft upon the vitality of the patient had been made than was supposed ; and in its last agony, eighteen months later, Biddle's bank helped to blast Van Buren's political ambition.

# CHAPTER X

PRESIDENT. — CANADIAN INSURRECTION. — TEXAS. — SEMINOLE WAR. — DEFEAT FOR REËLECTION

ANOTHER unpopular duty fell to Van Buren during his presidency, a duty but for which New York might have been saved to him in 1840. In the Lower and Upper Canadas popular discontent and political tumult resulted late in 1837 in violence, so often the only means by which English dependencies have brought their imperial mistress to a respect for their complaints.[1] The liberality of the Whigs, then lately triumphant in England, was not broad enough to include these distant colonists. The provincial legislature in each of the Canadas consisted of a Lower House or assembly chosen by popular vote, and an Upper House or council appointed by the governor, who himself was appointed by and represented the crown.

---

[1] I cannot refrain in this revised edition to note that England, although not always a ready scholar, has in later years learned a farseeing wisdom which in colonial administration makes her the teacher of the world. The modern policy of deference to local sentiment and of finding her own advantage in the independent prosperity of the colony, has bound continents, islands, races, religions, to the English empire, and brought from them wealth to England, as the old rule of force never did.

Reforms after reforms, proposed by the popular houses, were rejected by the council. In Lower Canada the popular opposition was among the French, who had never been embittered towards the United States. In Upper Canada its strength was among settlers who had come since the war closed in 1815. Lower Canada demanded in vain that the council be made elective. Its assembly, weary of the effectual opposition of the council to popular measures, began in 1832 to refuse votes of supplies unless their grievances were redressed; and by 1837 government charges had accrued to the amount of £142,100. On April 14, 1837, Lord John Russell, still wearing the laurel of a victor for popular rights, procured from the imperial parliament permission, without the assent of the colonial parliament, to apply to these charges the money in the hands of the receiver-general of Lower Canada. This extraordinary grant passed the House of Commons by 269 to 46. A far less flagitious case of taxation without representation had begun the American Revolution. The money had been raised under laws which provided for its expenditure by vote of a local representative body. It was expended by the vote of a body at Westminster, three thousand miles away, but few of whose members knew or cared anything for the bleak stretch of seventeenth-century France on the lower St. Lawrence, and none of whom had contributed a penny of it. To even Gladstone, lately the under-secretary for the colonies and then a

" rising hope of unbending Tories," there seemed nothing involved but the embarrassment of faithful servants of the crown. This thoroughly British disregard of sentiment among other people roused a deep opposition which was headed by Papineau, eloquent and a hero among the French. An insurrection broke out in November, 1837, and blood was shed in engagements at St. Denis and St. Charles, not far from Montreal. But the insurgents were quickly defeated, and within three weeks the insurrection in Lower Canada was ended.

In Upper Canada there was considerable Republican sentiment, and the party of popular rights had among its leaders men of a high order of ability. One of them, Marshall S. Bidwell, through the magnanimity or procurement of the governor, escaped from Canada to become one of the most honored and stately figures at the bar of New York. Early in 1836, Sir Francis B. Head, a clever and not ill-natured man, arrived as governor. He himself wrote the unconscious Anglicism that "the great danger " he "had to avoid was the slightest attempt to conciliate any party." It was assumed with the usual insufferable affectation of omniscience that these hardy Western settlers were merely children who did not know what was best for them. Even the suggestions of concession sent him from England were not respected. In an election for the Assembly he had the issue announced as one of separation from England;

and by the use, it was said, of his power and patronage, the colonial Tories carried a majority of the House. Hopeless of any redress, and fired by the rumors of the revolt in Lower Canada, an insurrection took place early in December near Toronto. It was speedily suppressed. One of the leaders, Mackenzie, escaped to Buffalo. Others were captured and punished, some of them capitally.

The mass of the Canadians were doubtless opposed to the insurrection. But there was among them a widespread and reasonable discontent, with which the Americans, and especially the people of northern and western New York, warmly sympathized. It was natural and traditional to believe England an oppressor; and there was every reason in this case to believe the Canadians right in their ill-feeling. The refugees who had fled to New York met with an enthusiastic reception, and, in the security of a foreign land, prepared to advance their rebellion. On the long frontier of river, lake, and wilderness, it was difficult, with the meagre force regularly at the disposal of the United States, to prevent depredations. This difficulty became enhanced by a culpable though not unnatural invasion of American territory by British troops. On December 12, 1837, Mackenzie, who had the day before arrived with a price of $4000 set upon his head, addressed a large audience at Buffalo. Volunteers were called for; and the next day, with twenty-five men, commanded by Van

Rensselaer, an American, he seized Navy Island in the Niagara River, but a short distance above the cataract, and belonging to Canada. He there established a provisional government, with a flag and a great seal; and that the new State might be complete, paper money was issued. By January, 1838, there were several hundred men on the island, largely Americans, with arms and provisions chiefly obtained from the American side.

On the night of December 29, 1837, a party of Canadian militia crossed the Niagara to seize the Caroline, a steamer in the service of the rebels. It happened, however, that the steamer, instead of being at Navy Island, was at Schlosser, on the American shore. The Canadians seized the vessel, killing several men in the affray, and after setting her on fire, loosened her from the shore, to go blazing down the river and over the falls. This invasion of American territory caused indignant excitement through the United States. Van Buren had promptly sought to prevent hostility from our territory. On January 5, 1838, he had issued a proclamation reciting the seizure of Navy Island by a force, partly Americans, under the command of an American, with arms and supplies procured in the United States, and declared that the neutrality laws would be rigidly enforced and the offenders punished. Nor would they receive aid or countenance from the United States, into whatever difficulties they might be thrown by their violation of friendly territory. On the same day Van Buren

sent General Winfield Scott to the frontier, and
by special message asked from Congress power to
prevent such offenses in advance, as well as afterwards to punish them, — a request to which Congress, in spite of the excitement over the invasion
at Schlosser, soon acceded. The militia of New
York were, on this invasion, called out by Governor Marcy, and placed under General Scott's
command. But there was little danger. On January 13 the insurgents abandoned Navy Island.
The war, for the time, was over, although excitement and disorder continued on the border and
the lakes as far as Detroit; and in the fall of 1838
other incursions were made from American territory. But they were fruitless and short-lived
Nearly nine hundred arrests were made by the
Canadian authorities. Many death sentences were
imposed and several executed, and many more
offenders were sentenced to transportation.

England, in her then usual fashion, was duly
waked to duty by actual bloodshed. Sir Francis
B. Head left Canada, and the Melbourne ministry
sent over the Earl of Durham, one of the finest
characters in English public life, to be governor-
general over the five colonies; to redress their
wrongs; to conciliate, and perhaps yield to demands
for self-government: all which might far better
have been done five years before. Lord Durham
used a wise mercy towards the rebels. He made
rapid progress in the reforms, and, best and first
of all, he won the confidence and affection of the

people. But England used to distrust an English statesman who practiced this kind of rule towards a dependency. A malevolent attack of Lord Brougham was successful, and Lord Durham returned to ministerial disgrace, though to a wiser popular applause, soon to die in what ought to have been but an early year in his generous and splendid career. Although punishing her benefactor, England was shrewd enough to accept the benefit. The concessions which Lord Durham had begun were continued, and Canada became and has remained loyal. Before leaving Canada, Lord Durham was invited by a very complimentary letter of Van Buren to visit Washington, but the invitation was courteously declined.

Mackenzie was arrested at Buffalo and indicted. After his indictment he addressed many public meetings through the United States in behalf of his cause, one at Washington itself. In 1839, however, he was tried and convicted. Van Buren, justly refusing to pardon him until he had served in prison two thirds of his sentence, thus made for himself a persistent and vindictive enemy.

Upon renewed raids late in 1838, the President, by a proclamation, called upon misguided or deluded Americans to abandon projects dangerous to their own country and fatal to those whom they professed a desire to relieve ; and, after various appeals to good sense and patriotism, warned them that, if taken in Canada, they would be left to the policy and justice of the government whose dominions they had, "without the shadow of justification or excuse, nefariously invaded." This had no uncertain sound. Van Buren was promptly declared to be a British tool. The plain facts were ignored that the great majority of the Canadians, however much displeased with their rulers, were hostile to Republican institutions and to a separation from England, and that the majority in Canada had the same right to be governed in their own fashion as the majority here. There was seen, however, in this firm performance of international obligations, only additional proof of Van Buren's coldness towards popular rights, and of his sycophancy to power.

The system of allowing to actual settlers, at the minimum price, a preëmption of public lands already occupied by them, was adopted at the long session of 1837–38. Webster joined the Democrats in favoring the bill, against the hot opposition of Clay, who declared it "a grant of the property of the whole people to a small part of the people." The dominant party was now wisely committed to the policy of using the public domain for settlers, and not as mere property to be turned into money. But a year or two before, the latter system had in practice wasted the national estate and corrupted the public with a debauchery of speculation.

The war between Mexico and the American settlers in her revolted northeast province began in 1835. Early in 1836 the heroic defense of the

Alamo against several thousand Mexicans by less than two hundred Americans, and among them Davy Crockett, Van Buren's biographer, and the butchery of all but three of the Americans, had consecrated the old building, still proudly preserved by the stirring but now peaceful and pleasing city of San Antonio, and had roused in Texas a fierce and resolute hatred of Mexico. In April, 1836, Houston overwhelmed the Mexicans at San Jacinto, and captured their president, Santa Anna.

In his message of December 21, 1836, Jackson, although he announced these successes of the Texans and their expulsion of Mexican civil authority, still pointed out to Congress the disparity of physical force on the side of Texas, and declared it prudent that we should stand aloof until either Mexico itself or one of the great powers should have recognized Texan independence, or at least until the ability of Texas should have been proved beyond cavil. The Senate had then passed a resolution for recognition of Texan independence. But the House had not concurred; and before Van Buren's inauguration Congress had done no more than authorize the appointment of a diplomatic agent to Texas whenever the President should be satisfied of its independence. In August, 1837, the Texan representative at Washington laid before Van Buren a plan of annexation of the revolted Mexican state. The offer was refused; and it was declared that the United States desired to remain neutral, and perceived that annexation would necessarily lead to war with Mexico. In December, 1837, petitions were presented in Congress against the annexation of Texas, now much agitated at the South; and Preston, Calhoun's senatorial associate from South Carolina, offered a resolution for annexation. Some debate on the question was had in 1838, in which both the pro-slavery character of the movement and the anti-slavery character of the opposition clearly appeared. But this danger to Van Buren was delayed several years. Nor was he yet a character in the drama of the slavery conflict which by 1837 was well opened. The agitation over abolition petitions and the murder of Lovejoy the abolitionist are now readily enough seen to have been the most deeply significant occurrences in America between Van Buren's inauguration and his defeat; but they were as little part of his presidency as the arrival at New York from Liverpool on April 22 and 23, 1838, of the Sirius and the Great Western, the first transatlantic steamships. In Washington the slavery question did not get beyond the halls of Congress. The White House remained for several years free from both the dangers and the duties of the question accompanying the discussion.

Van Buren's administration pressed upon Mexico claims arising out of wrongs to American citizens and property which had long been a grievance. Jackson had thought it our duty, in view of the "embarrassed condition" of that republic, to "act with both wisdom and moderation by giving to Mexico one more opportunity to atone for the past."

In December, 1837, Van Buren, tired of Mexican procrastination, referred the matter to Congress, with some menace in his tone. In 1840 a treaty was at last made for an arbitration of the claims, the king of Prussia being the umpire. John Quincy Adams vehemently assailed the American assertion of these claims, as intended to " breed a war with Mexico," and " as machinery for the annexation of Texas ; " and his violent denunciations have obtained some credit. But Adams himself had been pretty vigorous in the maintenance of American rights. And the plain and well known facts are, that after several years of negotiation the claims were with perfect moderation submitted for decision to a disinterested tribunal ; that they were never made the occasion of war ; and that Van Buren opposed annexation.

In June, 1838, James K. Paulding, long the navy agent at New York, was made secretary of the navy in place of Mahlon Dickerson of New Jersey, who now resigned. Paulding seems to us rather a literary than a political figure. Besides the authorship of part of " Salmagundi," of " The Dutchman's Fireside," and of other and agreeable writings grateful to Americans in the days when the sting of the question, " Who reads an American book ? " lay rather in its truth than in its ili-nature, Paulding's pen had aided the Republican party as early as Madison's presidency. Our politics have always, even at home, paid some honor to the muses, without requiring them to descend very far into the partisan arena. A curious illustration was the nomination of Edwin Forrest, the famous tragedian, for Congress by the Democrats of New York in 1838, a nomination which was more sensibly declined than made. An almost equally curious instance was the tender Van Buren made of the secretaryship of the navy to Washington Irving before he offered it to Paulding, who was a connection by marriage of Irving's brother. Van Buren had, it will be remembered, become intimately acquainted with Irving abroad; and others than Van Buren strangely enough had thought of him for political service. The Jacksonians had wanted him to run for Congress; and Tammany Hall had offered him a nomination for mayor of New York. Van Buren wrote to Irving that the latter had " in an eminent degree those peculiar qualities which should distinguish the head of the department," and that this opinion of his had been confirmed by Irving's friends, Paulding and Kemble, the former of whom it was intimated was "particularly informed in regard to the services to be rendered." But one cannot doubt that in writing this the President had in mind the sort of service to the public, and the personal pleasure and rest to himself, to be brought by a delightful and accomplished man of letters, who was no mere recluse, but long practiced in polished and brilliant life abroad, rather than any business or executive or political ability. Irving wisely replied that he should delight in full occupation, and should take peculiar interest in the navy department; but that he shrank from the harsh turmoils of life at Washington, and the bitter personal hostility and the slanders of the press. A short career at Washington would, he said, render him "mentally and physically a perfect wreck." Paulding's appointment to the cabinet portfolio assigned to New York was not agreeable to the politicians; and they afterwards declared that, if Marcy had been chosen instead, the result in 1840 might have been different. The next Democratic president gave the same place to another famous man of letters, George Bancroft.

On June 6, 1837, Louis Napoleon wrote the President from New York that the dangerous illness of his mother recalled him to the old world; and that he stated the reason for his departure lest the President might "have given credence to the calumnious surmises respecting" him. The famous adventurer used one of those many phrases of his which, if they had not for years imposed on the world, no wise man would believe could ever have obtained respect. Van Buren, as the ruler of a free people, ought to be advised, the prince wrote, that, bearing the name he did, it was impossible for him "to depart for an instant from the path pointed out to me by my conscience, my honor, and my duty."

The elections of 1838 showed a recovery from the defeat in 1837, a recovery which would perhaps have been permanent if the financial crisis had been really over. Maine wheeled back into

the Van Buren ranks; and Maryland and Ohio
now joined her. In New Jersey and Massachusetts the Whig majorities were reduced; and in
New York, where Seward and Weed had established a political management quite equal to the
Regency, the former was chosen governor by a
majority of over 10,000, but still less by 5000
than the Whig majority of 1837. The Democrats
now reaped the unpopularity of Van Buren's upright neutrality in the Canadian troubles. Northern and western New York gave heavy Whig
majorities. Jefferson county on the very border,
which had stood by Van Buren even in 1837, went
over to the Whigs.

Van Buren met Congress in December, 1838,
with more cheerful words. The harvest had been
bountiful, he said, and industry again prospered.
The first half century of our Constitution was
about to expire, after proving the advantage of a
government " entirely dependent on the continual
exercise of the popular will." He returned firmly
to his lecture on economics and the currency, drawing happily, but too soon, a lesson from the short
duration of the suspension of specie payments in
1837 and the length of that in 1814. We had
been saved, he said, the mortification of seeing our
distresses used to fasten again upon us so " dangerous an institution " as a national bank. The treasury would be able in the coming year to pay off the
$8,000,000 outstanding of the $10,000,000 of treasury notes authorized at the extra session. Texas

had withdrawn its application for admission to the
Union. The final removal of the Indian tribes to
the west of the Mississippi in accordance with the
Democratic policy was almost accomplished. There
were but two blemishes on the fair record the White
House sent to the Capitol. Swartwout, Jackson's
collector of New York, was found, after his super-
session by Jesse Hoyt, to be a defaulter on a vast
scale. His defalcations, the President carefully
pointed out, had gone on for seven years, as well
while public moneys were kept with the United
States Bank and while they were kept with state
banks, as while they were kept by public officers.
It was broadly intimated that this disgrace was
not unrelated to the general theory which had
so long connected the collection and custody of
public moneys with the advancement of private interests; and the President asked for a law making
it a felony to apply public moneys to private uses.
Swartwout's appointment in 1829, as has been said,
was strenuously opposed by Van Buren as unfit to
be made. After a year or two Jackson returned
to Van Buren his written protest, saying that time
had proved his belief in Swartwout's unfitness to
be a mistake. Van Buren's own appointment to
the place was, however, far from an ideal one.
Jesse Hoyt was shown by his published correspondence — a veritable instance, by the way, of "*stolen
sweets*" — to have been a shrewd, able man, who
enjoyed the strangely varied confidence of many
distinguished, discreet, and honorable men, and of

many very different persons, ranging through a
singular gamut of religion, morals, statesmanship,
economics, politics, patronage, banking, trade, stock
gambling, and betting. The respectability of some
of Hoyt's friends and his possession of some ability
palliate, but do not excuse, his appointment to a
great post.

The second Florida war still dragged out its slow
and murderous length. The Seminoles under pressure had yielded to Jackson's firm policy of removing all the Indian tribes to the west of the Mississippi. The policy seemed, or rather it was, often
cruel, as is so much of the progress of civilization.
But the removal was wise and necessary. Tribal
and independent governments by nomadic savages
could not be tolerated within regions devoted to the
arts and the government of white men. Whatever
the theoretical rights of property in land, no civilized race near vast areas of lands fit for the tillage
of a crowding population has ever permitted them
to remain mere hunting grounds for savages.
The Seminoles in 1832, 1833, and 1834 agreed to
go west upon terms like those accepted by other
Indians. The removal was to take place, one third
of the tribe in each of the three years 1833, 1834,
and 1835 ; but the dark-skinned men, as their white
brothers would have done, found or invented ex-
cuses for not keeping their promise of voluntary
expatriation. Late in 1835, when coercion, although it had not yet been employed against the
Seminoles, was still feared by them, they rose under

their famous leader, the half-breed Powell, better known as Osceola, and massacred the federal agent and Major Dade, and 107 out of 111 soldiers under him. Then followed a series of butcheries and outrages upon white men of which we have heard, and doubtless of crimes enough upon Indians of which we have not heard. Among the everglades, the swamps and lakes of Florida, its scorching sands and impenetrable thickets, a difficult, tedious, inglorious, and costly contest went on. Military evolutions and tactics were of little value; it was a war of ambushes and assassination. Osceola, coming with a flag of truce, was taken by General Jessup, the defense for his capture being his violation of a former parole. He was sent to Fort Moultrie, in Charleston harbor, and there died, after furnishing recitations to generations of schoolboys, and sentiment to many of their elders. Van Buren had been compelled to ask $1,600,000 from Congress at the extra session. Before his administration was ended nearly $14,000,000 had been spent; and not until 1842 did the war end. It was one of the burdens of the administration which served to irritate a people already uneasy for deeper and more general reasons. The prowess of the Indian chief, his eloquence, his pathetic end, the miseries and wrongs of the aborigines, the cost and delay of the war, all reënforced the denunciation of Van Buren by men who made no allowance for embarrassments which could be surmounted by no ability, because they were inevitable to the settlement by a

civilized race of lands used by savages. Time,
however, has vindicated the justice and mercy, as
well as the policy of the removal, and of the establishment of the Indian Territory.

A few days before the close of the session Van
Buren asked Congress to consider the dispute with
Great Britain over the northeast boundary. Both
Maine and New Brunswick threatened, by rival
military occupations of the disputed territory, to
precipitate war. Van Buren permitted the civil
authorities of Maine to protect the forests from
destruction; but disapproved any military seizure,
and told the state authorities that he should propose arbitration to Great Britain. If, however,
New Brunswick sought a military occupation, he
should defend the territory as part of the State.
Congress at once authorized the President to call
out 50,000 volunteers, and put at his disposal a
credit of $10,000,000. Van Buren persisted in
his great effort peacefully to adjust the claims of
our chronically belligerent northeastern patriots, —
in Maine as in New York finding his fate in his duty
firmly and calmly to restrain a local sentiment inspiring voters of great political importance to him.
The "news from Maine" in 1840 told of the angry
contempt the hardy lumbermen felt for the President's perfectly statesmanlike treatment of the
question.

In the summer of 1839 Van Buren visited his
old home at Kinderhook; and on his way there
and back enjoyed a burst of enthusiasm at York,

Harrisburg, Lebanon, Reading, and Easton in
Pennsylvania, at Newark and Jersey City in New
Jersey, and at New York, Hudson, and Albany in
his own State. There were salutes of artillery,
pealing of bells, mounted escorts in blue and white
scarfs, assemblings of "youth and beauty," the
complimentary addresses, the thronging of citizens
"to grasp the hand of the man whom they had
delighted to honor," and all the rest that makes
up the ovations of Americans to their black-coated
rulers. He landed in New York at Castle Garden, amid the salutes of the forts on Bedloe's,
Governor's, and Staten Islands, and of a " seventy-
four," whose yards were covered with white uni-
formed sailors. After the reception in Castle
Garden he mounted a spirited black horse and
reviewed six thousand troops assembled on the
Battery ; and then went in procession along Broadway to Chatham Street, thence to the Bowery, and
through Broome Street and Broadway back to the
City Hall Park. Not since Lafayette's visit had
there been so fine a reception. At Kinderhook he
was overwhelmed with the affectionate pride of his
old neighbors. He declined public dinners, and
by the simple manner of his travel offered disproof
of the stories about his " English servants, horses
and carriages." The journey was not, however,
like the good-natured and unpartisan presidential
journeys of our time. The Whigs often churlishly
refused to help in what they said was an electioneering tour. Seward publicly refused the invita-

tion of the common council of New York to participate in the President's reception, because the
State had honored him with the office of governor
for his disapproval of Van Buren's political character and public policy, and because an acceptance of the invitation " would afford evidence of
inconsistency and insincerity." Van Buren's own
friends gave a party air to much of the welcome.
Democratic committees were conspicuous in the
ceremonies ; and in many of the addresses much
that was said of his administration was fairly in a
dispute certain to last until the next year's election
was over. Van Buren could hardly have objected
to the coldness of the Whigs, for his own speeches,
though decorous and respectful to the last degree
to those who differed from him, were undisguised
appeals for popular support of his financial policy.
At New York he referred to the threatening dis-
satisfaction in his own State concerning his firm
treatment of the Canadian troubles. But he was
persuaded, he said, that good sense and ultimately
just feeling would give short duration to these unfavorable impressions.

The President was too experienced and cool in
judgment to exaggerate the significance of superficial demonstrations like these, which often seemed
conclusive to his exuberant rival Clay. He was
encouraged, however, by the elections of 1839. In
Ohio the Whigs were " pretty essentially used up,"
though unfortunately not to remain so a twelve-
month. In Massachusetts Morton, the Van Buren

candidate for governor, was elected by just one vote more than a majority of the 102,066 votes cast. Georgia, New Jersey, and Mississippi gave administration majorities. In New York the adverse majority which in 1837 had been over 15,000, and in 1838 over 10,000, was now less than 4000, in spite of the disaffection along the border counties. It was not an unsatisfactory result, although for the first time since 1818 the legislature was completely lost. Another year, Van Buren now hoped, would bring a complete recovery from the blow of 1837. But the autumn of 1839 had also brought a blast, to grow more and more chilling and disastrous.

In the early fall the Bank of the United States agreed to loan Pennsylvania $2,000,000; and for the loan obtained the privilege of issuing $5 notes, having before been restricted to notes of $20 and upwards. "Thus has the Van Buren State of Pennsylvania," it was boasted, "enabled the banks to overcome the reckless system of a Van Buren national administration." The price of cotton, which had risen to 16 cents a pound, fell in the summer of 1839, and in 1840 touched as low a point as 5 cents. In the Northwest many banks had not yet resumed since 1837. To avoid execution sales it was said that two hundred plantations had been abandoned and their slaves taken to Texas. The sheriff, instead of the ancient return, *nulla bona*, was said, in the grim sport of the frontier, to indorse on the fruitless writs " G. T.,"

meaning " Gone to Texas." A money stringency
again appeared in England, in 1839. Its expor-
tation of goods and money to America had again
become enormous. The customs duties collected
in 1839 were over $23,000,000, and about the
same as they had been in 1836, having fallen in
1837 to $11,000,000, and afterwards in 1840 fall-
ing to $13,000,000. Speculation revived, the land
sales exceeding $7,000,000 in 1839, while they had
been $3,700,000 in 1838, and afterwards fell to
$3,000,000 in 1840. Under the pressure from
England the Bank of the United States sank
with a crash. The " Philadelphia Gazette," complacently ignoring the plain reasons for months
set before its eyes, said that the disaster had " its
chief cause in the revulsion of the opium trade
with the Chinese ; " that upon the news that the
Orientals would no longer admit the drug the
Bank of England had " fairly reeled ; " and that,
the balance of trade being against us, we had to
dishonor our paper. Explanations of like frivolity
got wide credence. The Philadelphia banks suspended on October 9, 1839, the banks of Baltimore
the next day, and in a few days the banks in the
North and West followed. The banks of New
York and New England, except those of Providence, continued firm. Although the excitement
of 1839 did not equal that of 1837, there was a
duller and completer despondency. It was at last
known that the recuperative power of even our
own proud and bounding country had limits.

Years were yet necessary to a recovery. But the presidential election would not, alas! wait years. With no faltering, however, Van Buren met Congress in December, 1839. He began his message with a regret that he could not announce a year of "unalloyed prosperity." There ought never, as presidential messages had run, to be any alloy in the prosperity of the American people. But the harvest, he said, had been exuberant, and after all (for the grapes of trade and manufacture were a little sour), the steady devotion of the husbandman was the surest source of national prosperity. A part of the $10,000,000 of treasury notes was still outstanding, and he hoped that they might be paid. We must not resort to the ruinous practice of supplying supposed necessities by new loans; a permanent debt was an evil with no equivalent. The expenditures for 1838, the first year over whose appropriations Van Buren had had control, had been less than those of 1837. In 1839 they had been $6,000,000 less than in 1838; and for 1840 they would be $5,000,000 less than in 1839. The collection and disbursement of public moneys by public officers rather than by banks had, since the bank suspensions in 1837, been carried on with unexpected cheapness and ease; and legislation was alone wanting to insure to the system the highest security and facility. Nothing daunted by the second disaster so lately clouding his political future, Van Buren sounded another blast against the banks. With unusual abundance of harvests,

with manufactures richly rewarded, with our gra-
naries and storehouses filled with surplus for
export, with no foreign war, with nothing indeed
to endanger well-managed banks, this banking disaster had come. The government ought not to
be dependent on banks as its depositories, for the
banks outside of New York and Philadelphia were
dependent upon the banks in those great cities,
and the latter banks in turn upon London, " the
centre of the credit system." With some truth,
but still with a touch of demagogy, venial perhaps
in the face of the blatant and silly outcries against
him from very intelligent and respectable people,
he said that the founding of a new bank in a distant American village placed its business " within
the influence of the money power of England."
Let us then, he argued, have gold and silver and
not bank-notes, at least in our public transactions ;
let us keep public moneys out of the banks. Again
he attacked the national bank scheme. In 1817
and 1818, in 1823, in 1831, and in 1834 the United
States Bank had swelled and maddened the tides
of banking, but had seldom allayed or safely directed them. Turning with seemingly cool resolution, but with hidden anxiety, to the menacing
distresses of the American voters, he did not
flinch or look for fair or flattering words. We
must not turn for relief, he said, to gigantic banks,
or splendid though profitless railroads and canals.
Relief was to be sought, not by the increase, but
by the diminution of debt. The faith of States

already pledged was to be punctiliously kept; but
we must be chary of further pledges. The bounties of Providence had come to reduce the consequences of past errors. "But let it be indelibly
engraved on our minds," he said, "that relief is
not to be found in expedients. Indebtedness cannot be lessened by borrowing more money, or by
changing the form of the debt."

The House of Representatives was so divided
that its control depended upon whether five Whig
or five Democratic congressmen from New Jersey
should be admitted. They had been voted for
upon a general ticket through the whole State; and
the Whig governor and council had given the certificate of election to the Whigs by acquiescing in
the actions of the two county clerks who had, for
irregularities, thrown out the Democratic districts
of South Amboy and Millville. A collision arose
curiously like the dispute over the electoral returns
from Florida and Louisiana in 1877. This exclusion of the two districts the Democrats insisted to
have been wrongful; and not improbably with reason, for at the next election in 1839· the State,
upon the popular vote, gave a substantial majority
against the Whigs, although by the district division
of the State a majority of the legislature were
Whigs and reëlected the Whig governor. The
clerk of the national House had, according to usage,
prepared a roll of members, which he proceeded to
call. He seems to have placed on the roll the
names of the New Jersey representatives holding

the governor's certificates. But before calling their names, he stated to the House that there were rival credentials ; that he felt that he had no power to decide upon the contested rights ; and that, if the House approved, he would pass over the names until the call of the other States was finished. The rival credentials included a record of the votes upon which the governor's certificate was presumed to be based. Objection was made to passing New Jersey, and one of the governor's certificates was read. The New Jerseymen with certificates insisted that their names should be called. The clerk declined to take any step without the authority of the House, holding that he was in no sense a chairman. He behaved in the case with modesty and decorum, and the savage criticisms upon him seem to have no foundation except this refusal of his to decide upon the *prima facie* right to the New Jersey seats, or to act as chairman except upon unanimous consent. He was clearly right. He had no power. The very roll he prepared, and his reading it, had no force except such as the House chose to give them. Upon any other theory he would practically wield an enormous power justified neither by the Constitution nor by any law. On the fourth day of tumult a simple and lawful remedy was discovered to be at hand. Any member could himself act as chairman to put his own motion for the appointment of a temporary speaker ; and if a majority acquiesced, there was at once an organization without the clerk's aid. This was

in precise accord with the attitude of the clerk,
hotly abused as he was by Adams and others who
adopted his position.  So Adams proposed himself
to put the question on his own motion to call the
roll with the members holding certificates.  Further
confusion then ensued, which was terminated by
Rhett of South Carolina, who moved that John
Quincy Adams act as chairman until a speaker
should be chosen.  Rhett put his own motion, and
it was carried.  Adams took the chair, rules were
adopted, and order succeeded chaos.  None of the
New Jerseymen were permitted to vote for speaker,
but a few Calhoun Democrats refused to vote for
the administration candidate.  Most of the administration members offered to accept a Calhoun man ;
but a few of them, naturally angry at South Carolina dictation, refused, under Benton's advice, to
vote for him.  At last the Whigs joined the Calhoun men, and ended this extraordinary contest.
The speaker, Robert M. T. Hunter, was a so-called
states-rights man, and a supporter of the independent treasury scheme.  He had the fortune, after a
singularly varied and even important career in the
United States and the Confederate States, to be
appointed by President Cleveland to the petty
place of collector of customs at Tappahannock, in
Virginia, and to live among Americans who were
familiar with his prominence fifty years ago, but
supposed him long since dead.  The clerk, Hugh
A. Garland, was reëlected, in spite of what Adams
in his diary, after his picturesque but utterly

unjustifiable fashion, called the "baseness of his treachery to his trust." The Whig New Jerseymen were refused seats, and the apparent perversion of the popular vote was rightly defeated by seating their rivals. The Whigs posed as defenders of the sanctity of state authority, and sought, upon that political issue, to force the Van Buren men to be the apologists for centralization.

It was at this session that the sub-treasury bill was passed. As a sort of new declaration of independence Van Buren signed it on July 4, 1840. His long and honorable and his greatest battle was won. It was the triumph of a really great cause. The people, by their labor and capital, were to support the federal government as a mere agency for limited purposes. That government was not, in this way at least, to support or direct or control either the people or their labor or capital. But the captain fell at the time of his victory. The financial disaster of 1839 had exhausted the good-nature and patience of the people. Dissertations on finance and economics, however wise, now served to irritate and disgust. These cool admonitions to economy and a minding of one's business were popularly believed to be heartless and repulsive.

In 1840 took place the most extraordinary of presidential campaigns. While Congress was wrangling over the New Jersey episode in December, 1839, the Whig national convention again nominated Harrison for President. Tyler was taken from the ranks of seceding Democrats as the can-

didate for Vice-President. The slaughter of Henry
Clay, the father of the Whig party, had been
effected by the now formidable Whig politicians
of New York, cunningly marshaled by Thurlow
Weed. Availability had its first complete triumph
in our national politics. They had not come, Governor Barbour of Virginia, the president of the
Whig convention, said, to whine after the flesh-
pots of Egypt, but to give perpetuity to Republican
institutions. To reach this end (not very explicitly
or intelligibly defined), it mattered not what letters
of the alphabet spelled the name of the candidate;
for his part, he could sing Hosanna to any alpha-
betical combination. No platform or declaration
of principles was adopted, lest some of those dis-
contented with Van Buren should find there a
counter-irritant. The candidates, in accepting their
nominations, refrained from political discussion.
Harrison stood for the plain, honest citizen, coming, as one of the New York conventions said,
"like another Cincinnatus from his plough," resolute for a generous administration, and ready to
diffuse prosperity and to end hard times. Tyler,
formerly a strict constructionist member of the
Jackson party, was nominated to catch votes, in
spite of his perfectly well known opposition to the
whole Whig theory of government.

The Democratic, or Democratic-Republican, convention met at Baltimore on May 5, 1840. The
party name was now definitely and exclusively
adopted. Among the delegates were men long

afterwards famous in the later Republican party, John A. Dix, Hannibal Hamlin, Simon Cameron. There was an air of despondency about the convention, for the enthusiasm over "log cabin and hard cider" was already abroad. But the convention without wavering announced its belief in a limited federal power, in the separation of public moneys from banking institutions; and its opposition to internal improvements by the nation, to the federal assumption of state debts, to the fostering of one industry so as to injure another, to raising more money than was required for necessary expenses of government, and to a national bank. Slavery now took for a long time its place in the party platform. The convention declared the constitutional inability of Congress to interfere with slavery in the States, and that all efforts of abolitionists to induce Congress to interfere with slavery were alarming and dangerous to the Union. An elaborate address to the people was issued. It began with a clear, and for a political campaign a reasonably moderate, defense of Van Buren's administration; it renewed the well-worn arguments for the limited activity of government; it made a silly assertion that Harrison was a Federalist, and an insinuation that the glory of his military career was doubtful; it denounced the abolitionists, whose fanaticism it charged the Whigs with enlisting in their cause. In closing, it recalled the Democratic revolution of 1800 which broke the "iron rod of Federal rule," and contrasted the "costly and

stately pageants addressed merely to the senses "
by the Whigs with the truth and reason of the
Democracy.

During the canvass Van Buren submitted to
frequent interrogation. In a fashion that would
seem fatal to a modern candidate, he wrote to
political friends and enemies alike, letter after letter, restating his political opinions. Especially
was it sought to arouse Southern distrust of him.
He was accused, with fire-eating anger, of having
approved a sentence of a court-martial against a
naval lieutenant which was based upon the testimony of negroes. He reiterated what he had
already said upon slavery ; but late in the canvass
he went one step further. When asked his opinion
as to the treatment by Congress of the abolition
petitions, he replied, justly enough, that the President could have no concern with that matter ; but
lest he should be charged with " non-committalism," he declared that Congress was fully justified
in adopting the " gag " rule. For years the petitions had been received and referred. On one
occasion in each House the subject had been considered upon a report of a committee, and decided
against the petitioners with almost entire unanimity. The rule had been adopted only after it
was clear that the petitioners simply sought to
make Congress an instrument of an agitation which
might lead to a dissolution of the Union. It was
thus that Van Buren made his extreme concession to the slavocracy. And there was obvious a

material excuse. No president while in office could approve the perversion of legislative procedure from the making of laws to be a mere stimulant of moral excitement. To encourage or justify petitions intended to inflame public sentiment against a wrong might be legitimate for some men, however well they knew, as Adams said he knew, that the body addressed ought not to grant the petitioners' prayers. Such a course might be noble and praiseworthy for a private citizen, or possibly for a member of Congress representing the exalted moral sentiment of a single district. It would be highly illegitimate for a man holding a great public office, and there representing the entire people and its established system of laws. John Quincy Adams, under his sense of duty as president, had in 1828 pressed the humiliating claim that England should surrender American slaves escaped to English freedom; and there is little reason to doubt that, if he had remained in the field of responsible and executive public life, he would have agreed with Van Buren in his treatment of the matter of the abolition petitions, or rather in his expressions from the White House about them.

Harrison hastened to clear his skirts of abolitionism. Congress could not, he declared, abolish slavery in the District of Columbia without the consent of Virginia and Maryland and of the District itself. For, as he argued, ignobly applying, as well as misquoting, the American words solemnly lauded by Lord Chatham in his speech on Quartering Soldiers in Boston, "what a man has honestly acquired is absolutely his own, which he may freely give, but which cannot be taken from him without his consent." He denounced as a slander the charge that he was an abolitionist, or that the vote he had given against anti-slavery restriction in Missouri had violated his conscience. He declared for the right of petition, which indeed nobody disputed ; but he did not say what course should be taken with the anti-slavery petitions, which was the real question to be answered. The discussion by the citizens of the free States of slavery in the slave States was not, he said, "sanctioned by the Constitution." "Methinks," he said at Dayton, "I hear a soft voice asking, Are you in favor of paper money? I am;" and to that there were "shouts of applause."

In no presidential canvass in America has there been, as Mr. Schurz well says in his life of Henry Clay, "more enthusiasm and less thought" than in the Whig canvass of 1840. The people were rushing as from a long restraint. Wise saws about the duties of government had become nauseating. A plain every-day man administering a paternal and affectionate government was the ruling text, while Tyler and his strict construction quietly served their turn with some of the doctrinaires at the South. The nation, Clay said, was "like the ocean when convulsed by some terrible storm." There was what he called a "rabid appetite for public discussions."

Webster's campaign speeches probably marked
the height of the splendid and effectual flood of
eloquence now poured over the land. The breeze
of popular excitement, he said, with satisfactory
magniloquence, was flowing everywhere; it fanned
the air in Alabama and the Carolinas; and cross-
ing the Potomac and the Alleghanies, to mingle
with the gales of the Empire State and the mountain blasts of New England, would blow a perfect
hurricane. "Every breeze," he declared, "says
change; the cry, the universal cry, is for a change."
He had not, indeed, been born in a log cabin, but
his elder brothers and sisters had; he wept to
think of those who had left it; and if he failed in
affectionate veneration for him who raised it, then
might his name and the name of his posterity be
blotted from the memory of mankind. He touched
the bank question lightly; he denounced the sub-
treasury as "the first in a new series of ruthless
experiments," and declared that Van Buren's
"abandonment of the currency" was fatal. Forgetting who had supported and who had opposed
the continued distribution of surplus revenues
among the States, he condemned the President
for the low state of the treasury; and notwithstanding it declared his approval of a generous
policy of internal improvements. He would not
accuse the President of seeking to play the part of
Cæsar or Cromwell because Mr. Poinsett, his secretary of war, had recommended a federal organization of militia, the necessity or convenience of

which, it was supposed, had been demonstrated by
the Canadian troubles; but the plan, he said, was
expensive, unconstitutional, and dangerous to our
liberties. He was careful to say nothing of slavery
or the right of petition. Only in brief and casual
sentences did he even touch the charges that Van
Buren had treated political contests as " rightfully
struggles for office and emolument," and that federal officers had been assessed in proportion to
their salaries for partisan purposes. The President
was pictured as full of cynical and selfish disregard of the people; he had disparaged the credit
of the States; he had accused Madison, and, monstrous sacrilege, even Washington, of corruption.
" I may forgive this," Webster slowly said to the
appalled audience, " but I shall not forget it; "
such " abominable violations of the truth of history " filled his bosom with " burning scorn."
This was a highly imaginative allusion to Van
Buren's statement that the national bank had been
originally devised by the friends of privileged
orders. Nor need the South, even Webster intimated, have any fear of the Whigs about slavery.
Could the South believe that Harrison would " lay
ruthless hands on the institutions among which he
was born and educated? " No, indeed, for Washington and Hancock, Virginia and Massachusetts,
had joined their thoughts, their hopes, their feelings. " How many bones of Northern men," he
asked with majestic pathos, " lie at Yorktown? "
Senator Rives, now one of the Conservatives, said

that Van Buren was indeed "mild, smooth, affable, smiling;" but humility was "young and old ambition's ladder." The militia project meant military usurpation. Look at Cromwell, he said; look at Bonaparte. Were their usurpations not in the name of the people? Preston of South Carolina said that Van Buren had advocated diminished wages to others; now he should himself receive diminished wages. Harrison was, he said "a Southern man with Southern principles." As for Van Buren, this "Northern man with Southern principles," did he not come "from beyond the Hudson," had he not been "a friend of Rufus King, a Missouri restrictionist, a friend and advocate of free negro suffrage?" Clay said that it was no time "to argue;" a rule his party for the moment well observed. The nation had already pronounced upon the ravages Van Buren had brought upon the land, the general and widespread ruin, the broken hopes. With the mere fact of Harrison's election, "without reference to the measures of his administration," he told the Virginians at Hanover, "confidence will immediately revive, credit be restored, active business will return, prices of products will rise; and the people will feel and know that, instead of their servants being occupied in devising measures for their ruin and destruction, they will be assiduously employed in promoting their welfare and prosperity."

All this was far more glorious than the brutally

true advice of the old man with a broad-axe on his
shoulders, whom the Democrats quoted. When
asked what was to become of everybody in the
heavy distress of the panic, he answered, "Damn
the panic! If you would all work as I do, you
would have no panic." The people no longer
cared about "the interested few who desire to en-
rich themselves by the use of public money." If,
as the Democrats said, the interested few had been
thwarted, an almost universal poverty had for
some reason or other come with their defeat.
Perhaps the reflecting citizen thought that he
might become, if he were not already, one of the
"interested few." Nor was the demagogy all on
the side of the Whigs, although they enjoyed the
more popular quality of the quadrennial product.
Van Buren himself, in the futile fashion of aging
parties which suppose that their ancient victories
still stir the popular heart, recalled "the reign of
terror" of the elder Adams, and how the "Samson
of Democracy burst the cords which were already
bound around its limbs," how "a web more art-
fully contrived, composed of a high protective
tariff, a system of internal improvements, and a
national bank, was then twined around the sleeping giant" until he was "roused by the warning
voice of the honest and intrepid Jackson." Harrison's own numerous speeches were awkward and
indefinite enough; but still they showed an honest and sincere man, and in the enthusiasm of the
day they did him no harm.

The revolts against the severe party discipline of the Democracy, aided by the popular distress, were serious. Calhoun, indeed, had returned; but all his supporters did not return with him. The Southern defection headed by White in 1836 was still most formidable, and was now reënforced by the Conservative secession North and South. Even Major Eaton forgot Van Buren's gallantry ten years before, and joined the enemy. The talk of " spoils " was amply justified; but the abuses of patronage had not prevented Jackson's popularity, and under Van Buren they were far less serious. This cry did not yet touch the American people. The most serious danger of " spoils " still lay in the future. Patronage abuses had injured the efficiency of the public service, but they had not yet begun to defeat the popular will. Jackson came resolutely to Van Buren's aid in the fashionable letter-writing. " The Rives Conservatives, the Abolitionists and Federalists " had combined, the ex-President vivaciously said, to obtain power " by falsehood and slander of the basest kind ; " but the " virtue of the people," he declared in what from other lips would have seemed cant, would defeat " the money power." Van Buren's firmness and ability entitled him, he thought, to a rank not inferior to Jefferson or Madison, while he rather unhandsomely added that he had never admired Harrison as a military man.

The Whig campaign was highly picturesque. Meetings were measured by " acres of men."

They gathered on the field of Tippecanoe. Revolutionary soldiers marched in venerable processions. Wives and daughters came with their husbands and fathers. There were the barrel of cider, the coon-skins, and the log cabin with the live raccoon running over it and the latch-string hung out; for Harrison had told his soldiers when he left them, that never should his door be shut, "or the string of the latch pulled in." Van Buren meantime, with an aristocratic sneer upon his face, was seated in an English carriage, after feeding himself from the famous gold spoons bought for the White House. Harrison was a hunter who had caught a fox before and would again; one of the county processions from Pennsylvania boasted, "Old Mother Cumberland — she'll bag the fox." Illinois would "teach the palace slaves to respect the log cabin." "Down with the wages, say the administration." "Matty's policy, fifty cents a day and French soup; our policy, two dollars a day and roastbeef." Newspapers were full of advertisements like this: "The subscriber will pay $5 a hundred for pork if Harrison is elected, and $2.50 if Van Buren is."

But the songs were most interesting. The ball, which Benton had said in his last speech on the expunging resolution that he "solitary and alone" had put in motion, was a mine of similes. They sang:

> "With heart and soul
> This ball we roll."

> "As rolls the ball,
> Van's reign does fall,
> And he may look
> To Kinderhook."

> "The gathering ball is rolling still,
> And still gathering as it rolls."

Harrison's battle with the Indians gave the effective cry of "Tippecanoe and Tyler too." And so they sang:

> "Farewell, dear Van,
> You're not our man;
> To guard the ship,
> We'll try old Tip."

> "With Tip and Tyler
> We'll burst Van's biler."

> "Old Tip he wears a homespun suit,
> He has no ruffled shirt — wirt — wirt;
> But Mat he has the golden plate,
> And he's a little squirt — wirt — wirt."

When the election returns began to come from the August and September States, the joyful excitement passed all bounds. Then the new Whigs found a new Lilliburlero. To the tune of the "Little Pig's Tail" they sang:

> "What has caused this great commotion, motion, motion,
> Our country through?
> It is the ball a-rolling on,
> For Tippecanoe and Tyler too, Tippecanoe and Tyler too!

> "And with them we'll beat little Van, Van;
> Van is a used-up man.
> Oh, have you heard the news from Maine, Maine, Maine,
> All honest and true?
> One thousand for Kent and seven thousand gain
> For Tippecanoe," etc.

And then Joe Hoxie would close the meetings
by singing " Up Salt River."

The result was pretty plain before November.
New Hampshire, Connecticut, Rhode Island, and
Virginia voted for state officers in the spring.   All
had voted for Van Buren in 1836 ; all now gave
Whig majorities, except New Hampshire, where
the Democratic majority was greatly reduced.   In
August North Carolina was added to the Whig
column, though in Missouri and Illinois there was
little change.   But when in September Maine,
which had given Van Buren nearly eight thousand
majority, and had since remained steadfast, " went
hell-bent for Governor Kent " and gave a slight
Whig majority, the administration's doom was
sealed.

Harrison received 234 electoral votes, and Van
Buren 60.   New York gave Harrison 13,300 votes
more than Van Buren ; but a large part of this
plurality, perhaps all, came from the counties on
the northern and western borders.   Only one
Northern State, Illinois, voted for Van Buren.   Of
the slave States, five, Virginia, South Carolina,
Alabama, Missouri, and Arkansas, were for Van
Buren ; the other eight for Harrison.   There was
a popular majority in the slave States of about
55,000 against Van Buren in a total vote of about
695,000, and in the free States, of about 90,000 in
a total vote of about 1,700,000, still showing, therefore, his greater popular strength in the free States.
The increase in the popular vote was the most

extraordinary the country has ever known, proving
the depth and universality of the feeling. This
vote had been about 1,500,000 in 1836; it reached
about 2,400,000 in 1840, an increase of 900,000,
while from 1840 to the Clay canvass of 1844 it
increased only 300,000. Van Buren, as a defeated
candidate in 1840, received about 350,000 votes
more than elected him in 1836; and the growth of
population in the four years was probably less, not
greater, than usual. There were cries of "fraud
and corruption" because of this enormously increased vote, cries which Benton long afterwards
seriously heeded; but there seems to be no good
reason to treat them otherwise than as one of the
many expressions of Democratic anguish.

Van Buren received the seemingly crushing defeat with dignity and composure. While the cries
of "Van, Van, he's a used-up man," were coming
with some of the sting of truth through the White
House windows, he prepared the final message with
which he met Congress in December, 1840. The
year, he said, had been one of "health, plenty,
and peace." Again he declared the dangers of a
national debt, and the equal dangers of too much
money in the treasury; for "practical economy in
the management of public affairs," he said, "can
have no adverse influence to contend with more
powerful than a large surplus revenue." Again
he attacked the national bank scheme. During
four years of the greatest pecuniary embarrassments ever known in time of peace, with a decreas-

ing public revenue, with a formidable opposition, his administration had been able punctually to meet every obligation without a bank, without a permanent national debt, and without incurring any liability which the ordinary resources of the government would not speedily discharge. If the public service had been thus independently sustained without either of these fruitful sources of discord, had we not a right to expect that this policy would " receive the final sanction of a people whose unbiased and fairly elicited judgment upon public affairs is never ultimately wrong?" Again with a clear emphasis he declared against any attempt of the government to repair private losses sustained in private business, either by direct appropriations or by legislation designed to secure exclusive privileges to individuals or classes. In the very last words of this, his last message, he gave an account of his efforts to suppress the slave trade, and to prevent " the prostitution of the American flag to this inhuman purpose," asking Congress, by a prohibition of the American trade which took supplies to the slave factories on the African coast, to break up " those dens of iniquity."

The short session of Congress was hardly more than a jubilee of the Whigs, happily ignorant of the complete chagrin and frustration of their hopes which a few months would bring. Some new bank suspensions occurred in Philadelphia, and among banks closely connected with that city. The Bank of the United States, after a resumption for twenty days, succumbed amid its own loud protestations of solvency, its final disgrace and ruin being, however, deferred a little longer.

Van Buren's cabinet had somewhat changed since his inauguration. In 1838 his old friend and ally, and one of the chief champions of his policy, Benjamin F. Butler, resigned the office of attorney-general, but without any break political or personal, as was seen in his fine and arduous labors in the canvass of 1840 and in the Democratic convention of 1844. Felix Grundy of Tennessee then held the place until late in 1839, when he resigned. Van Buren offered it, though without much heartiness, to James Buchanan, who preferred, however, to retain his seat in the Senate; and Henry D. Gilpin, another Pennsylvanian, was appointed. Amos Kendall's enormous industry and singular equipment of doctrinaire convictions, narrow prejudices, executive ability, and practical political skill and craft, were lost to the administration through the failure of his health in the midst of the campaign of 1840. In an address to the public he gave a curious proof that for him work was more wearing in public than in private service. He stated that as he was poor he should resort to private employment suitable to his health; and that he proposed, therefore, during the canvass to write for the "Globe" in defense of the President, in whose integrity, principles, and firmness his confidence, he said, had increased. In 1838, when his health had threatened to be unequal to his work, Van Buren had offered him the mission to Spain, if it should become vacant. John M. Niles, formerly a Democratic senator from Connecticut, took Kendall's place in the post-office.

Van Buren welcomed Harrison to the White House, and before the inauguration entertained him there as a guest, with the easy and dignified courtesy so natural to him, and in marked contrast to the absence of social amenities on either side at the great change twelve years before. Under Van Buren indeed the executive mansion was administered with elevated grace. There was about it, while he was its master, the unostentatious elegance suited to the dwelling of the chief magistrate of the great republic. There were many flings at him for his great economy, and what was called his parsimony ; but he was accused as well of undemocratic luxury. The talk seemed never to end over the gold spoons. The contradictory charges point out the truth. Van Buren was an eminently prudent man. He did not indulge in the careless and useless waste which impoverished Jefferson and Jackson. By sensible and honorable economy he is said to have saved one half of the salary of $25,000 a year then paid to the President.[1] Returning to private life, he was spared the humiliation of pecuniary trouble, which had dis-

[1] It should be remembered that several great expenses of the White House were then and are now met by special and additional appropriations.

tressed three at least of his predecessors. But
with his exquisite sense of propriety, he had not
failed to order the White House with fitting decorum and a modest state. His son Abraham
Van Buren was his private secretary ; and after
the latter's marriage, in November, 1838, to Miss
Singleton of South Carolina, a niece of Andrew
Stevenson, and a relation of Mrs. Madison, he and
his wife formed the presidential family. In 1841
they accompanied the ex-President to his retirement at Lindenwald.

Under Andrew Jackson the social air of the
White House had suffered from his ill-health and
the bitterness of his partisanship ; and in this respect the change to his successor was most pleasing. Van Buren used an agreeable tact with even
his strongest opponents ; and about his levees and
receptions there were a charm and a grace by no
means usual in the dwellings of American public
men. He had, we are told in the Recollections of
Sargent, a political adversary of his, " the high
art of blending dignity with ease and gravity."
He introduced the custom of dining with the heads
of departments and foreign ministers, although
with that exception he observed the etiquette of
never being the guest of others at Washington.
Judge Story mentions the " splendid dinner " given
by the President to the judges in January, 1839.

John Quincy Adams's diary bears unintended
testimony to Van Buren's admirable personal bearing in office. From the time he reached Washing-

ton as secretary of state, he had treated Adams in
his defeat with marked distinction and deference,
which Adams, as he records, accepted in his own
house, in the White House, and elsewhere. At a
social party the President, he said, " was, as usual,
courteous to all, and particularly to me." Van
Buren had therefore every reason to suppose that
there was between himself and Adams a not unfriendly personal esteem. But Adams, in his churl-
ish, bitter temper, apparently found in these wise
and generous civilities only evidence of a mean
spirit. After one visit at the White House during
the height of the crisis of 1837, he recorded that
he found Van Buren looking, not wretched, as he
had been told, but composed and tranquil. Returning home from this observation of the President's
" calmness, his gentleness of manner, his easy and
conciliatory temper," this often unmannerly pen
described besides " his obsequiousness, his sycophancy, his profound dissimulation and duplicity,
. . . his fawning civility." In a passage which
was remarkable in that time of political bitterness
so largely personal, Clay said, in his parliamentary
duel with Calhoun, after the latter rejoined the
Democratic party, that he remembered Calhoun
attributing to the President the qualities of " the
most crafty, most skulking, and the meanest of the
quadruped tribe." Saying that he had not shared
Calhoun's opinion, he then added of Van Buren : —

" I have always found him in his manner and deport-
ment, civil, courteous, and gentlemanly; and he dis-

penses in the noble mansion which he now occupies, one worthy the residence of the chief magistrate of a great people, a generous and liberal hospitality. An acquaintance with him of more than twenty years' duration has inspired me with a respect for the man, although I regret to be compelled to say, I detest the magistrate."

# CHAPTER XI

VAN BUREN loitered at Washington a few days after his presidency was over, and on his way home stopped at Baltimore, Philadelphia, and New York. At New York he was finely welcomed. Amid great crowds he was taken to the City Hall in a procession headed by Captain Brown's corps of lancers and a body of armed firemen. He reached Kinderhook on May 15, 1841, there to make his home until his death. He had, after the seemly and pleasing fashion of many men in American public life, lately purchased, near this village among the hills of Columbia county, the residence of William P. Van Ness, where Irving had thirty years before lived in seclusion after the death of his betrothed, and had put the last touches to his Knickerbocker. It was an old estate, whose lands had been rented for twenty years and under culti- vation for a hundred and sixty, and from which Van Buren now managed to secure a profit. To this seat he gave the name of Lindenwald, a name which in secret he probably hoped the American

people would come to group with Monticello, Mont-
pellier, and the Hermitage. But this could not be.
Van Buren had served but half the presidential
term of honor. He was not a sage, but still a candidate for the presidency. Before the electoral
votes were counted in 1841, Benton declared for
his renomination in 1844: and until the latter
year he again held the interesting and powerful
but critical place of the probable candidate of his
party for the presidency. He remained easily the
chief figure in the Democratic ranks. His defeat
had not taken from him that honor which is the
property of the statesman standing for a cause
whose righteousness and promise belong to the
assured future. His defeat signified no personal,
no political fault. It had come to him from a widespread convulsion for which, perhaps less than any
great American of his time, he was responsible.
His party could not abandon its battle for a limited
and non-paternal government and against the use
of public moneys by private persons. It could
not therefore abandon him; for more than any
other man who had not now finally retired he
represented these causes in his own person. But
his easy composure of manner did not altogether
hide that eating and restless anxiety which so often
attends the supreme ambition of the American.

Two days after leaving the White House, Van
Buren said, in reply to complimentary resolutions
of the legislature of Missouri, that he did not utterly lament the bitter attacks upon him; for expe-

rience had taught him that few political men were praised by their foes until they were about abandoning their friends. With a pleasing frankness he admitted that to be worthy of the presidency and to reach it had been the object of his " most earnest desire ; " but he said that the selection of the next Democratic candidate must be decided by its probable effect upon the principles for which they had just fought, and not upon any supposition that he had been wounded or embittered by his defeat in their defense. His description of a candidate meant himself, however, and rightly enough. In November, 1841, he wrote of the "apparent success of last year's buffoonery ; " and intimated that, though he would take no step to be a candidate, it was not true that he had said he should decline a nomination.

Early in 1842, the ex-President made a trip through the South, in company with James K. Paulding, visiting on his return Clay at Ashland, and Jackson at the Hermitage. He was one of the very few men on personally friendly terms with both those long-time enemies. At Ashland, doubtless, Texas was talked over, even if a bargain were not made, as has been fancied, that Clay and Van Buren should remove the troublesome question from politics. In a fashion very different from that of modern candidates, he now wrote, from time to time, able, long, and explicit, but somewhat tedious letters on political questions. In one of them he touched protection more clearly than ever before.

He favored, he said in February, 1843, a tariff for revenue only; the "incidental protection" which that must give many American manufacturers was all the protection which should be permitted; the mechanics and laborers had been the chief sufferers from a "high protective tariff." He was at last and definitely "a low tariff man." He declared that he should support the Democratic candidate of 1844; for he believed it to be impossible that a selection from that source should not accord with his views. He did not perhaps realize to how extreme a test his sincerity would be put. He added words which four years later read strangely enough. "My name and pretensions," he said, "however subordinate in importance, shall never be at the disposal of any person whatever, for the purpose of creating distractions or divisions in the Democratic party."

The party was indeed known as the "Van Buren party" until 1844, so nearly universal was the supposition that he was to be renominated, and so plainly was he its leader. The disasters which had now overtaken the Whigs made his return to power seem probable enough. The utterly incongruous elements held together during the sharp discontent and wonderful but inarticulate enthusiasm of 1840 had quickly fallen apart. While on his way to Kinderhook Van Buren was the chief figure in the obsequies at New York of his successful competitor. This honest man, of whom John Quincy Adams said, with his usual savage exagge

ration, that his dull sayings were repeated for wit
and his grave inanity passed off for wisdom, had
already quarreled with the splendid leader whose
place he was too conscious of usurping. Tyler's
accession was the first, but not the last illustration,
which American politicians have had of the danger
of securing the presidency by an award of the
second place to a known opponent of the principles
whose success they seek. Tyler had not before his
nomination concealed his narrow and Democratic
views of government. The Whigs had ostenta-
tiously refused to declare any principles when they
nominated him. In technical conscientiousness he
marched with a step by no means cowardly to un-
honored political isolation, as a quarter of a century
later marched another vice-president nominated by
a party in whose ranks he too was a new recruit.

Upon Tyler's veto of the bill for a national bank,
an outcry of agony went up from the Whigs; the
whole cabinet, except Webster, resigned; a new
cabinet was formed, partly from the Conservatives;
and by 1844, Tyler was a forlorn candidate for the
Democratic nomination, which he claimed for his
support of the annexation of Texas.

Upon this first of the great pro-slavery movements Van Buren was defeated for the Democratic
nomination in 1844, although it seemed assured to
him by every consideration of party loyalty, obligation, and wise foresight. The relations of government to private business ceased to be the dominant
political question a few months and only a few

months too soon to enable Van Buren to complete his eight years. Slavery arose in place of economics.

No mistake is more common in the review of American history than to suppose that slavery was an active or definite force in organized American politics after the Missouri Compromise and before the struggle for the annexation of Texas under Tyler's administration. The appeals of the abolitionists to the simpler and deeper feelings of humanity were indeed at work before 1835; and from that year on they were profoundly stirring the American conscience and storing up tremendous moral energy. But slavery was not in partisan politics. In 1836 and 1840 there was upon slavery no real difference between the utterances of the candidates and other leaders, Whig and Democratic, whether North or South. Van Buren was supported by many abolitionists; the profoundest distrust of him was at the South. Upon no question touching slavery with which the president could have concern, did his opinions or his utterances differ from those of John Quincy Adams. Clay said in November, 1838, that the abolitionists denounced him as a slaveholder and the slaveholders denounced him as an abolitionist, while both united on Van Buren. The charge of truckling to the South, traditionally made against Van Buren, is justified by no utterance or act different from those made by all American public men of distinction at the time, except perhaps in two instances, — his vote as vice-president for Kendall's bill against sending inflammatory abolition circulars through the post-office to States which prohibited their circulation, and his approval of the rules in the Senate and House for tabling or refusing abolition petitions without reading them. But neither of these, as has been shown, was a decisive test. In the first case he met a political trick; and for his vote there was justly much to be said on the reason of the thing, apart from Southern wishes. As late as 1848, Webster, in criticising Van Buren's inconsistency, would say no more of the law than that it was one " of very doubtful propriety; " and declared that he himself should agree to legislation by Congress to protect the South " from incitements to insurrection." In the second case Van Buren's position in public life might of itself properly restrain him from acquiescing in an agitation in Congress for measures which, with all responsible public men, Adams included, he believed Congress ought not to pass.

The Democratic convention was to meet in May, 1844. The delegates had been very generally instructed for Van Buren; and two months before it assembled his nomination seemed beyond doubt. But the slave States were now fired with a barbarous enthusiasm to extend slavery by annexing Texas. To this Van Buren was supposed to be hostile. His Southern opponents, in February, 1843, skillfully procured from Jackson, innocent of the plan, a strong letter in favor of the annexation, to be used, it was said, just before the convention,

"to blow Van out of water." The letter was first
published in March, 1844. Van Buren was at
once put to a crucial test. His administration had
been adverse to annexation; his opinion was still
adverse. But a large, and not improbably a controlling section of his party, aided by Jackson's
wonderful prestige, deemed it the most important
of political causes. Van Buren was, according to
the plan, explicitly asked by a Southern delegate
to state, with distinct reference to the action of
the convention, what were his opinions.

The ex-President deeply desired the nomination;
and the nomination seemed conditioned upon his
surrender. It was at least assured if he now gave
no offense to the South. But he did not flinch.
He resorted to no safe generalizations. His views
upon the annexation were, he admitted, different
from those of many friends, political and personal; but in 1837 his administration after a careful
consideration had decided against annexation of the
State whose independence had lately been recognized by the United States; the situation had not
changed; immediate annexation would place a weapon in the hands of those who looked upon Americans and American institutions with distrustful and
envious eyes, and would do us far more real and
lasting injury than the new territory, however valuable, could repair. He intimated that there was
jobbery in some of the enthusiasm for the annexation. The argument that England might acquire
Texas was without force; when England sought

in Texas more than the usual commercial favors, it would be time for the United States to interfere. He was aware, he said, of the hazard to which he exposed his standing with his Southern fellow-citizens, " of whom it was aptly and appropriately said by one of their own number that ' they are the children of the sun and partake of its warmth.' " But whether we stand or fall, he said, it is always true wisdom as well as true morality to hold fast to the truth.   If to nourish enthusiasm were one of the effects of a genial climate, it seldom failed to give birth to a chivalrous spirit.   To preserve our national escutcheon untarnished had always been the unceasing solicitude of Southern statesmen. The only tempering he gave his refusal was to say that if, after the subject had been fully discussed, a Congress chosen with reference to the question showed the popular will to favor it, he would yield.[1]

[1] I must again complain of the curious though unintended unfairness of Professor Von Holst (*Const. Hist. of the U. S.* 1828–1846, Chicago, 1879, p. 663).  He treats this letter with great contempt.  He assumes indeed that Van Buren's declaration for annexation would have given him the nomination ; and admits that Van Buren declared himself "decidedly opposed to annexation."  After this sufficient proof of courage, for Van Buren could at least have simply promised to adopt the vote of Congress on the main question, it was not very sensible to declare " disgusting " Van Buren's efforts " to creep through the thorny hedge which shut him off from the party nomination."  Professor Von Holst's " disgust " seems particularly directed against the passage here annotated where, after his strong argument against annexation, he declared that he would not be influenced by sectional feeling, and would obey the wishes of a Congress chosen with reference to the question.  Few, I think, will consider this

Van Buren thus closed his letter: "Nor can I in any extremity be induced to cast a shade over the motives of my past life, by changes or conceal-ments of opinions maturely formed upon a great national question, for the unworthy purpose of in-creasing my chances for political promotion."

To a presidential candidate the eve of a national convention is dim with the self-deceiving twilight of sophistry; and the twilight deepens when a ques-tion is put upon which there is a division among those who are, or who may be, his supporters. He can keep silence, he can procure the questioning friend to withdraw the troublesome inquiry; he can ignore the question from an enemy; he can affect an enigmatical dignity. Van Buren did neither of these. His Texas letter was one of the finest and bravest pieces of political courage, and deserves from Americans a long admiration.

The danger of Van Buren's difference with Jack-son it was sought to avert. Butler visited Jackson at the Hermitage, and doubtless showed him for what a sinister end he had been used. Jackson did not withdraw his approval of annexation; but publicly declared his regard for Van Buren to be so great, his confidence in Van Buren's love of country to be so strengthened by long intimacy, that no difference about Texas could change his

promise with reference to such a question, either cowardly or "disgusting," made, as it was, by a candidate for the presidency, of a democratic republic, after clearly and firmly declaring his own views in advance of the congressional elections.

opinions.    Van Buren's nomination was again
widely supposed to be assured.    But the work of
Calhoun and Robert J. Walker had been too well
done.    The convention met at Baltimore on May
27, 1844.    George Bancroft headed the delegation
from Massachusetts.    Before the Rev. Dr. Johns
had "fervently addressed the Throne of Grace"
or the Rev. Mr. McJilton had "read a scrip-
ture lesson," the real contest took place over the
adoption of the rule requiring a two thirds vote
for a nomination.    For it was through this rule
that enough Southern members, chosen before Van
Buren's letter as they had been, were to escape
obedience to their instructions to vote for him.
Robert J. Walker, then a senator from Mississippi,
a man of interesting history and large ability, led
the Southerners.    He quoted the precedent of 1832,
when Van Buren had been nominated for the vice-
presidency under the two thirds rule, and that of
1835, when he had been nominated for the presidency.    These nominations had led to victory.    In
1840 the rule had not been adopted.    Without
this rule, he said amid angry excitement, the party
would yield to those whose motto seemed to be
"rule or ruin."    Butler, Daniel S. Dickinson, and
Marcus Morton led the Northern ranks.    Butler
regretted that any member should condescend to
the allusion to 1840.    That year, he said, had been
a debauchery of the nation's reason amid log cabins,
hard cider, and coon-skins ; and in an ecstasy of
painful excitement at the recollection and amid a

tremendous burst of applause " he leaped from the
floor and stamped . . . as if treading beneath his
feet the object of his loathing." The true Democratic rule, he continued, required the minority to
submit to the majority. Morton said that under
the majority rule Jefferson had been nominated;
that rule had governed state, county, and township
conventions. Butler admitted that under the rule
Van Buren would not be nominated, although a
majority of the convention was known to be for
him. In 1832 and 1835 the two thirds rule had
prevailed because it was certainly known who would
be nominated; and the rule operated to aid not to
defeat the majority. If the rule were adopted, it
would be by the votes of States which were not
Democratic, and would bring " dismemberment and
final breaking up of the party." Walker laughed
at Butler's " tall vaulting " from the floor; and,
refusing to shrink from the Van Buren issue, he
protested against New York dictation, and warningly said that, if Van Buren were nominated,
Clay would be elected. After the convention had
received with enthusiasm a floral gift from a Democratic lady whom the President declared to be
fairer than the flowers, the vote was taken. The
two thirds rule was adopted by 148 to 118. All
the negatives were Northerners, except 14 from
Missouri, Maryland, and North Carolina. Fifty-
eight true " Northern men with Southern principles " joined ninety Southerners in the affirmative.
It was really a vote on Van Buren, — or rather

upon the annexation of Texas, — or rather still
upon the extension of American slave territory. It
was the first battle, a sort of Bull Run, in the last
and great political campaign between the interests
of slavery and those of freedom.

On the first ballot for the candidate, Van Buren
had 146 votes, 13 more than a majority. If after
the vote on the two thirds rule anything more were
required to show that some of these votes were
given in mere formal obedience to instructions, the
second ballot brought the proof. Van Buren then
sank to 127, less than a majority; and on the
seventh ballot to 99. A motion was made to declare him the nominee as the choice of a majority
of the convention; and there followed a scene of
fury, the President bawling for order amid savage
taunts between North and South, and bitter denunciations of the treachery of some of those who
had pledged themselves for Van Buren. Samuel
Young of New York declared the "abominable
Texas question" to be the fire-brand thrown among
them by the "mongrel administration at Washington," whose hero was now doubtless fiddling while
Rome was burning. Nero seems to have been Calhoun, though between the god-like young devil of
antiquity wreathed with sensual frenzy and infamy,
and the solemn, even saturnine figure of the great
modern advocate of human slavery, the likeness
seemed rather slight. The motion was declared
out of order; and the name of James K. Polk was
presented as that of "a pure whole-hogged Demo-

crat." On the eighth ballot he had 44 votes. Then
followed the magnanimous scene of "union and
harmony" which has so often, after a conflict,
charmed a political body into unworthy surrender.
The great delegation from New York retired during
the ninth balloting; and returned to a convention
profoundly silent but thrilling with that bastard
sense of coming glory in which a lately tumultuous
and quarreling body waits the solution of its difficulties already known to be reached but not yet
declared. Butler quoted a letter which Van Buren
had given him authorizing the withdrawal of his
name if it were necessary for harmony; he eulo-
gized Polk as a strict constructionist, and closed
by reading a letter from Jackson fervently urging
Van Buren's nomination. Daniel S. Dickinson
said that "he loved this convention because it had
acted so like the masses," and cast New York's 35
votes for Polk. The latter's nomination was declared with the utmost joy, and sent to Washington over Morse's first telegraph line, just completed.
Silas Wright of New York, Van Buren's strong
friend and a known opponent of annexation, was,
in the fashion since followed, nominated for the
vice-presidency, to soothe the feelings and the conscience of the defeated. Wright peremptorily tele-
graphed his refusal. He told his friends that he
did "not choose to ride behind on the black pony."
George M. Dallas of Pennsylvania took his place.

The Democratic party now threw away all
advantage of the issue made by the undeserved

defeat four years before. Thirty-six years later it repeated the blunder in discarding Van Buren's famous neighbor and disciple. Polk's was the first nomination by the party of a man of the second or of even a lower rank. Polk was known to have ability inferior not only to that of Van Buren and Calhoun, but to Cass, Buchanan, Wright, and others. He was the first presidential "dark horse," and indeed hardly that. His own State of Tennessee had, by resolution, presented him as its choice for vice-president with Van Buren in the first place. He had been speaker of the national House, and later, governor of his State; but since holding these places had been twice defeated for governor. In accepting the nomination he declared, with an apparent fling at Van Buren, that, if elected, he should not accept a renomination, and should thus enable the party in 1848 to make " a free selection."

The nomination aroused disgust enough. "Polk! Great God, what a nomination!" Letcher, the Whig governor of Kentucky, wrote to Buchanan. But the experiment of 1840 with the Whigs had been disastrous; the people had swung back to the strict doctrines of the Democracy. Van Buren faithfully kept his promise to support the nomination; under his urgency Wright finally accepted the nomination for governor of New York. And by the vote of New York Henry Clay was defeated by a man vastly his inferior. Polk had 5000 plurality in that State; but Wright had

10,000. Had not James G. Birney, the abolitionist candidate who polled there 15,812 votes, been in the field, not even Van Buren's party loyalty would have prevented Clay's election. Van Buren's friends saved the State; but in doing so voted for annexation. In April, 1844, Clay had written a letter against annexation. As it appeared within a few days of Van Buren's letter, and as the personal relations between the two great party leaders were most friendly, some have inferred an arrangement between them to take the question out of politics. This would indeed have been an extraordinary occurrence. One might well wish to have overheard a negotiation between two rivals for the presidency to exclude a great question distasteful to both. After the Democratic convention, Tyler's treaty of annexation was rejected in the Senate by 35 to 16, six Democrats from the North, among them Wright of New York .and Benton of Missouri, voting against it. During the campaign Clay had weakly abandoned even the mild emphasis of his first opposition, and by flings at the abolitionists had openly bid for the pro-slavery vote; thus perhaps losing enough votes in New York to Birney to defeat him. After the election the current for annexation seemed too strong; and a resolution passed both Houses authorizing the admission of Texas as a State. The resolution provided for the formation of four additional States out of Texas. In any such additional State formed north of the

Missouri compromise line, slavery was to be prohibited; but in those south of it slavery was to be
permitted or prohibited as the inhabitants might
choose.

Slavery was now clearly before the political
conscience of the nation. Van Buren was the
conspicuous victim of the first encounter. The
Baltimore convention had in its platform compli-
mented "their illustrious fellow-citizen," "his inflexible fidelity to the Constitution," his "ability,
integrity, and firmness," and had tendered to him,
"in honorable retirement," the assurance of the
deeply-seated "confidence, affection, and respect
of the American Democracy." This sentence to
"honorable retirement" Van Buren, who was
only in his sixty-second year and in the amplitude
of his natural powers, received with outward complacency. On the eve of the election he pointed
out, probably referring to Cass, that the hostility
to him had not been in the interest of Polk, and
warmly said that, unless the Democratic creed
were a delusion, personal feelings ought to be
turned to nothing. Van Buren was, however,
profoundly affected by what he deemed the undeserved Southern hostility to himself. For he hardly
yet appreciated that his defeat was politically legitimate, and not the result of political treachery or
envy. Between him and the Southern politicians
had opened a true and deep division over the
greatest single question in American politics since
Jefferson's election.

With Polk's accession and the Mexican war, the schism in the Democratic ranks over the extension of American slave territory became plainer. Even during the canvass of 1844 a circular had been issued by William Cullen Bryant, David Dudley Field, John W. Edmonds, and other Van Buren men, supporting Polk, but urging the choice of congressmen opposed to annexation. Early in the new administration the division of New York Democrats into "Barnburners" and "Old Hunkers" appeared. The former were the strong pro-Van Buren, anti-Texas men, or "radical Democrats," who were likened to the farmer who burned his barn to clear it of rats. The latter were the "Northern men with Southern principles," the supporters of annexation, and the respectable, dull men of easy consciences, who were said to hanker after the offices. The Barnburners were led by men of really eminent ability and exalted character : Silas Wright, then governor, Benjamin F. Butler, John A. Dix, chosen in 1845 to the United States Senate, Azariah C. Flagg, the famous comptroller, and John Van Buren, the ex-President's son, and a singularly picturesque figure in politics, who was, in 1845, made attorney-general by the legislature. He had been familiarly called "Prince John" since his travels abroad during his father's presidency. Daniel S. Dickinson and William L. Marcy were the chief figures in the Hunker ranks. Polk seemed inclined, at the beginning, to favor or at least to placate, the Barnburners. He offered the Treasury to Wright, though he is said to have known that Wright could not leave the governorship. He offered Butler the War Department, but the latter's devotion to his profession, for which he had resigned the attorney-general's place in Van Buren's cabinet, made him prefer the freedom of the United States attorneyship at New York, and Marcy was finally given the New York place in the cabinet. Jackson's death in June, 1845, deprived the Van Buren men of the tremendous moral weight which his name carried, and which might have daunted Polk. It perhaps also helped to loosen the weight of party ties on the Van Buren men. After this the schism rapidly grew. In the fall election of 1845 the Barnburners pretty thoroughly controlled the Democratic party of the State in hostility to the Mexican war, which the annexation of Texas had now brought. Samuel J. Tilden of Columbia county, and a profound admirer of Van Buren, became one of their younger leaders.

Now arose the strife over the "Wilmot Proviso," in which was embodied the opposition to the extension of slavery into new Territories. Upon this proviso the modern Republican party was formed eight years later; upon it, fourteen years later, Abraham Lincoln was chosen president; and upon it began the war for the Union, out of whose throes came the vastly grander and unsought beneficence of complete emancipation. David Wilmot was a Democratic member of Congress from Pennsyl-

*Silas Wright*

vania ; in New York he would have been a Barnburner. In 1846 a bill was pending to appropriate
$2,000,000 for use by the President in a purchase
of territory from Mexico as part of a peace. Wilmot proposed an amendment that slavery should
be excluded from any territory so acquired. All
the Democratic members, as well as the Whigs
from New York, and most strongly the Van Buren
or Wright men, supported the proviso. The Democratic legislature approved it by the votes of the
Whigs with the Barnburners and the Soft Hunkers, the latter being Hunkers less friendly to slavery. It passed the House at Washington, but
was rejected by the Senate, not so quickly open to
popular sentiment. In the Democratic convention
of New York, in October, 1846, the " war for the
extension of slavery " was charged by the Barnburners on the Hunkers. The former were victorious, and Silas Wright was renominated for
governor, to be defeated, however, at the election.
Polk, Marcy, and Dickinson, angered at the Democratic opposition in New York to the pro-slavery
Mexican policy, now threw all the weight of federal patronage against the Barnburners, many of
whom believed the administration to have been
responsible for Wright's defeat. Van Buren and
his influence were completely separated from the
national administration. Just before the adjournment of Congress in 1847, the appropriation to
secure territory from Mexico was again proposed.
Again the Wilmot Proviso was added in the

House; again it was rejected in the Senate, to the defeat of the appropriation; and again Barnburners and Whigs carried in the New York legislature a resolution approving it, and directing the New York senators to support it.

The tide was rising. It seemed that Mexican law prohibited slavery in New Mexico and California, and that upon their cession the principles of international law would preserve their condition of freedom. Benton, therefore, deemed the Wilmot Proviso unnecessary; a "thing of nothing in itself, and seized upon to conflagrate the States and dissolve the Union." For the Supreme Court had not then pronounced slavery a necessary accompaniment of American supremacy. But the legal protection of freedom was practically unsubstantial, even if not technical; there could be no doubt of the determination of the South to carry slavery into these Territories, whatever might be the obligations of either municipal or international law; and their conquest, therefore, made imminent a decision of the vital question whether slavery should be still further extended.

At the Democratic convention at Syracuse, in September, 1847, the Hunkers, after a fierce struggle over contested seats, seized control of the body. David Dudley Field, for the Barnburners, proposed a resolution that, although the Democracy of New York would faithfully adhere to the compromises of the Constitution and maintain the reserved rights of the States, they would still declare, since the crisis had come, "their uncompromising hostility to the extension of slavery into territory now free." This was defeated. The Barnburners then seceded, and issued an address, in which Lawrence Van Buren, the ex-President's brother, joined. They protested that the anti-slavery resolution had been defeated by a fraudulent organization of the convention, and called a mass meeting at Herkimer, on October 26, "to avow their principles and consult as to future action." The Herkimer convention was really an important preliminary to the formation of the modern Republican party. It was a gathering of the ex-President's friends. Cambreleng, his old associate, presided; David Wilmot addressed the meeting; and John Van Buren, now very conspicuous in politics, reported the resolutions. In these the fraud at Syracuse was again denounced; a convention was called for Washington's birthday in 1848, to choose Barnburner delegates to contest the seats of those chosen by the Hunkers in the national Democratic convention. It was declared that the freemen of New York would not submit to slavery in the conquered provinces; and that, against the threat of Democrats at the South that they would support no candidate for the presidency who did not assent to the extension of slavery, the Democrats of New York would proclaim their determination to vote for no candidate who did so assent.

It was clear that Van Buren sympathized with all this. Relieved from the constraint of power, there strongly revived his old hostility to slavery; he recalled his vote twenty-eight years before against admitting Missouri otherwise than free. He now perceived how profound had really been the political division between him and the Southern Democrats when, in 1844, he wrote his Texas letter. Ignoring the legitimate character of the politics of Polk's administration in denying official recognition or reward to Barnburners, — legitimate if, as Van Buren had himself pretty uniformly maintained, patronage should go to friends rather than enemies, and if, as was obvious, there had arisen a true political division upon principles, — Van Buren was now touched with anger at the proscription of his friends. Excluded from the power which ought to have belonged to the chief of Democrats enjoying even in "honorable retirement" the "confidence, affection, and respect" of his party, independence rapidly grew less heinous in his eyes. One can hardly doubt that there now more freely welled up in his mind, to clarify its vision, the sense of personal wrong which, since Polk's nomination, had been so long held in magnanimous and dignified restraint, — though of this he was probably unconscious. Van Buren was not insincere when, in October, 1847, he wrote from Lindenwald to an enthusiastic Democratic editor in Pennsylvania, who had hoisted his name to the top of his columns for 1848. Whatever, he said, had been his aspirations in the past, he now had no desire to be President; every day confirmed

him in the political opinions to which he had adhered. Conscious of always having done his duty
to the people to the best of his ability, he had "no
heart burnings to be allayed and no resentments to
be gratified by a restoration of power." Life at
Lindenwald was entirely adapted to his taste ; and
he was (so he wrote, and so doubtless he had forced
himself to think) "sincerely and heartily desirous
to wear the honors and enjoyments of private life
uninterruptedly to the end." If tendered a unanimous Democratic support with the assurance of
the election it would bring, he should not "hesitate
respectfully and gratefully, but decidedly to decline it," adding, however, the proviso so precious
to public men, "consulting only my own feelings
and wishes." It was in the last degree improbable,
he said, — and so it was, — that any emergency
should arise in which this indulgence of his own
preferences would, in the opinion of his true and
faithful friends, conflict with his duty to the party
to which his whole life had been devoted, and to
which he owed any personal sacrifice. The Mexican war had, he said, been so completely sanctioned
by the government that it must be carried through ;
and, he ominously added, the propriety of there-
after instituting inquiries into the necessity of its
occurrence, so as to fix the just responsibility to
public opinion of public servants, was then out of
season. Not a word of praise did he speak of
Polk's administration ; in this he was for once
truly and grimly "non-committal."

In the New York canvass of 1847, the Barnburners, after their secession, " talked of indifferent
matters." The Whigs were therefore completely
successful. In the legislature the Barnburners, or
" Free-soilers " as they began to be called, outnumbered the Hunkers. Dickinson proposed in
the Senate at Washington a resolution, the precur-
sor of Douglas's " squatter sovereignty," — that
all questions concerning the domestic policy of the
Territories should be left to their legislatures to be
chosen by their people. Lewis Cass, now the coming candidate of the South, asserted in December,
1847, the same proposition, pointing out that, if
Congress could abolish the relation of master and
servant in the Territories, it might in like manner
treat the relation of husband and wife. After
this " Nicholson letter " of his, Cass might well
have been asked whether he would have approved
the admission of a State where the last relation
was forbidden, and where concubinage existed as
a " domestic institution." Dickinson's proposal
meant that the first settlers of each Territory should
determine it to freedom or to slavery; it meant
that in admitting new States the nation ought to
be indifferent to their laws on slavery. If slavery
were a mere incident in the polity of the State, a
matter of taste or convenience, the proposition
would have been true enough. But euphemistic
talk about " domestic institutions " blinded none
but theorists or lovers of slavery to the truth that
slavery was a fearful and barbarous power, and

that it must become paramount in any new Southern State, monstrous and corrupting in its tendencies towards savagery, unyielding, wasteful, and
ruinous, — a power whose corruption and savagery,
whose waste and ruin, debauched and enfeebled
all communities closely allied to the States which
maintained it, — a power in whose rapid growth,
in whose affirmative and dictatorial arrogance, and
in the intellectual ability and even the moral ex-
cellences of the aristocracy which administered it
at the South, there was an appalling menace. As
well might one propose the admission to political
intimacy and national unity of a State whose laws
encouraged leprosy or required the funeral obla-
tions of the suttee. If there were already slave
States in the confederacy, it was no less true that
the nation had profoundly suffered from their
slavery. Nor could all the phrases of constitutional lawyers make the slave-block, the black laws,
and all the practices of this barbarism mere local
peculiarities, distasteful perhaps to the North but
not concerning it, peculiarities to be ranked with
laws of descent or judicial procedure. Cass and
Dickinson for their surrender to the South were
now called " dough-faces " and " slavocrats " by
the Democratic Free-soilers. They were the true
" Northern men with Southern principles."

The Barnburners met at Utica on February 16,
an earlier day than that first appointed, John Van
Buren again being the chief figure. The convention praised John A. Dix for supporting the Wil-

mot Proviso; and declared that Benton, a senator from a slave State, but now a sturdy opponent of extending the evil, and long the warm friend and admirer of Van Buren, had "won a proud preëminence among the statesmen of the day." Delegates were chosen to the national convention to oppose the Hunkers. In April, 1848, the Barnburner members of the legislature issued an address, the authors of which were long afterwards disclosed by Samuel J. Tilden to be himself and Martin and John Van Buren. At great length it demonstrated the Free-soil principles of the Democratic fathers.

The national convention assembled in May, 1848. It offered to admit the Barnburner and Hunker delegations together to cast the vote of the State. The Barnburners rejected the compromise as a simple nullification of the vote of the State, and then withdrew. Lewis Cass was nominated for president, the Wilmot Proviso being thus emphatically condemned. For Cass had declared in favor of letting the new Territories themselves decide upon slavery. The Barnburners, returning to a great meeting in the City Hall Park at New York, cried, "The lash has resounded through the halls of the Capitol!" and condemned the cowardice of Northern senators who had voted with the South. Among the letters read was one from Franklin Pierce, who had in 1844 voted against annexation, a letter which years afterwards was, with a reference to his famous friend and biographer, called the "Scarlet Letter." The delegates

issued an address written by Tilden, fearlessly
calling Democrats to independent action. In June
a Barnburner convention met at Utica. Its president, Samuel Young, who had refused at the convention at Baltimore in 1844 to vote for Polk
when the rest of his delegation surrendered, said
that if the convention did its duty, a clap of political thunder would in November "make the
propagandists of slavery shake like Belshazzar."
Butler, John Van Buren, and Preston King, afterwards a Republican senator, were there. David
Dudley Field read an explicit declaration from the
ex-President against the action and the candidates
of the national convention. This letter, whose prolixity is an extreme illustration of Van Buren's
literary fault, created a profound impression. He
declared his "unchangeable determination never
again to be a candidate for public office." The
requirement by the national convention that the
New York delegates should pledge themselves to
vote for any candidate who might be nominated
was, he said, an indignity of the rankest character.
The Virginia delegates had been permitted, without incurring a threat of exclusion, to declare that
they would not support a certain nominee. The
convention had not allowed the Democrats of New
York fair representation, and its acts did not therefore bind them.

The point of political regularity, when discussed
upon a technical basis, was, however, by no means
clear. The real question was whether the surren-

der of the power of Congress over the Territories, and the refusal to use that power to exclude slavery, accorded with Democratic principles. On this Van Buren was most explicit. Jefferson had proposed freedom for the Northwest Territories; and all the representatives from the slaveholding States had voted for the ordinance. Not only Washington and the elder and younger Adams had signed bills imposing freedom as the condition of admitting new Territories or States, but those undoubted Democrats, Jefferson, Madison, Monroe, and Jackson, had signed such bills; and so had he himself in 1838 in the case of Iowa. This power of Congress was part of "the compromises of the Constitution," compromises which, "deeply penetrated" as he had been "by the convictions that slavery was the only subject that could endanger our blessed Union," he had, he was aware, gone further to sustain against Northern attacks than many of his best friends approved. He would go no further. As the national convention had rejected this old doctrine of the Democracy, he should not vote for its candidate, General Cass; and if there were no other candidate but General Taylor, he should not vote for president. If our ancestors, when the opinion and conduct of the world about slavery were very different, had rescued from slavery the territory now making five great States, should we, he asked, in these later days, after the gigantic efforts of Great Britain for freedom, and when nearly all mankind were

convinced of its evils, doom to slavery a territory
from which as many more new States might be
made. He counseled moderation and forbearance,
but still a firm resistance to injustice.

This powerful declaration from the old chief of
the Democracy was decisive with the convention.
Van Buren was nominated for president, and
Henry Dodge, a Democratic senator of Wisconsin,
for vice - president. Dodge, however, declined,
proud though he would be, as he said, to have his
name under other circumstances associated with
Van Buren's. But his State had been represented
in the Baltimore convention ; and as one of its
citizens he cordially concurred in the nomination
of Cass. A national convention was called to
meet at Buffalo on August 9, 1848.

Charles Francis Adams, the son of John Quincy
Adams, presided at the Buffalo convention ; and
in it Joshua R. Giddings, the famous abolitionist,
and Salmon P. Chase were conspicuous. To the
unspeakable horror of every Hunker there participated in the deliberations a negro, the Rev. Mr.
Ward. Butler reported the resolutions in words
whose inspiration is still fresh and ringing. They
were assembled, it was said, " to secure free soil
for a free people ; " the Democratic and Whig
organizations had been dissolved, the one by sti-
fling the voice of a great constituency, the other
by abandoning its principles for mere availability.
Remembering the example of their fathers in the
first declaration of independence, they now, put-

ting their trust in God, planted themselves on the national platform of freedom in opposition to the sectional platform of slavery; they proposed no interference with slavery in any State, but its prohibition in the Territories then free ; for Congress, they said, had " no more power to make a slave than to make a king." There must be no more compromises with slavery. They accepted the issue forced upon them by the slave power; and to its demand for more slave States and more slave Territories, their calm and final answer was, " no more slave States and no more slave territory." At the close were the stirring and memorable words : " We inscribe on our banner, Free Soil, Free Speech, Free Labor, and Free Men ; and under it we will fight on and fight ever, until a triumphant victory shall reward our exertions."

Joshua Leavitt of Massachusetts, one of the " blackest " of abolitionists, reported to the convention the name of Martin Van Buren for president. After the convention was over, even Gerrit Smith, the ultra-abolitionist candidate, declared that, of all the candidates whom there was the least reason to believe the convention would nominate, Van Buren was his preference. The nomination was enthusiastically made by acclamation, after Van Buren had on an informal ballot received 159 votes to 129 cast for John P. Hale. A brief letter from Van Buren was read, declaring that his nomination at Utica had been against his earnest wishes ; that he had yielded because his obligation to the friends, who had now gone so far, required him to abide by their decision that his name was necessary to enable " the ever faithful Democracy of New York to sustain themselves in the extraordinary position into which they have been driven by the injustice of others; " but that the abandonment at Buffalo of his Utica nomination would be most satisfactory to his feelings and wishes. The exclusion of slavery from the Territories was an object, he said, " sacred in the sight of heaven, the accomplishment of which is due to the memories of the great and just men long since, we trust, made perfect in its courts." Charles Francis Adams was nominated for vice-president; and dazzled and incredulous eyes beheld on a presidential ticket with Martin Van Buren the son of one of his oldest and bitterest adversaries. That adversary had died a few months before, the best of his honors being his latest, those won in a querulous but valiant old age, in a fiery fight for freedom.

In September, John A. Dix, then a Democratic senator, accepted the Free-soil nomination for governor of New York. The Democratic party was aghast. The schismatics had suddenly gained great dignity and importance. Martin Van Buren, the venerable leader of the party, its most famous and distinguished member, this courtly, cautious statesman, — could it be he rushing from that " honorable retirement," to whose safe retreat his party had committed him with so deep an affec-

tion, to consort with long-haired and wild-eyed
abolitionists! He was the arch "apostate," leading fiends of disunion who would rather rule in
hell than serve in heaven. Where now was his
boasted loyalty to the party? Rage struggled
with loathing. All the ancient stories told of him
by Whig enemies were revived, and believed by
those who had long treated them with contempt.
It is clear, however, that Van Buren's attitude was
in no wise inconsistent with his record. His party
had never pronounced for the extension of slavery;
nor had he. The Buffalo convention was silent
upon abolition in the District of Columbia. There
was for the time in politics but one question, and
that was born of the annexation of Texas, — Shall
slavery go into free territory? As amid the clash
of arms the laws are stilled, so in the great fight
for human freedom, the independent treasury, the
tariff, and internal improvements could no longer
divide Americans.

The Whigs had in June nominated Taylor, one
of the two heroes of the Mexican war. It is a
curious fact that Taylor had been authoritatively
sounded by the Free-soil leaders as to an acceptance of their nomination. Clay and Webster were
now discarded by their party for this bluff soldier,
a Louisiana slaveholder of unknown politics; and
with entire propriety and perfect caution the Whigs
made no platform. A declaration against the
extension of slavery was voted down. Webster
said at Marshfield, after indignation at Taylor's

nomination had a little worn away, that for "the leader of the Free-*spoil* party" to "become the leader of the Free-soil party would be a joke to shake his sides and mine." The anti-slavery Whigs hesitated for a time; but Seward of New York and Horace Greeley in the New York "Tribune" finally led most of them to Taylor rather than, as Seward said, engage in "guerrilla warfare" under Van Buren. Whigs must not, he added, leave the ranks because of the Whig affront to Clay and Webster. "Is it not," he finely, though for the occasion sophistically, said, "by popular injustice that greatness is burnished?" This launching of the modern Republican party was, strangely enough, to include in New York few besides Democrats. In November, 1847, the Liberty or Abolition party nominated John P. Hale for president; but upon Van Buren's nomination he was withdrawn.

Upon the popular vote in November, 1848, Van Buren received 291,263 votes, while there were 1,220,544 for Cass and 1,360,099 for Taylor. Van Buren had no electoral votes. In no State did he receive as many votes as Taylor; but in New York, Massachusetts, and Vermont he had more than Cass. The vote of New York was an extraordinary tribute to his personal power; he had 120,510 votes to 114,318 for Cass; and it was clear that nearly all the former came from the Democratic party. In Ohio he had 35,354 votes, most of which were probably drawn from the Whig abolitionists.

In Massachusetts he had 38,058 votes, in no small part owing to the early splendor, the moral austerity and elevation of Charles Sumner's eloquence. "It is not," he said, "for the Van Buren of 1838 that we are to vote; but for the Van Buren of to-day, — the veteran statesman, sagacious, determined, experienced, who, at an age when most men are rejoicing to put off their armor, girds himself anew and enters the lists as champion of Freedom." Taylor had 163 electoral votes and Cass 127.

The political career of Van Buren was now ended. It is mere speculation whether he had thought his election a possible thing. That he should think so was very unlikely. Few men had a cooler judgment of political probabilities; few knew better how powerful was party discipline in the Democratic ranks, for no one had done more to create it; few could have appreciated more truly the Whig hatred of himself. Still the wakening rush of moral sentiment was so strong, the bitterness of Van Buren's Ohio and New York supporters had been so great at his defeat in 1844, that it seemed not utterly absurd that those two States might vote for him. If they did, that dream of every third party in America might come true, — the failure of either of the two great parties to obtain a majority in the electoral college, and the consequent choice of president in the House, where each of them might prefer the third party to its greater rival. Ambition to reënter the White

House could indeed have had but the slightest influence with him when he accepted the Free-soil
nomination.    Nor was his acceptance an act of revenge, as has very commonly been said.    The motives of a public man in such a case are subtle and
recondite even to himself.    No distinguished political leader with strong and publicly declared opinions, however exalted his temper, can help uniting
in his mind the cause for which he has fought with
his own political fortunes.    If he be attacked, he
is certain to honestly believe the attack made upon
the cause as well as upon himself.    When his party
drives him from a leadership already occupied by
him, he may submit without a murmur; but he will
surely harbor the belief that his party is playing
false with its principles.    In 1848 there was a great
and new cause for which Van Buren stood, and
upon which his party took the wrong side; but
doubtless his zeal burned somewhat hotter, the edge
of his temper was somewhat keener, for what he
thought the indignities to himself and his immediate political friends.    To say this is simply to
pronounce him human.    His acceptance of the
nomination was given largely out of loyalty to
those friends whose advice was strong and urgent.
It was the mistake which any old leader of a political party, who has enjoyed its honors, makes in
the seeming effort — and every such political candidacy at least seems to be such an effort — to
gratify his personal ambition at its expense.    Van
Buren and his friends should have made another

take the nomination, to which his support, however vigorous, should have gone sorrowfully and reluctantly; and the form as well as the substance of his relations to the canvass should have been without personal interest.

Had Van Buren died just after the election of 1848 his reputation to-day would be far higher. He had stood firmly, he had suffered politically, for a clear, practical, and philosophical method and limitation of government; he had adhered with strict loyalty to the party committed to this method, until there had arisen the cause of human freedom, which far transcended any question still open upon the method or limits of government. With this cause newly risen, a cause surely not to leave the political field except in victory, he was now closely united. He might therefore have safely trusted to the judgment of later days and of wiser and truer-sighted men, growing in number and influence every year. His offense could never be pardoned by his former associates at the South and their allies at the North. No confession of error, though it were full of humiliation, no new and affectionate return to party allegiance, could make them forget what they sincerely deemed astounding treason and disastrous sacrilege. Loyal remembrance of his incomparable party services had irretrievably gone, to be brought back by no reasoning and by no persuasion. If he were to live, he should not have wavered from his last position. Its righteousness was to be plainer and plainer with the passing years.

Van Buren did live, however, long after his honorable battle and defeat; and lived to dim its honor by the faltering of mistaken patriotism. In 1849, John Van Buren, during the efforts to unite the Democratic party in New York, declared it his wish to make it "the great anti-slavery party of the Union." Early in 1850 and when the compromise was threatened at Washington, he wrote to the Free-soil convention of Connecticut that there had never been a time when the opponents of slavery extension were more urgently called to act with energy and decision or to hold their representatives to a rigid responsibility, if they faltered or betrayed their trust. With little doubt his father approved these utterances. A year later, however, the ex-President, with nearly all Northern men, yielded to the soporific which Clay in his old age administered to the American people. In their support of the great compromise between slavery and freedom, Webster and Clay forfeited much of their fame, and justly. For though the cause of humanity gained a vast political advantage in the admission of California as a free State, the advantage, it was plain, could not have been long delayed had there been no compromise. But the rest of the new territory was thrown into a struggle among its settlers, although the power of Congress over the Territories was not yet denied; and a fugitive-slave law of singular atrocity was passed. All the famous Northern Whigs were now true "doughfaces." Fillmore, president through Taylor's death, one of the most dignified and timid of their number, signed the compromise bills.

The compromise being passed, Van Buren with almost the entire North submissively sought to believe slavery at last expelled from politics. It would have been a wise heroism, it would have given Van Buren a clearer, a far higher place with posterity, if after 1848 he had even done no more than remain completely aloof from the timid politics of the time, if he had at least refused acquiescence in any compromise by which concessions were made to slavery. But he was an old man. He shared with his ancient and famous Whig rivals that intense love and almost adoration of the Union, upon which the arrogant leaders of the South so long and so successfully played. The compromise was accomplished. It would perhaps be the last concession to the furious advance of the cruel barbarism. The free settlers in the new Territories would, he hoped, by their number and hardihood, defeat the incoming slave-owners, and even under " squatter sovereignty " save their homes from slavery. If the Union should now stand without further disturbance, all might still come right without civil war. Economic laws, the inexorable and beneficent progress of civilization, would perhaps begin, slowly indeed but surely, to press to its death this remnant of ancient savagery. But if the Union were to be broken by a violation of the compromise, a vast and irremediable catastrophe and ruin would undo all the patriotic labors of sixty years, would dismiss to lasting unreality the dreams of three generations of great men who had loved their country. It seemed too appalling a responsibility.

Upon all this reasoning there is much unfair modern judgment. The small number of resolute abolitionists, who cared little for the Union in comparison with the one cause of human rights, and whose moral fervor found in the compromises of the Constitution, so dear and sacred to all American statesmen, only a covenant with hell, may for the moment be ignored. Among them there was not a public man occupying politically responsible or widely influential place. The vast body of Northern sentiment was in two great classes. The one was led by men like Seward, and even Benton, who considered the South a great bully. They believed that to a firm front against the extension of slavery the South would, after many fire-eating words, surrender in peace. The other class included most of the influential men of the day, some of them greater men, some lesser, and some little men. Webster, Clay, Cass, Buchanan, Marcy, Douglas, Fillmore, Dickinson, were now joined by Van Buren and by many Free-soil men of 1848 daunted at the seeming slowness with which the divine mills were grinding. They believed that the South, to assert the fancied "rights" of their monstrous wrong, would accept disunion and even more, that in this cause it would fiercely accept all the terrors of a civil war and its

limitless devastation. The event proved the first
men utterly in the wrong; and it was fortunate
that their mistake was not visible until in 1861 the
battle was irreversibly joined. The second and
more numerous class were right. There had to be
yielding, unless such evils were to be let loose,
unless Webster's "ideas, so full of all that is horrid
and horrible," were to come true. The anxiety
not to offend the South was perhaps most strikingly
shown after the election of Lincoln. A distinguished statesman of the modern Republican party
has recently pointed out [1] that in February, 1861,
the Republican members of Congress, and among
them Charles Sumner and Thaddeus Stevens, acquiesced in the organization of the new Territories of Colorado, Dakota, and Nevada, without
any prohibition of slavery, thus ignoring the very
principle and the only principle upon which their
great battle had been fought and their great victory won.

Complete truth dwelt only with the small and
hated abolitionist minority. Without honored and
influential leaders in political life they alone saw
that war with all these horrors was better, or even
a successful secession was better, than further surrender of human rights, a surrender whose corruption and barbarism would cloud all the glories,
and destroy all the beneficence of the Union. No
historical judgment has been more unjust and
partial than the implied condemnation of Van

[1] James G. Blaine's *Twenty Years*, vol. i. pp. 269, 272.

Buren for his acquiescence in Clay's compromise, while only gentle words have chided the great statesmen whose eloquence was more splendid and inspiring but whose devotion to the Union was never more supreme than Van Buren's, — statesmen who had made no sacrifice like his in 1844, who in their whitening years had taken no bold step like his in 1848, and who had in 1850 actively promoted the surrender to which Van Buren did no more than submit after it was accomplished.

In 1852 the overwhelming agreement to the compromise brought on a colorless presidential campaign, fought in a sort of fool's paradise. Its character was well represented by Franklin Pierce, the second Democratic mediocrity raised to the first place in the party and the land, and by the absurd political figure of General Scott, fitly enough the last candidate of the decayed Whig party. Both parties heartily approved the compromise, but it mattered little which of the two candidates were chosen. The votes cast for John P. Hale, the Free-soil candidate, were as much more significant and honorable as they were fewer than those cast for Pierce or Scott. Van Buren, in a note to a meeting in New York, declared that time and circumstances had issued edicts against his attendance, but that he earnestly wished for Pierce's election. He attempted no argument in this, perhaps the shortest political letter he ever wrote. But John Van Buren, in a speech at Albany, gave some reasons which prevent much condemnation of his father's perfunctory acquiescence in the action of his party. The movement of 1848, he said, had been intended to prevent the extension of slavery. Since then, California had come in, a Free State, and not, as the South had desired, a slave State; and "the abolition of the slave market in the District of Columbia was another great point gained." The poverty of reasons was shown in the eager insistence that every member of Congress from New Hampshire had voted against slavery extension, and that the Democratic party now took its candidate from that State "without any pledges whatever."

After this election Van Buren spent two years in Europe. President Pierce tendered him the position of the American arbitrator upon the British-American claims commission established under the treaty of February 8, 1853, but he declined. During his absence the South secured the Kansas-Nebraska bill, the repeal of the Missouri Compromise, and the practical opening to slavery of the new Territories north of the line of 36° 30'. If the settlers of Kansas, which lay wholly on the free side of that compromise line, desired slavery, they were to have it. But even this was not sufficient. The hardy settlers of this frontier, separated though they were by the slave State of Missouri from free soil and free influences, would, it now seemed, pretty certainly favor freedom. The ermine of the Supreme Court had, therefore, to be used to sanctify with the Dred Scott decision

the last demand of slavery, inconsistent though it
was with the claims of the South from the time
when it secured the Missouri Compromise until
Calhoun grimly advanced his monstrous propositions. Slavery was to be decreed a constitutional
right in all Territories, whose exercise in them Congress was without power to prohibit, and which
could not be prevented even by the majority of
their settlers until they were admitted as States.

Van Buren came back to America when there
was still secret within the judicial breast the mo-
mentous decision that the American flag carried
human slavery with it to conquered territory as a
necessary incident of its stars and stripes, and that
Congress could not, if it would, save the land to
freedom. Van Buren voted for Buchanan ; a vote
essentially inconsistent with his Free-soil position,
a vote deeply to be regretted. He still thought
that free settlers would defeat the intention of the
Kansas-Nebraska act, and bring in, as they afterwards did, a free though bleeding Kansas. There
was something crude and menacing in this new
Republican party, and in its enormous and growing
enthusiasm. It was hard to believe that its candidate had been seriously selected for chief magistrate of the United States. Fremont probably
seemed to Van Buren a picturesque sentimentalist
leading the way to civil war, which, if it were to
come, ought, so it seemed to this former senator
and minister and president, to be led in by serious
and disciplined statesmen. The new party was

repulsive to him as a body chiefly of Whigs; old
and bitter adversaries whom he distrusted, with
hosts of camp-followers smelling the coming spoils.
All this a young man might endure, when he
saw the clear fact that the Republican convention,
ignoring for the time all former differences, had
pronounced not a word inconsistent with the Democratic platform of 1840, and had made only the
one declaration essential to American freedom and
right, that slavery should not go into the Territories. Van Buren was not, however, a young man,
or one of the few old men in whom a fiery sense of
morality, and an eager and buoyant resolution, are
unchilled by thinner and slower blood, and indomi-
tably overcome the conservative influences of age.
A bold outcry from him, even now, would have
placed him for posterity in one of the few niches set
apart to the very greatest Americans. But since
1848 Van Buren had come to seventy-four years.

Invited to the Tammany Hall celebration of Independence Day, he wrote, on June 28, 1856, a
letter in behalf of Buchanan. There was no diminution in explicit clearness ; but hope was nearly
gone ; the peril of the Union obscured every other
danger ; the South was so threatening that patriotism seemed to him to require at the least a surrender to all that had passed ; and for the future our
best reliance would be upon a fair vote in Kansas
between freedom and slavery. He could not come
to its meeting, he told Tammany Hall, because of
his age. He had left one invitation unanswered ;

and if he were so to leave another, he might be suspected of a desire to conceal his sentiments. But this letter should be his last, as it was his first, appearance in the canvass. He was glad of the Democratic reunion ; for although not always perfectly right, in no other party had there been " such exclusive regard and devotion to the maintenance of human rights and the happiness and welfare of the masses of the people." There was a touch of age in his fond recitals of the long services of that party since, in Jefferson's days, it had its origin with " the root-and-branch friends of the Republican system ; " of its support of the war of 1812 ; of its destruction of the national bank ; of its establishment of an independent treasury. But slavery, he admitted, was now the living issue. Upon that he had no regrets for his course. He had always preferred the method of dealing with that institution practiced by the founders of the government. He lamented the recent departure from that method ; no one was more sincerely opposed than himself to the repeal of the Missouri Compromise. He had heard of it, and condemned it in a foreign land ; he had there foreseen the disastrous reopening of the slavery agitation. But the measure was now accomplished ; there was no more left than to decide what was the best now to do. The Kansas-Nebraska act had, he said, gradually become less obnoxious to him ; though this impression, he admitted, might result from the unanimous acquiescence in it of the party in which he had been reared. Its operation, he trusted, would be beneficial; and he had now come to believe that the feelings and opinions of the free States would be more respected under its provisions than by specific congressional interference. He did not doubt the power of Congress to enable the people of a Territory to exclude slavery. Buchanan's pledge to use the presidential power to restore harmony among the sister States could be redeemed in but one way; and that was, to secure to the actual settlers of the Territory a "full, free, and practical enjoyment" of the rights of suffrage on the slavery question conferred by the act. He praised Buchanan, if not exuberantly, still sufficiently. He must, Van Buren thought, be solicitous for his reputation in the near "evening of his life." He believed that Buchanan would redeem his pledge, and should therefore cheerfully support him. If Buchanan were elected, there were " good grounds for hope " that the Union might be saved. Such was this saddening and despondent letter. It was a defense of a vote which it was rather sorry work that he should have needed to make. But the tramp of armies and the conflagration of American institutions were heard and seen in the sky with terrifying vividness. The letter secured, however, no forgiveness from the angry South. The " Richmond Whig " said : " If there is a man within the limits of the Republic who is cordially abhorred and detested by intelligent and patriotic men of all parties at the South, that man is Martin Van Buren."

Many of the best Americans shared Van Buren's distrust of Fremont and of those who supported Fremont; they shared his love of peace and his fear of that bloodshed, North and South, which seemed the dismal El Dorado to which the "pathfinder's" feet were surely tending. So the majority of the Northern voters thought; for those north of Mason and Dixon's line who divided themselves between Buchanan and Fillmore, the candidate of the "Silver Gray" Whigs, considerably outnumbered the voters for Fremont.

In 1860 Van Buren voted for the union electoral ticket which represented in New York the combined opposition to Lincoln. Every motive which had influenced him in 1856 had now increased even more than his years. The Republican party was not only now come bringing, it seemed, the torch in full flame to light an awful conflagration; but in its second national convention there became obvious upon the tariff question the preponderance of the Whig elements, which made up the larger though not the more earnest or efficient body of its supporters.

After Van Buren's return from Europe in 1855, he lived in dignified and gracious repose. This complete and final escape from the rush about him had often seemed in his busy strenuous years full of delight. But doubtless now in the peaceful pleasures of Lindenwald and in the occasional glimpses of the more crowded social life of New York which was glad to honor him, there were the regrets and slowly dying impatience, the sense of isolation, which must at the best touch with some sadness the later and well-earned and even the best-crowned years. At this time he began writing memoirs of his life and times, which were brought down to the years 1833–1834 ; but they were never revised by him and have not been published. Out of this work grew a sketch of the early growth of American parties, which was edited by his sons and printed in 1867. Its pages do not exhibit the firm and logical order which was so characteristic of Van Buren's political compositions. It was rather the reminiscence of the political philosophy which had completely governed him. With some repetitions, but in an easy and interesting way, he recalled the far-reaching political differences between Jefferson and Hamilton. In these chapters of his old age are plain the profound and varied influences which had been exercised over him by the great founder of his party, and his unquenchable animosity towards " the money power " from the days of the first secretary of the treasury to its victory of " buffoonery " in 1840. In one chapter, with words rather courtly but still not to be mistaken, he condemns Buchanan for a violation of the principles of Jefferson and Jackson in accepting the Dred Scott decision as a rule of political action ; and this the more because its main conclusion was unnecessary to adjudge Dred Scott's rights in that suit, and because its announcement was part of a political scheme. Chief Justice

Taney and Buchanan, Van Buren pointed out, though raised to power by the Democratic party, had joined it late in life, " with opinions formed and matured in an antagonist school." Both had come from the Federalist ranks, whose political heresy Van Buren believed to be hopelessly incurable.

At the opening of the civil war Van Buren's animosity to Buchanan's behavior became more and more marked. He strongly sympathized with the uprising of the North ; and sustained the early measures of Lincoln's administration. But he was not to see the dreadful but lasting and benign solution of the problem of American slavery. His life ended when the fortunes of the nation were at their darkest ; when McClellan's seven days' battle from the Chickahominy to the James was just over, and the North was waiting in terror lest his troops might not return in time to save the capital. For several months he suffered from an asthmatic attack, which finally became a malignant catarrh, causing him much anguish. In the latter days of his sickness his mind wandered ; but when sensible and collected he still showed a keen interest in public affairs, expressed his confidence in President Lincoln and General McClellan, and declared his faith that the rebellion would end without lasting damage to the Union.

On July 24, 1862, he died, nearly eighty years old, in the quiet summer air at Lindenwald, the noise of battle far away from his green lawns and clumps of trees. In the ancient Dutch church at Kinderhook the simple funeral was performed; and a great rustic gathering paid the last and best honor of honest and respectful grief to their old friend and neighbor. For his fame had brought its chief honor to this village of his birth, the village to which in happy ending of his earthly career he returned, and where through years of well-ordered thrift, of a gentle and friendly hospitality, and of interesting and not embittered reminiscence, he had been permitted

> "To husband out life's taper at the close,
> And keep the flame from wasting by repose."

# CHAPTER XII

VAN BUREN'S CHARACTER AND PLACE IN HISTORY

IN the engraved portrait of Van Buren in old age, prefixed to his "History of Parties," are plainly to be seen some of his traits, — the alert outlooking upon men, the bright, easy good-humor, the firm, self-reliant judgment. Inman's painting, now in the City Hall of New York,[1] gives the face in the prime of life, — the same shrewd, kindly expression, but more positively touched with that half cynical doubt of men which almost inevitably belongs to those in great places. The deep wrinkles of the old and retired ex-president were hardly yet incipient in the smooth, prosperous, almost complacent countenance of the governor. In the earlier picture the locks flared outwards from the face, as they did later; as yet, however, they were dark and a bit curling. His form was always slender and erect, but hardly reached the middle height, so that to his political enemies it was endless delight to call him "Little Van."

In the older picture one sees a scrupulous daintiness about the ruffled shirt and immaculate neck-

[1] An engraving of this portrait accompanies Holland's biography, written for the campaign of 1836.

erchief; for Van Buren was fond of the elegance of life. The Whigs used to declare him an aristocrat, given to un-American, to positively British splendor. Very certainly he never affected contempt for the gracious and stately refinement suited to his long held place of public honor, that contempt which a silly underrating of American good sense has occasionally commended to our statesmen. At Lindenwald, among books and guests and rural cares, he led what in the best and truest sense was the life of a country gentleman, not set like an urban exotic among the farmers, but fond of his neighbors as they were fond of him, and unaffectedly sharing without loss of distinction or elegance their thrifty and homely cares. When he retired to this home he was able, without undignified or humiliating shifts, to live in ease and even affluence. For in 1841 his fortune of perhaps $200,000 was a generous one. His last days were not, like those of Jefferson and Monroe and Jackson, embittered by money anxieties, the penalty of the careless profusion the temptation to which, felt even by men wise in the affairs of others, is often greater than the certain danger and unwisdom of its indulgence. But no suggestion was breathed against his pecuniary integrity, public or private. Nor was there heard of him any story of wrong or oppression or ungenerous dealing.

Van Buren's extraordinary command of himself was apparent in his manners. They are finely described from intimate acquaintance by William

Allen Butler, the son of Van Buren's long-time friend, in his charming and appreciative sketch printed just after Van Buren's death. They had, Mr. Butler said, a neatness and polish which served every turn of domestic, social, and public intercourse. "As you saw him once, you saw him always — always punctilious, always polite, always cheerful, always self-possessed. It seemed to any. one who studied this phase of his character as if, in some early moment of destiny, his whole nature had been bathed in a cool, clear, and unruffled depth, from which it drew this life-long serenity and self-control." An accomplished English traveler, " the author of 'Cyril Thornton,'" who saw him while secretary of state, and before he had been abroad, said that he had more of " the manner of the world " than any other of the distinguished men at Washington ; that in conversation he was " full of anecdote and vivacity." Chevalier, one of our French critics, in his letters from America described him as setting up " for the American Talleyrand." John Quincy Adams, as has been said, sourly mistook all this, and even the especial courtesy Van Buren paid him after his political downfall, as mere proof of insincerity ; and he more than once compared Van Buren to Aaron Burr, a comparison of which many Democrats were fond after 1848. In his better-natured moments, however, Adams saw in his adversary a resemblance to the conciliatory and philosophic Madison. For his " extreme caution in avoiding and averting personal collisions," he called him another Sosie of Molière's "Amphitryon," "ami de tout le monde."

Van Buren's skill in dealing with men was indeed extraordinary. It doubtless came from this temper of amity, and from an inborn genius for society; but it had been wonderfully sharpened in the unrivaled school of New York's early politics. When he was minister at London, he wrote that he was making it his business to be cordial with prominent men on both sides; a branch of duty, he said, in which he was not at home, because he had all his life been "wholly on one side." But he was jocosely unjust to himself. He was, for the politics of his day, abundantly fair to his adversaries. Sometimes indeed he saw too much of what might be said on the other side. Had he seen less, he would sometimes have been briefer, less indulgent in formal caution. Nor did he fail to avoid the unnecessary misery caused to many public men, the obstacles needlessly raised in their way, by personal disputes, or by letting into negotiations matters of controversy irrelevant to the thing to be done. Patience in listening, a steady and singularly acute observance of the real end he sought, and a quick, keen reading of men, saved him this wearing unhappiness so widespread in public life. Once he thus criticised his friend Cambreleng: "There is more in small matters than he is always aware of, although he is a really sensible and useful man." In this maxim of lesser things Van Buren was carefully practiced. During the Jackson-Adams campaign, the younger Hamilton was about sending to some important person an account of the general. Van Buren, knowing of this, wrote to Hamilton, and, after signing his letter, added : " P. S. — Does the old gentleman have prayers in his own house ? If so, mention it modestly."

His self-command was not stilted or unduly precise or correct. He was very human. A candidate for governor of New York would to-day hardly write to another public man, however friendly to him, as Van Buren in August and September, 1828, wrote to Hamilton. " Bet on Kentucky, Indiana, and Illinois," he said, " jointly if you can, or any two of them ; don't forget to bet all you can." But this was the fashion of the day.[1] His life was entirely free from the charges of dissipation or of irregular habits, then so commonly, and often truly, made against great men. This very correctness was part of the offense he gave his rivals and their followers. It would hardly be accurate to describe him, even in younger years, as jovial with his friends ; but he was perfectly companionable. Of

[1] The mania for election betting among public men was very curious. In the letters and memoranda printed by Mackenzie, the bets of John Van Buren and Jesse Hoyt are given in detail. They ranged from $5000 to $50; from " three cases of champagne " or " two bales of cotton," to " boots, $7," or " a ham, $3." They were made with the younger Alexander Hamilton, James Watson Webb, Moses H. Grinnell, John A. King, George F. Talman, Dudley Selden, and other notable men of the time.

a social and cheerful temper, he not only liked the
decorous gaiety of receptions and public entertain-
ment, but was delighted and delightful in closer
and easier conversation and in the chat of familiar
friends. His reminiscences of men are said to have
been full of the charm which flows from a strong
natural sense of humor, and a correct and vivid
memory of human action and character.

There are many apocryphal stories of Van Buren's craft or cunning or selfishness in politics. It
is a curious appreciation with which reputable historians have received such stories from irresponsible or anonymous sources; for they deserve as little credence as those told of Lincoln's frivolity or
indecency. To them all may not only be pleaded
the absence of any proof deserving respect, but
they are refuted by positive proof, such as from
earliest times has been deemed the best which private character can in its own behalf offer to history. In politics Van Buren enjoyed as much
strong and constant friendship as he encountered
strong and constant hatred. Nothing points more
surely to the essential soundness of life and the
generosity of a public man than the near and long-
continued friendship of other able, upright, and
honorably ambitious men. It was an extraordinary measure in which Van Buren enjoyed friendship of this quality. With all the light upon his
character, Jackson was too shrewd to suffer long
from imposition. His intimacy with Van Buren
for twenty years and more was really affectionate;

his admiration for the younger statesman was profound. The explanation is both unnecessary and
unworthy, which ascribes to hatred of Clay all
Jackson's ardor in the canvass of 1840 or his almost pathetic anxiety for Van Buren's nomination
in 1844. Their peculiar and continuous associa-
tion for six years at Washington had so powerfully
established Van Buren in his love and respect,
that neither distant separation nor disease nor the
nearer intrigues and devices of rivals could abate
them. Those who were especially known as Van
Buren men, those who not only stood with him in
the party but who went with him out of it, were
men of great talents and of the highest character.
Butler's career closely accompanied Van Buren's.
Both were born at Kinderhook; they were together
in Hudson, in Albany, in Washington; they were
together as Bucktails, as Jacksonian Democrats, as
Free-soil men; they were close to one another from
Butler's boyhood until, more than a half-century
later, they were parted by death. To this strong-
headed and sound-hearted statesman, we are told
by William Allen Butler, in a fine and weilnigh
sufficient eulogy, that Van Buren was the object
of an affection true and steadfast, faithful through
good report and evil report, loyal to its own high
sense of duty and affection, tender and generous.
Benton, liberal and sane a slaveholder though he
was, did not approve the Wilmot Proviso, or join
the Free-soil revolt. But in retirement and old
age, reviewing his "Thirty Years," during twenty

of which he and Van Buren had, spite of many differences, remained on closely intimate terms, he showed a deep liking for the man. Silas Wright, Azariah C. Flagg, and John A. Dix, all strong and famous characters in the public life of New York, were among the others of those steadily faithful in loyal and unwavering regard for this political and personal chief. Nor were they deceived. Jackson and Butler, Wright and Flagg and Dix, sturdy, upright, skillful, experienced men of affairs, were not held in true and lifelong friendship and admiration by the insinuating manners, the clever management, the selfish and timid aims, which make the Machiavellian caricature of Van Buren so often drawn. No American in public life has shown firmer and longer devotion to his friends. His reputation for statesmanship must doubtless rest upon the indisputable facts of his career. But for his integrity of life, for his sincerity, for his fidelity to those obligations of political, party, and personal friendship, within which lies so much of the usefulness as well as of the singular charm of public life, his relations with these men make a proof not to be questioned, and surely not to be weakened by the malicious or anonymous stories of political warfare.

For the absurdly sinister touch which his political enemies gave to his character, it is difficult now to find any just reason. It may be that the cool and imperturbable appearance of good-nature, with which he received the savage and malevolent

attacks so continually made upon him, to many
seemed so impossible to be real as to be sheer hypocrisy ;[1] and from the fancy of such hypocrisy it
was easy for the imagination to infer all the arts
and characteristics of deceit. Doubtless the caution of Van Buren's political papers irritated impatient and angry opponents. They found them
full of elaborate and subtle reservations, as they
fancied, against future political contingencies; a
charge, it ought to be remembered, which is continually made against the ripest, bravest, and
greatest character in English politics of to-day or
of the century.[2] Van Buren's reasoning was perfectly clear, and his style highly finished. But he
had not the sort of genius which in a few phrases
states and lights up a political problem. The complexity of human affairs, the danger of short and
sweeping assertions, pressed upon him as he wrote;
and the amplitude of his arguments, sometimes
tending to prolixity, seemed timid and lawyer-like
to those who disliked his conclusions.

[1] One of the latest and most important historians of the time,
after saying that "nothing ruffled" Van Buren, is contented with
a different explanation from mine. Professor Sumner says that
"he was thick-skinned, elastic, and tough ; he did not win confidence from anybody." But within another sentence or two the
historian adds, as if effect did not always need adequate cause,
that "as president he showed the honorable desire to have a
statesmanlike and high-toned administration." (Sumner's *Jackson*, p. 451.)

[2] Here again I spoke of Gladstone, to whom, as this revised
edition is going to press, the civilized world is bringing, in his
death, a noble and fitting tribute.

Van Buren was not, however, an unpopular man, except as toward the last his politics were unpopular as politics out of sympathy with those of either of the great parties, and except also at the South, where he was soon suspected and afterwards hated as an anti-slavery man. He was on the whole a strong candidate at the polls. In his own State and at the Northeast his strength with the people grew more and more until his defeat by the slaveholders in 1844. Perhaps the most striking proof of this strength was the canvass of 1848, when in New York he was able to take fully half of his party with him into irregular opposition, a feat with hardly a precedent in our political history. And there was complete reciprocity. Van Buren was profoundly democratic in his convictions. He thoroughly, honestly, and without demagogy believed in the common people and in their competence to deal wisely with political difficulties. Even when his faith was tried by what he deemed the mistakes of popular elections, he still trusted to what in a famous phrase of his he called "the sober second thought of the people." [1]

However widely the student of history may differ from the politics of Van Buren's associates, the politics of Benton, Wright, Butler, and Dix, and in a later rank of his New York disciples, of Sam-

---

[1] This expression was not original with Van Buren, as has been supposed. It was used by Fisher Ames in 1788; and Bartlett's *Quotations* also gives a still earlier use of part of it by Matthew Henry in 1710.

uel J. Tilden and Sanford E. Church, it is impossible not to see that their political purpose was at the least as long and steady as their friendship for Van Buren. Love for the Union, a belief in a simple, economical, and even unheroic government, a jealousy of taking money from the people, and a scrupulous restriction upon the use of public moneys for any but public purposes, a strict limitation of federal powers, a dislike of slavery and an opposition to its extension, — these made up one of the great and fruitful political creeds of America, a creed which had ardent and hopeful apostles a half century ago, and which, save in the articles which touched slavery and are now happily obsolete, will doubtless find apostles no less ardent and hopeful a half century hence. Each of its assertions has been found in other creeds ; but the entire creed with all its articles made the peculiar and powerful faith only of the Van Buren men. As history gradually sets reputations aright, the leader of these men must justly wear the laurel of a statesman who, apart from his personal and party relations and ambitions, has stood clearly for a powerful and largely triumphant cause.

No vague, no thoughtless rush of popular sentiment touched or shook this faith of Van Buren. Had there been indeed a readier emphasis about him, a heartier and quicker sympathy with the temper of the day, he would perhaps have aroused a popular enthusiasm, he might perhaps have been the hero which in fact he never was. But his intellectual perceptions did not permit the subtle self-deceit, the enthusiastic surrender to current sentiment, to which the striking figures that delight the masses of men are so apt to yield. Van Buren was steadfast from the beginning to the end, save when the war threats of slavery alarmed his old age and the sober second thought of a really patient and resolute people seemed a long time coming. Two years before his death Jefferson wrote to Van Buren an elaborate sketch of his relations with Hamilton and of our first party division. Two years before his own death Van Buren was finishing a history of the same political division written upon the theory and in the tone running through Jefferson's writings. It was composed by Van Buren in the very same temper in which he had respectfully read the weighty epistle from the great apostle of Democracy. Between the ending life at Monticello and that at Lindenwald, the political faith of the older man had been steadily followed by the younger.

The rise of the " spoils " system, and the late coming, but steadily increasing perception of its corruptions and dangers, have seriously and justly dimmed Van Buren's fame. But history should be not less indulgent to him than to other great Americans. The practical politics which he first knew had been saturated with the abuse. He did no more than adopt accustomed means of political warfare. Neither he nor other men of his time perceived the kind of evil which political proscrip-

tion of men in unpolitical places must yield.
They saw the undoubted rightfulness of shattering
the ancient idea that in offices there was a property
right. They saw but too clearly the apparent help
which the powerful love of holding office brings to
any political cause, and which has been used by
every great minister of state the world over. Van
Buren had, however, no love of patronage in itself.
The use of a party as a mere agency to distribute
offices would have seemed to him contemptible.
In neither of the great executive places which he
held, as governor, secretary of state, or president,
did he put into an extreme practice the proscriptive rules which were far more rigorously adopted
about him. To his personal temper not less than
to his conceptions of public duty the inevitable
meanness and wrong of the system were distasteful.

Chief among the elements of Van Buren's public
character ought to be ranked his moral courage
and the explicitness of his political utterances, —
the two qualities which, curiously enough, were
most angrily denied him by his enemies. His well-
known Shocco Springs letter of 1832 on the tariff
was indeed lacking in these qualities; but he was
then not chiefly interested. There was only a
secondary reponsibility upon him. But it is not
too much to say that no American in responsible
and public station, since the days when Washington returned from his walk among the miserable
huts at Valley Forge to write to the Continental

Congress, or to face the petty imbecilities of the jealous colonists, has shown so complete a political courage as that with which Van Buren faced the crisis of 1837, or in which he wrote his famous Texas letter. Nor did any American, stirred with ambition, conscious of great powers, as was this captain of politicians, and bringing all his political fortunes, as he must do, to the risks of universal suffrage, ever meet living issues dangerously dividing men ready to vote for him if he would but remain quiet, with clearer or more decided answers than did Van Buren in his Sherrod Williams letter of 1836 and in most of his chief public utterances from that year until 1844. The courtesies of his manner, his failure in trenchant brevity, and even the almost complete absence of invective or extravagance from his papers or speeches, have obscured these capital virtues of his character. He saw too many dangers; and he sometimes made it too clear that he saw them. But upon legitimate issues he was among the least timid and the most explicit of great Americans. No president of ours has in office been more courageous or more direct.

It is perhaps an interesting, it is at least a harmless speculation, to look for Van Buren's place of honor in the varied succession of men who have reached the first office, though not always the first place, in American public life. Every student will be powerfully, even when unconsciously, influenced in this judgment by the measure of strength or beneficence he accords to different political tendencies. With this warning the present writer will, however, venture upon an opinion.

Van Buren very clearly does not belong among the mediocrities or accidents of the White House, — among Monroe, Harrison, Tyler, Polk, Taylor, Fillmore, and Pierce, not to meddle with the years since the civil war whose party disputes are still part of contemporary politics. Van Buren reached the presidency by political abilities and public services of the first order, as the most distinguished active member of his party, and with a universal popular recognition for years before his promotion that he was among the three or four Americans from whom a president would be naturally chosen. Buchanan's experience in public life was perhaps as great as Van Buren's, and his political skill and distinction made his accession to the presidency by no means unworthy. But he never led, he never stood for a cause ; he never led men ; he was never chief in his party ; and in his great office he sank with timidity before the slaveholding aggressors, as they strove with vengeance to suppress freedom in Kansas, and before the menaces and open plunderings of disunion. Van Buren showed no such timidity in a place of equal difficulty.

Jackson stands in a rank by himself. He had a stronger and more vivid personality than Van Buren. But useful as he was to the creation of a powerful sentiment for union and of a hostility to the schemes of a paternal government, it is clear that in those qualities of steady wisdom, foresight,

patience, which of right belong to the chief magistracy of a republic, he was far inferior to his less
picturesque and less forceful successor. The first
Adams, a man of very superior parts, competent
and singularly patriotic, was deep in too many
personal collisions within and without his party,
and his presidency incurred too complete and lasting, and it must be added, too just a popular condemnation, to permit it high rank, though very
certainly he belonged among neither the mediocrities nor the accidents of the White House.

If to the highest rank of American presidents
be assigned Washington, and if after him in it
come Jefferson and perhaps Lincoln (though more
than a quarter of a century must go to make
the enduring measure of his fame), the second
rank would seem to include Madison, the younger
Adams, and Van Buren. Between the first and
the last of these, the second of them, as has been
said, saw much resemblance. But if Madison had
a mellower mind, more obedient to the exigencies
of the time and of a wider scholarship, Van Buren
had a firmer and more direct courage, a steadier
loyalty to his political creed, and far greater resolution and efficiency in the performance of executive duties. If one were to imitate Plutarch in
behalf of John Quincy Adams and Van Buren, he
would need largely to compare their rival political
creeds. But leaving these, it will not be unjust to
say that in virile and indomitable continuance of
moral purpose after official power had let go its

trammels, and when the harassments and feebleness
of age were inexorable, and though the heavens
were to fall, the younger Adams was the greater;
that in executive success they were closely together
in a high rank; but that in skill and power of
political leadership, in breadth of political purpose,
in freedom from political vagaries, in personal
generosity and political loyalty, Van Buren was
easily the greater man.

Van Buren did not have the massive and forcible
eloquence of Webster, or the more captivating
though fleeting speech of Clay, or the delightful
warmth of the latter's leadership, or the strength
and glory which their very persons and careers
gave to American nationality. But in the persistent and fruitful adherence to a political creed
fitted to the time and to the genius of the American
people, in that noble art which gathers and binds
to one another and to a creed the elements of a
political party, the art which disciplines and guides
the party, when formed, to clear and definite purposes, without wavering and without weakness or
demagogy, Van Buren was a greater master than
either of those men, in many things more interesting as they were. In this exalted art of the politician, this consummate art of the statesman, Van
Buren was close to the greatest of American party
leaders, close to Jefferson and to Hamilton.

In his very last years the stir and rumbling of
war left Van Buren in quiet recollection and anxious loyalty at Lindenwald. As his growing ill-

ness now and then spared him moments of ease, his mind must sometimes have turned back to the steps of his career, senator of his State, senator of the United States, governor, first cabinet minister, foreign envoy, vice-president, and president. There must again have sounded in his ears the hardly remembered jargon of Lewisites and Burrites, Clintonians and Livingstonians, Republicans and Federalists, Bucktails and Jacksonians and National Republicans, Democrats and Whigs, Loco-focos and Conservatives, Barnburners and Hunkers. There must rapidly though dimly have shifted before him the long series of his struggles, — struggles over the second war with England, over internal improvements, the Bank, nullification, the divorce of bank and state, the resistance to slavery extension. Through them all there had run, and this at least his memory clearly recalled, the one strong faith of his politics and statesmanship. In all his labors of office, in all his multifarious strifes, he never faltered in upholding the Union. But not less firmly would this true disciple of Jefferson restrain the activities of the federal government. Whatever wisdom, whatever integrity of purpose might belong to ministers and legislators at Washington, — though the strength of the United States might be theirs, and though they were panoplied in the august prestige rightly ascribed by American patriotism to that sovereign title of our nation, — still Van Buren was resolute that they should not do for the people what the States or the people themselves could do as well. To his eyes there was clear and undimmed from the beginning to the close of his career, the idea of government as an instrument of useful public service, rather than an object of superstitious veneration, the idea but two years after his death clothed with memo- rable words by a master in brief speech, the demo- cratic idea of a " government of the people, by the people, for the people."

# INDEX

York merchants to remonstrate against specie circular, 317.

Derby, Earl of, compared as parliamentarian to Van Buren, 123.

De Tocqueville, Alexis de, on lawyers in America, 35.

Dickerson, Mahlon, condemns too much diplomacy, 129; votes against Panama congress, 131; supports tariff of 1828, 143; secretary of navy under Van Buren, 283; resigns, 300.

Dickinson, Daniel S., at Democratic Convention of 1844, 408, 411; leads Hunkers, 415; uses federal patronage against Barnburners, 417; suggests idea of squatter sovereignty, 422; supports compromise of 1850, 437.

Diplomatic history, conduct of State Department by Van Buren, 215; negotiations leading to payment of French spoliation claims, 216; payment of Danish spoliation claims, 217; other commercial treaties, 217; negotiations relative to British West India trade, 217–222; Gallatin's mission to England, 219; American claims abandoned by Van Buren, 220; mutual concessions open trade, 222; Van Buren's mission to England, 224–228; rejection of Texas treaty, 413.

Disraeli, Benjamin, his Jingo policy compared to Clay's and Adams's, 126.

District of Columbia, question of abolition of slavery in, raised, 272, 273; general understanding that this was impossible, 273, 274; opinion of Van Buren concerning, 274, 275.

Dix, John A., his desire to be one of Albany Regency, 112; at Democratic convention of 1840, 379; leads Barnburners, 415; praised by Utica convention of 1847, 423; accepts Free-soil nomination for governor, 429; his friendship for Van Buren, 456.

Dix, Dr. Morgan, describes honesty of Albany Regency, 112.

Dodge, Henry, nominated by Barnburners for vice-presidency, 427; declines to abandon Cass, 427.

Douglas, Stephen A., supports compromise of 1850, 437.

Dudley, Charles E., member of Albany Regency, 111; offers to surrender seat in Senate to Van Buren, 236.

Duer, John, refusal of Van Buren to secure his removal from office, 209.

Duer, William, joins Bucktail Republicans, 73.

Durham, Earl of, sent to Canada, his character, 355; his successful rule, 355; recalled, 356; declines invitation to visit Washington, 356.

Dutch, in New York, Americanized in eighteenth century, 14.

Eaton, John H., supports tariff of 1828, 143; secretary of war, 179; marries Peggy Timberlake, 181; repeats remarks about Calhoun to Jackson, 186; resigns secretaryship, 199; succeeds Barry as minister to Spain, 199; opposes Van Buren in 1840, 387.

Eaton, Mrs. "Peggy," scandals concerning, 181; upheld by Jackson, 181, 182; ostracized by Washington society, 182; treated politely by Van Buren, 183, 184.

Eden, Joseph, in suit for Medcef Eden's property, 28.

Eden, Medcef, suit concerning his will, 28–30.

Edmonds, John W., issues circular opposing Texas but supporting Polk, 415.

Election of 1824, nominations for, discussed in Senate, 105; candidates for, 106–109; lack of principles in, 108; nomination of Crawford by caucus, 114; action of Adams men in New York throws out Clay, 115; discussion of outcome of vote in House, 116; its result used in 1828 to condemn Adams, 164.

Election of 1828, a legitimate canvass, 153; broad principles at stake in, 153, 154; propriety of opposition to Adams and Clay, 159, 160; founds principles of both parties until present day, 161; saves country from dangers of centralization, 162; slanderous character of, 162, 163; the

leader, 273 , his murder not of political interest, 359.

Lundy's Lane, battle of, 62.

McJilton, Rev. ——, at Democratic Convention of 1844, 408.

McKean, Samuel, complains to Kendall of political activity of postmasters, 261.

McLane, Louis, secretary of treasury, 199; Van Buren's instructions to him when minister to England, 219–221; his successful negotiations regarding West India trade, 222; wishes to return, 223; mentioned as candidate for vice-presidency, 238; wishes removal of deposits postponed, 250; disapproving of removal of deposits, resigns State Department, 255.

McLean, John T., appointed to Supreme Court, 179; refuses to proscribe postmasters, 207; wishes Anti-Masonic nomination for presidency, 245.

Mackenzie, William L., quoted by Von Holst, 326 n.; his character, 326; leads an insurrection in Upper Canada, 353; flies to Buffalo and plans a raid, 353; indicted and convicted, 356; on Van Buren's refusal to pardon him, becomes a bitter enemy, 356.

Madison, James, member of land-owning class, 33; his foreign policy attacked by Federalists, 39; voted against by Van Buren in 1812, 58; his incapacity as war leader, 59; criticised by Van Buren for sanctioning Bank of United States, 146; compared to Van Buren in regard to ability, 464.

Maine, threatens war over disputed boundary, 367; angered at Van Buren's peaceful measures, 367.

Manley, Dr., refusal of Van Buren to remove from office, 174.

Manning, Daniel, member of Albany Regency, 112, 192 n.

Marcy, William L., aids Van Buren, in behalf of King's election to Senate, 69; member of Albany Regency, 111, 112; appointed a judge by Van

Buren, 174; defends spoils system, his famous phrase, 232; warns against over-speculation in 1836, 302, 303; calls out New York militia to prevent raids into Canada, 335; leads Hunkers, 415, 417; supports compromise of 1850, 437.

Marshall, John, on Jefferson's political principles, 6; his legal fame, 19.

Massachusetts, supports Webster for president in 1836, 260.

Meigs, Henry, urged by Van Buren to remove postmasters, 75.

Mexico, its war with Texas, 357; neutrality toward, declared by Van Buren, 358; claims against, pressed by Van Buren, 359, 360.

Missouri, legislature of, compliments Van Buren, 399.

Missouri question, in New York, 73, 74; its slight effect on national complacency, 90, 91.

Monroe, James, member of land-owning class, 33; reëlected president, 72; voted for by Van Buren in 1820, 75; his message of 1820, 88; his character, 89; his tour in New England, 89; views on party government, 89, 90; vetoes internal improvement bill, 95, 96, 121; discussion in his cabinet over Jackson's action in Seminole matter, 185; complimentary dinner to, in 1829, 186; inferior as president to Van Buren, 463.

Monroe doctrine, its relation to Panama congress, 124.

Moore, Gabriel, remark of Benton to, on Van Buren, 234.

Morgan, William, his Masonic revelations and abduction, 167.

Morton, Marcus, elected governor of Massachusetts by one vote, 370; leads Northern Democrats at convention of 1844, 408; opposes two-thirds rule, 409.

Napoleon III., explains to Van Buren his reasons for returning to Europe, 362.

National Republicans, attacked by Van Buren, 145, 146; organized in